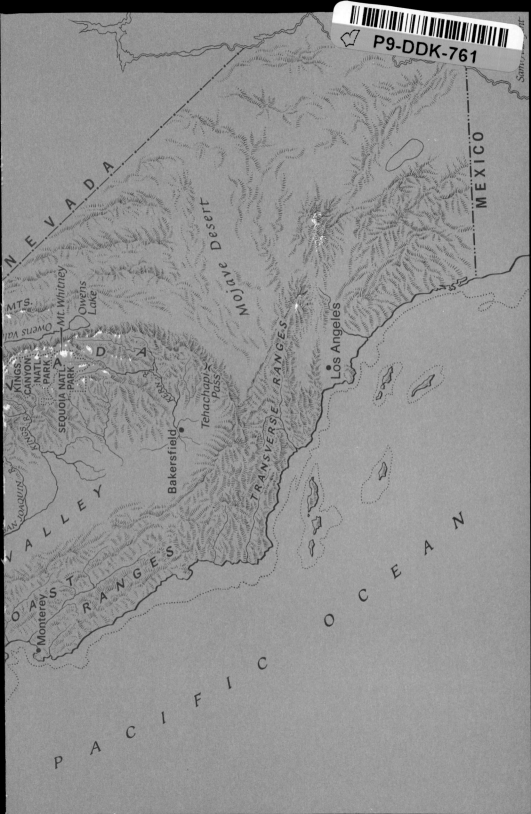

NEVADA

MEXICO

Mojave Desert

MTS.

Owens Valley

Mt. Whitney

Owens Lake

S I E R R A   N E V A D A

KINGS CANYON NATL. PARK

KINGS R.

SEQUOIA NATL. PARK

SAN JOAQUIN R.

VALLEY

Tehachapi Pass

Bakersfield

TRANSVERSE RANGES

Los Angeles

C O A S T   R A N G E S

Monterey

P A C I F I C   O C E A N

SIERRA NEVADA

SIERRA

The Naturalist's America

NEVADA

BY VERNA R. JOHNSTON

*Illustrated with photographs
by the author and maps by
Samuel H. Bryant*

1970
HOUGHTON MIFFLIN COMPANY BOSTON

THE NATURALIST'S AMERICA

First Printing **w**

Library of Congress Catalog Card Number: 79–96064
Printed in the United States of America

To Amber

Editors' Preface

WE PRESENT HERE the second volume in a series designed to inform North Americans about the wildlife, plants, and geology of their continent. It is also the purpose of this series, inspired by a similar series in England (The New Naturalist), to recapture the inquiring spirit of the old naturalists. In our preface to the first volume of the series, *The Appalachians* by Maurice Brooks, we pointed out that in this era of the highly trained biologist there has been a tendency to lose the feeling of wonder and of beauty and to focus, sometimes myopically, on too narrow segments of the natural scene. However, one notes a growing effort to close the gap between science and interpretation, and the Ph.D. who writes his papers in the formal clichés of his discipline is now finding that he might also express himself gracefully and that there is no stigma attached to writing well.

The author of this book, Verna Johnston, has had a long intimacy with the Sierra Nevada extending over a period of twenty years. For that reason as well as for her lucid way with words she was selected to tell the story of this beautiful mountain range.

John Muir, who explored every inch of Yosemite on foot and also much of the rest of the Sierra, would, if he were alive, have mixed feelings about the highways that now make these mountains accessible to the tourist. But it was he, in a sense, who brought the automobile to Yosemite and to the other Sierran parks by his untiring efforts in publicizing them so as to gain public support for these national treasures.

Verna Johnston puts things into perspective by assessing the conflicting values of the past and the present — on the one hand the destruction of Hetch Hetchy, the slaughter of the indigenous megafauna, the felling of the big groves, and the pollution of Tahoe; and on the other hand the creation of national parks and the attempt to reverse the appalling turn-of-the-century devastation.

In the Sierra everything is big. Here are the world's largest trees, many of the highest waterfalls, and perhaps the biggest exposed monolithic rocks. To quote James Fisher, the distinguished British naturalist who visited Yosemite in 1953: "A conspiracy of climate, geology, and history has made the western side of the Sierras, between 5000 and 8000 feet above the sea, the theater of organic size."

In contrast to the Appalachians the Sierra is a young range, lifted skyward almost yesterday. The Appalachians are among the oldest mountains on earth; their parent rocks were first raised up more than 250 million years ago, and their peaks, once as rugged and massive as any in the Alps or the Rockies, have been worn down by weather and erosion to gentle green mountains with soft, almost feminine contours. The Sierra Nevada, however, as we see it now is a mere one to two million years old. From his Olympian lookout on any of the snow-covered peaks, the climber observes that the Sierra has a long slope to the moist west and a very abrupt drop to the arid east. It is a 400-mile-long slab of the earth's crust that has slipped and tilted, its depressed "hinge" in the great California valleys and its up-thrust eastern edge poised high over the Nevada desert.

The traveler is aware, if he is a naturalist, that plant life is zoned, lying in altitudinal belts around these mountains, and that animal life is tied in with those belts. No one is more aware of this vertical zonation than the bird watcher who sees little else than rosy finches ("refrigerator birds") in the high peaks that dominate the windswept roof of the range. Descending from the environment that is usually called the Arctic-alpine Zone into the fringe of hemlocks, lodgepoles, and whitebark pines just below timberline (the Hudsonian Zone), he finds many of the same birds that he would see were he in the boreal forests of Canada — three-toed woodpeckers, pine grosbeaks, white-crowned sparrows, and others. Farther down, in the more luxurious evergreen forests of the Canadian Zone, olive-sided flycatchers and hermit thrushes sing in the summer, while sooty grouse intone their muffled hoots from the shadows.

The trend in the mountains is from conifers higher up to oaks and chaparral below. The belt where they meet and mix is called, appropriately, the Transition Zone. Here, where yellow pines dominate, big dark Steller's jays dash through the shady groves and western tanagers and solitary vireos voice their short musical phrases. Where the landscape flattens out into low foothills, live oaks, blue oaks, and digger pines take over. Here, in the Upper Sonoran Zone, the crestless scrub jay replaces the crested Steller's jay. California thrashers and brown towhees rummage among the dry leaves. On the eastern flank of the Sierra, where slopes drop more precipitously, there is an additional life zone, the Lower Sonoran Zone — hot, dry desert country.

But let Verna Johnston tell about these things. The superb photographs that illustrate this book are her own, and they give us a visual impression to supplement her prose.

ROGER TORY PETERSON
JOHN A. LIVINGSTON

Acknowledgments

WHEN Harold Biswell, Professor of Forestry at the University of California, Berkeley, asked me early in the work on this book what it aimed to do, I answered: to tell the story of Sierra Nevada wildlife in terms of the plant communities in which the animals live — red fir forests, foothill woodland, chaparral, yellow pine forests, and the rest — with full consideration of how fire, geology, man, history, and evolution have shaped the ecology of the range. I hoped the book would be such intriguing reading that if he picked it up on a winter night by the fireplace he wouldn't be able to put it down. Months later, after Harold had read the first draft of the fire ecology chapter, he wrote, "When I started reading it, I wanted to keep on." If the book can do this, it will have achieved its purpose.

The material has come from many sources: my own field experiences during parts of more than twenty years in the Sierra; the field observations of others, from John Muir and the University of California natural history surveys of the early 1900s to current ecologists and geneticists, entomologists, and foresters; and that vast body of accumulated knowledge — the literature.

The generously given ideas and suggestions of many fellow biologists have gone into this book. I am especially grateful to Elizabeth McClintock of the California Academy of Sciences, who read the entire manuscript, and to the following who read individual chapters: G. Ledyard Stebbins and Daniel I. Axelrod, University of California, Davis; A. Starker Leopold, Donald L. Dahlsten, and Harold H. Biswell, University of California, Berkeley; William P. Dasmann and Edward R. Schneegas, U.S. Forest Service; George E. Lawrence, Bakersfield College; Richard J. Hartesveldt, San Jose State College; Lloyd G. Ingles; Robert T. Orr, California Academy of Sciences.

Many individuals supplied specific needed information: Russell K. Grater, Chief Park Naturalist, Sequoia and Kings Canyon National Parks; George Briggs, Park Forester, Yosemite National Park; Douglass Hubbard, former Park Naturalist at Yosemite; James O. Keith, Wildlife Research Station, Davis, California; Robert C. Stebbins and Edward C. Stone, University of California, Berkeley; George Seymour and Floyd V. Koontz, California Department of Fish and Game; Grant A. Morse, William P. Dasmann, George R. Struble, and Edward R. Schneegas, U.S. Forest Service; Richard J. Hartesveldt, San Jose State College.

San Joaquin Delta College granted the leaves of absence from teaching which made the research and writing possible. My parents, John F. and Mabel Johnston, assisted in a number of ways. My good friends Amber Ellis and Blanche McDaniel provided the frankness and understanding that helped keep the manuscript and me rolling; Amber's aid freed many essential hours for writing; without her the book could not have been written. Editorial help was given readily by Paul Brooks, John Livingston, Ruth Hapgood, Helen Phillips, and Roger Tory Peterson of Houghton Mifflin Company. To all of these and to unnamed others my deepest thanks.

The nomenclature in this book is taken from the following

authorities; these works are not repeated in the Principal References at the back of the book:

A California Flora by Philip A. Munz and David D. Keck (Berkeley: University of California Press, 1959)

Supplement to A California Flora by Philip A. Munz (Berkeley: University of California Press, 1968)

A List of Common and Scientific Names of Fishes from the United States and Canada, 2nd edition. American Fisheries Society, Special Publication No. 2 (Ann Arbor, 1960)

A Field Guide to Western Reptiles and Amphibians by Robert C. Stebbins (Boston: Houghton Mifflin, 1966)

A Field Guide to Western Birds by Roger Tory Peterson (Boston: Houghton Mifflin, 1961)

A Field Guide to the Mammals, 2nd edition, by William H. Burt and Richard P. Grossenheider (Boston: Houghton Mifflin, 1964)

Sierra Nevada Natural History by Tracy I. Storer and Robert L. Usinger (Berkeley: University of California Press, 1963) for butterflies and others not covered in the preceding sources, and in a few instances for common names of plants.

Special acknowledgment must go to John Muir. His writings are often the only detailed source of early Sierran natural history. Muir once bemoaned taking a month of precious time away from his mountains to slave over a chapter that someone could read in twenty minutes. I know how he felt. But without his records there would be a huge informational vacuum; without his fighting pen there would be far less unexploited Sierra Nevada to roam today.

VERNA R. JOHNSTON

Stockton, California

Contents

Illustrations

SIERRA NEVADA

1. The Range

ON CLEAR, COLD WINTER MORNINGS in the Central Valley of California, you can look west to the rolling outline of the Coast Ranges, east to the snow-covered crest of the Sierra Nevada. It is roughly one hundred miles from the valley floor to closest Sierran summits; at this distance, the mighty mountains stand low against the skyline.

It was a view much like this that inspired the naming of the Sierra. The Anza expedition of Spanish soldiers, peasants, and friars which plodded north from Mexico into the "wilds" of central California in 1776 included a Franciscan missionary, Pedro Font. While exploring a hill in the San Francisco inner bay region one April morning, Font looked off to the northeast. "We saw an immense treeless plain," he wrote in his diary, ". . . at the opposite end of this extensive plain, about forty leagues off, we saw a great snow-covered range [*una gran sierra nevada*], which seemed to me to run from south-southeast to north-northwest." [1]

On his map, in a location east of the wide plain, Font sketched in the contours of a long jagged range and drew at its crest overlapping cumulus clouds terminating in peaks. Adjacent he printed the words SIERRA NEVADA — the first named and mapped record of this singular North American range.

The Sierra Nevada is the middle range of three major mountain barriers that extend roughly north-south and nearly parallel in the western United States. A thousand miles of Great Basin desert separate its eastern flank from the Rocky Mountains — an arid, desolate land whitened by salt-encrusted lakes, interspersed with sharp-peaked mountains whose lower slopes harbor spotted forests of pinyon pine and juniper. In the opposite direction, approximately 180 miles west of Sierra Nevada summits, the Coast Ranges fringe the Pacific Ocean. Between Coast and Sierra lies the Central Valley of California, most of it less than 100 feet above sea level. Originally an arid semigrassland, the valley is today a fertile farming, fruit-growing beneficiary of Sierran waters.

To the north the Sierra Nevada merges with the Cascade Range just south of Lassen National Park in northern California. At their border the two ranges are similar in vegetation, but show their different geological origins increasingly as they spread apart: the volcanic Cascades north to form the picturesque cones of Mounts Rainier, Hood, Adams, and Jefferson in Oregon and Washington; the predominantly granitic Sierra Nevada south along the eastern California border to culminate in one of the boldest mountain escarpments in the world. South of this, the Sierra Nevada bends in to meet the Coast Ranges near Tehachapi Pass.

The Cascades and the Rockies are more extensive mountain chains, cut up into many separate ranges. The Sierra Nevada stands alone as the longest, highest single-block mountain range in the United States. It is slightly over 400 miles long and 50 to 80 miles wide. Pushed up as a single tilted block of rock from a "hinge" in the Central Valley, it slopes gradually on the west, steeply on the east. From heights of 9000 feet in the north, its peaks rise to 13,000 feet in the central region and to the 14,495-foot climax of Mount Whitney in the southern Sierra. Around Whitney, twelve peaks of more than 14,000 feet pierce the sky; some of them drop off precipitously nearly two miles to the Great Basin desert below.

This great eastern escarpment ranks as one of the awesome geological features of its kind in the world, a two-mile-high wall formed primarily by a monumental uplift of the Sierran block along a fault in the earth's crust. Sierran geologist François Matthes has recounted that "Albrecht Penck, the dean of European geomorphologists, upon viewing this stupendous mountain front, was visibly affected by its grandeur and begged his guide to leave him for several hours that he might contemplate and study it in solitude." [2]

The Sierra Nevada in its present form is a young range. Along with the Rocky Mountains and Cascades, the Alps and Himalayas, it rose to its current heights in the Tertiary mountain building of 2,000,000 to 25,000,000 years ago. Its geologically new saw-toothed profiles contrast sharply with the rounded, worn-down contours of more ancient chains such as the Appalachians of the eastern United States, which are more than 250,000,000 years old.

Many of the range's most striking features owe their character to the Pleistocene glaciers that blanketed the subalpine heights and flowed down the river canyons, sculpturing cliffs, spires, and domes, broadening valleys into "yosemites" with leaping waterfalls, and pocketing the high country with numberless little rockbound lakes, or tarns. The plants and animals that thrived in this unique complex of soil, rock, climate, and topography showed a diversity unusual in temperate zone coniferous forests. Along with the variety came a magnetic beauty.

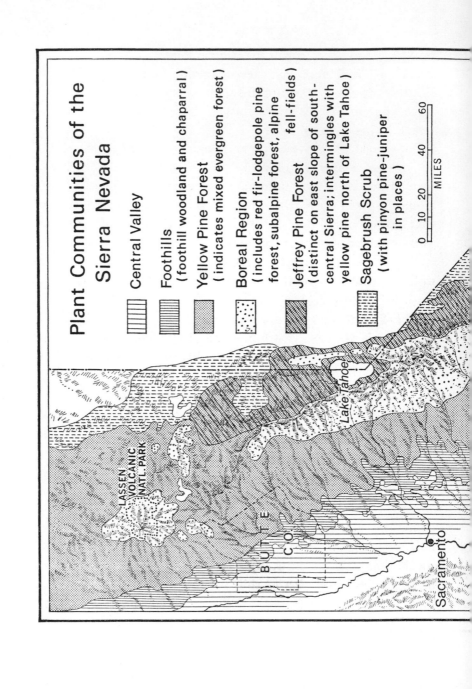

Plant Communities of the Sierra Nevada

Central Valley

Foothills
(foothill woodland and chaparral)

Yellow Pine Forest
(indicates mixed evergreen forest)

Boreal Region
(includes red fir-lodgepole pine
forest, subalpine forest, alpine
fell-fields)

Jeffrey Pine Forest
(distinct on east slope of south-
central Sierra; intermingles with
yellow pine north of Lake Tahoe)

Sagebrush Scrub
(with pinyon pine-juniper
in places)

0 10 20   40   60
MILES

LASSEN
VOLCANIC
NATL. PARK

BUTTE
CO.

Lake Tahoe

Sacramento

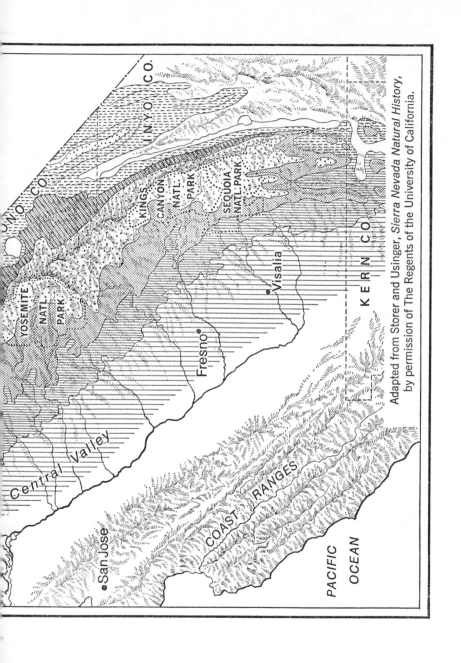

MONO CO.   INYO CO.

KINGS
CANYON
NATL.
PARK

SEQUOIA
NATL. PARK

YOSEMITE
NATL.
PARK

•Visalia

Fresno•

Central Valley

KERN CO.

COAST RANGES

•San Jose

PACIFIC OCEAN

Adapted from Storer and Usinger, *Sierra Nevada Natural History*, by permission of The Regents of the University of California.

Neither of these was lost on John Muir. From the day in 1868 when the young Scottish naturalist walked into the Sierra Nevada until his death in 1914, he sang the praises of the range. From its tawny foothills through its pine and fir forests to timberline, the Sierra was for him a radiant world. From its cone-dropping tree squirrels to black bears met as fellow berry-pickers at brambles, it was an unpredictable, lively world. As he swung in a Douglas fir at the height of a mountain storm, as he slid down into Yosemite Valley on a snow avalanche, as he listened to the song of the dipper on a wild winter morning, as he lay in a mountain meadow watching bees pollinate flowers, Muir felt the joyous pulse of the mountains. He never ceased to feel it: "And after ten years spent in the heart of it, rejoicing and wondering, bathing in its glorious floods of light, seeing the sunbursts of morning among the icy peaks, the noonday radiance on the trees and rocks and snow, the flush of the alpenglow, and a thousand dashing waterfalls with their marvelous abundance of irised spray, it still seems to me above all others the Range of Light, the most divinely beautiful of all the mountain-chains I have ever seen." [3]

Muir's writings largely unveiled the range to the world. His militant fight to preserve its natural beauty was a major national influence in the critical period around the turn of the century, when parks and forest reserves were new ideas that hung by tenuous threads. The Sierra Club, which Muir helped found in 1892, has kept a vigilant eye on trespass of the range's treasures — and, increasingly, the nation's — ever since.

Today's Sierra Nevada contains three national parks (Yosemite, Sequoia, and Kings Canyon), one national monument, (Devils Postpile), nine national forests, and ten state parks. The high southern Sierra above 8000 feet is a vast panoramic wilderness, the roadless haven of summer backpackers and family burro parties. Lower, easier passes broach the northern and central crest, following trails earlier trod by Indians and pioneers, now crossed by highways. A trip up and over these cross-mountain roads from June through October unfolds a succession of changing scenes, different on each pass but similar in the plant belts appearing at equivalent levels.

All high mountains of the world show plant belts, or "life zones," that vary with elevation. The zones are actually intricate plant and animal communities living at altitudes where temperature, moisture, soil, slope, and other environmental conditions meet their needs — and where circumstances of history and evolution have put them. In the Sierra all but the highest communities are accessible by road.[4]

For a close look at the wildlife communities of the range, we shall climb up and over: up the western slope through foothill woodlands of digger pine and oak and thickets of chaparral into the midmountain forests of yellow and sugar pine — and groves of giant sequoias — higher through red firs and lodgepole pines to subalpine forests that lead to timberline, beyond trees to alpine crests, and then down the steep east side into a land mightily different from the one where we began.

2. The Western Foothills

THE SUN SHINES three hundred days out of the year, on an average, in the western foothills of the Sierra Nevada. In winter, when the Central Valley below lies locked in fog, sunshine is frequent above the 1000-foot level; the remainder of the year it is practically guaranteed. Foothill plants are well adapted to their sunny habitats. From lower levels of 200 to 400 feet, where the foothills begin, to their merger with the midmountain forests several thousand feet above they form two distinct plant communities — foothill woodland and chaparral. Through a belt of hills and ravines running the length of the range, twenty or more straight-line miles across, these two communities appear and disappear and intermingle as tightly packed shrub jungles of chaparral alternating irregularly with the open stands of trees and grasses that form the woodlands.

The role of grasses is a unique and historically interesting one in the foothills. In summer, grasses roll in nearly continuous golden-brown waves up the gentle lower slopes from the valley, under the oaks and pine of the woodlands, around the slanting tombstonelike rocks, past the chaparral, all the way to the denser shade of the yellow pine forests at 3000 feet or higher.

This is the hot season. The sun bears down unimpeded day after day, bringing temperatures mostly in the nineties and above. The relative humidity hovers around 20 percent. In this dry, hot atmosphere the woodland grasses and forbs (broad-leaved herbs) drop their seeds early but retain luminous stalks and empty seedcases that sway in the parching breezes all summer. To the casual eye this low growth looks like a well-adapted native ground cover. Well adapted it is; but natural as the ground cover appears, 50 to 90 percent of it is alien. From the time of the Spanish missions, California's grasslands have been prime targets of foreign invasions.

It was probably a nearly virgin flora that greeted the eyes of Father Junipero Serra and his companions when in May 1769 they reached San Diego to begin the conquest of Alta California for the Holy Church and the Spanish crown. The few previous explorers had arrived by sea and had made only transient landings. But, as S. B. Parish describes it, "the followers of Saint Francis brought with them flocks and herds, and in the careful preparations for their expedition they had been particularly charged to provide themselves with a store of seeds of useful plants." [1]

Step by step the long chain of missions stretched northward till the last one was founded near Sonoma in the San Francisco Bay region in 1823. "Everywhere, one of the first proceedings was the planting of gardens and the sowing of fields; and the neophytes, as they gathered in, were taught to be farmers and herdsmen, so that each mission speedily became a hive of industry, based on its wide acres and countless herds." This was the beginning of the end for the native grasses that once covered California's valleys and foothills, the fields "tall in the wind" which Spanish horsemen called the finest pasture, enough for all their flocks and herds. The native grasses, both perennial and annual, along with the wildflowers that splashed yellow, purple, and orange over the hills in spring, formed a uniquely Californian range. Throughout the centuries they had evolved on western soils; they had held their own against the sharp teeth of antelope, deer, elk, and rodents; they had withstood the vagaries of the climate. They had never met the degree of grazing pressure and seed invasion that came with the advent of white men.

The invading seeds arrived in the wool of sheep, in hay carried aboard ships for cattle feed, in droppings of domestic animals, in clothing, on implements, mixed with seeds of garden crops. Once established on the trampled ground around missions or at the edges of fields cleared for farming, the exotic grasses and weeds held on until opportunity favored their spread into the native vegetation of the open range. Nearly all of the invading plants were annuals. Each year they would bear fruit and die, leaving buried in the soil seeds that could resist extreme dryness and germinate when the rains finally came.

Most of the native perennial grasses were well adapted to withstand drought. Like the foothill pine bluegrass (*Poa scabrella*), they could remain dormant from May to November, when rains would stimulate the root clumps to sprout anew. But consecutive years of low rainfall weakened them severely. Early and late heavy grazing reduced further their ability to tolerate drought. When excessive grazing by thousands of longhorn Spanish cattle and long-legged sheep combined with rainless years, as in the great drought of 1828–1830, the native perennials succumbed by the millions, and the great wave of invading plants began its takeover.

Developed in lands with a climate similar to that of their new home in the foothills, the immigrants thrived in competition with the natives, both annual and perennial. Some of them produced good forage; some became pests; most of them, grasses like wild oats (*Avena*), the bromes (*Bromus*), and foxtails (*Hordeum*) — and legumes such as bur clover (*Medicago hispida*) — had the advantage of being self-fertilized. Those first well-adapted individuals that moved into available niches quickly built up large, homogeneous, highly reproductive populations. Through occasional outbreeding, they produced enough genetic variability to infiltrate a wide range of diverse habitats. During the mission period, aliens as common now as ripgut grass (*Bromus rigidus*), foxtail grass, bur clover, wild oats, star thistle (*Centaurea*), and filaree (*Erodium*) spread over the state. Gold Rush days and the increasing arrival of travelers from all parts of the globe brought additional plant introductions, some deliberate, many inadvertent.

The livestock boom of 1850–1870 produced more domestic droves than had ever before descended on the bourgeoning state's grasslands, a peak of 3,000,000 head of cattle and close to 6,000,000 sheep. They fed almost where they pleased. The range country was impossible to fence in those pre-barbed-wire days, and the state's publicly owned lands were wide open to whoever got there first. Sheep migrating up the foothills to the higher Sierra Nevada meadows for summer forage sometimes nibbled the ground bare en route.

All abuse seemed to aid the invading annuals at the expense of the natives. The kind of constant grazing pressure and trampling applied by large numbers of domestic animals proved entirely different from that of wild animals such as antelope and elk. The native grasses had never been exposed to such grazing pressure, and were not adapted to it. Here the introduced Mediterranean annuals held an advantage. Having evolved over thousands of years in direct association with man's flocks and herds, they had become adapted to them.

There was soon hardly a piece of virgin grassland left in California. The Nature Conservancy, a nonprofit organization that preserves samples of American habitats, has tried in vain to purchase one plot of original California grassland.

. . .

Today a cosmopolitan grass and forb population from Europe, Asia, South Africa, Australia, South America, and the eastern United States dominates the California natives still left in foothill grasslands: nearly four hundred foreigners that have taken out apparently permanent residence in the state. The most common central foothill grasses are now annuals — slender wild oat, soft chess (*Bromus mollis*), ripgut grass, common foxtail, red brome (*Bromus rubens*) — and they all are aliens. Among the prominent forbs, broadleaf filaree, bur clover, star thistle, annual clovers (*Trifolium*), and tarweeds predominate. Of these only the last two are native. Many native wildflowers hold their own, but new species are still arriving, undesirables like Medusa-head (*Elymus caput-medusa*), and Italian thistle (*Carduus pycnocephalus*). Even the specialized niche of the native tarweeds may be in danger of being usurped.

The tarweeds (*Hemizonia, Holocarpha*) spread a basal rosette of leaves at the surface of the ground in early spring, at the time when the spring annuals emerge. As the neighboring plants continue through their full blooming cycle, the tarweeds lapse into dormancy. In late summer, during drought and severe heat and in fields long since brown with the dried annuals, tarweeds resume growth at a rapid pace, shoot up viscid stalks and heads of resinous flowers. A more specific adaptation to foothill habitat would be hard to find, yet the tarweed's niche is, in some places, being stolen by yellow star thistle, an introduction from Europe. In the foothills the two plants often occupy complementary niches, the tarweed on relatively sterile soils that have been grazed but not cultivated and yellow star thistle in bottomlands that frequently have been previously cultivated.

Native or introduced, these hardy plants have made themselves at home in one of the rarer climates of the world. Hot dry summers and cool wet winters are unusual around the globe. They occur sparingly on all continents, principally in small areas between 30° and 42° latitude. Within this range lie the countries bordering the Mediterranean Sea, famous for this "Mediterranean" climate.

The western foothills of the Sierra Nevada follow a Mediterranean climatic rhythm that is different from anything in North America east of the Sierra. From May to October scarcely a drop of rain touches the land. Birds finish nesting early. Streams dry up. Flowers wither. Woodland trees nod quietly above the grasses. Only the tarweeds break the dormancy of late summer, thrusting pungent yellow heads above the baked earth. The hills are peaceful, quiet, warm, dry.

With the approach of November, the rains come: sometimes gently, soaking in every drop, sometimes in drenching downpour running brown in the newly awakened streams. Between November and May the land gathers all the moisture it will get to carry the plants through the long dry summer. This varies from eleven inches in the lower mesas to about forty inches in the higher, more forested woodlands. Snow whitens the higher hills for a few brief days most winters, but it is copious rain that kindles the new life.

Within weeks after the first rains, green shoots sprout everywhere. In wet years a layer of green velvet covers much of the summer's old brown by Christmas. Made up of leaf rosettes of filaree, basal leaves of the soap plant (*Chlorogalum pomeridianum*) and other herbs, it is the promise of flowers to come. Growth slows during the cold of December, January, and February, when night temperatures may near freezing. But with the onset of warmer weather in early March everything that grows comes alive.

Native wildflowers burst through the warming earth. Goldfields (*Baeria chrysostoma*), one of the pioneers, spreads its three-inch-high heads over the slopes in a golden blanket, carrying some of the pansy-faced Johnny-jump-ups (*Viola douglasii*) and curious closed flowers of butter-and-eggs (*Orthocarpus*) in its mantle. Tidytips (*Layia fremontii*) wave white-tipped yellow rays among fields of popcorn flowers (*Plagiobothrys*), birds-eye gilia (*Gilia tricolor*), and the miniature magenta clovers (*Trifolium*). The first of the spring succession of brodiaeas breaks ground, blue dicks (*Brodiaea pulchella*), sending up foot-high barren stalks topped by clusters of bluish-purple waxy flowers.

California poppies (*Eschscholzia californica*) no longer flame the hills with the massive color displays that brought the early name, *tierra del fuego*, land of fire; but their brilliant orange still brightens undisturbed roadsides, open flats, and slopes. Lupines are frequent companions, unfurling symmetrical racemes of seemingly endless species and shades of blue, bluish purple, and ivory. (The index of Munz and Keck's *A California Flora* requires two pages of three columns each to list the state's lupines.)

Perhaps the most spectacular of the early wave of wildflowers is meadowfoam (*Limnanthes alba*), which springs out of the pools and wet meadows of the foothills, literally, like a white foam. So close together do its flowers grow that at a distance they seem more like a snowdrift than thousands of white petals lined with bright pink nerves. Distinctively Californian, mead-owfoam requires wet feet and fades to a rose, later a brown, as the pools dry up.

In drier meadows baby blue-eyes (*Nemophila menziesii*) spill across the grass, opening inch-wide corollas of pale blue. Tall spurred delphiniums add a royal-blue touch. As the lower meadows fade the higher ones bloom, and monkey-flowers (*Mimulus*) outline the creeks in brilliant yellow. From March through May there is floral luxuriance somewhere in the foot-hills.

What Sierran foothill flowers were like before the Gold Rush, no one knows. One of the earliest descriptions was left by John Woodhouse Audubon, son of the famous artist-naturalist John James Audubon. Young Audubon, then thirty-seven years old, journeyed overland with a party to the goldfields of California in 1849–1850. In the spring of 1850 he jogged by mule through the Sierran foothills, visiting mining camps and Indian villages. On March 28, 1850, following a trail from Wood's diggings to Hawkin's Bar, not far from the present town of Sonora at the 2000-foot level, he met a foothill floral display at its zenith.

Every turn gives some vista of beauty in this Garden of Eden; the soft southerly breeze is perfumed with the delicate odor of millions of smaller varieties of prairie flowers, in some places so abundant as to color acres, whole hillsides, so thickly as to hide the ground, and my mule had to eat flowers rather than grass. One without home ties might well feel all his days could be passed in the beauties of these valleys, roseate yellow and blue, so soft that the purest sky cannot surpass the color for delicacy. Tangled masses of vines climb everywhere, hiding the hard surfaces of the quartz rocks, and beyond this exquisite vegetation always some view, wild and impressive, meets the eye.[2]

Foothill woodlands, in their higher isolated reaches, are still wild and impressive. The trees consist mainly of silvery green digger pines and a variety of evergreen and deciduous oaks. Occasionally their crowns meet in an enclosing canopy, and the tangles of vines and shrubs are sometimes dense.

The Sierran woodland's nearest counterparts grow in the inner California Coast Ranges, southern California, Arizona, and northern Mexico. Several of these are fairly distant areas with distinct topographic barriers. The Coast Ranges adjoin the Sierra at both ends, are separated from it in between by the 50-mile-wide Central Valley; southern California is cut off from the Sierra by several transverse ranges; Arizona and northern Mexico lie 600 to 1000 miles southwest across an arid desert. How does it happen that such relatively widespread geographic regions share oak woodlands that are much alike yet recognizably different? Studies of fossil plants throughout the western United States by Daniel I. Axelrod, Ralph W. Chaney, Harry D. MacGinitie, and others have turned up some significant clues.

In early Tertiary times, forty to sixty million years ago, the interior of western North America and of California was still inundated by an inland sea. The Sierra Nevada probably formed a low range of hills and harbored a vegetation much different from that growing there today. The forest was of subtropical broad-leaved evergreen trees like those now in the forests of central Mexico at 5000 to 6000 feet. There was ample rain, chiefly in the summers.

As the Tertiary wore on, important changes occurred in world climate; there was a chilling of the oceans and an increase in dry land areas. The Pacific Ocean off California cooled and the land dried inland; the combined effects of the two led gradually to the development of a new climate on the western coast. Winds blowing from a colder ocean onto a dry land were warmed and dried, with little of the former potential for rain in the warm season. By the end of the Tertiary, a Mediterranean climate of wet winters and dry summers had evolved.

Meanwhile, from at least early Tertiary times, a group of plants especially adapted to semiarid climate had been evolving in the dry lands of Arizona and northern Mexico. These plants, mostly small-leaved, drought-resistant shrubs and small trees, thrived under limited seasonal rain, hot summers, and prolonged sun. Some of them were deciduous, dropping their leaves in the driest part of the season. As dry climate expanded over western North America, these plants followed it — north, east, south, and west. By ten to fifteen million years ago they had invaded and dominated the Sierra Nevada western foothills.

Plant migrations such as these sound disarmingly rapid when viewed over a geological epoch; translated to rate per year, the speed of travel slows to a crawl. Daniel Axelrod calculated that these plants migrated the 600 miles from southeastern California to southern Oregon during approximately 16,000,000 years. This averages .0037 mile per century, or 2.37 inches per year.

The flora that had taken over Sierran foothills and much of the semiarid west in the middle and late Tertiary period was a mixture of woodland and chaparral which included many plants adapted to the summer rain and relatively warm climate still prevalent. Paleobotanists have named it the Madro-Tertiary geoflora, signifying a major plant type of wide geographic extent during Tertiary times, originating in the Sierra Madre of Mexico. Relicts of it still survive in the Sierra Madre as well as in limited areas of California.

As the Tertiary drew to a close, tremendous regional uplifts occurred in the western half of the continent. The Sierra Nevada, Cascades, Rocky Mountains, the Basin ranges of Nevada, and the Sierra Madre assumed their present heights. The high mountains and the increased cooling of the oceans brought about major changes in climate. Greater extremes of temperature developed throughout the region; deserts appeared; winter rains became the pattern in the far west.

Sierran woodland and chaparral began to change, by elimination. As summer rains vanished in the Sierran foothills, so did the plants that required them. As the region became colder in winter, plants that could not stand cold disappeared. Those that could adapt to the changes survived and became the nucleus of today's flora. Many of the warmer-weather, summer-rain species, formerly Sierran, are alive today in woodland and chaparral of southern California, in thorn scrub of northern Mexico, and in the Sierra Madrean woodland of the Southwest, where the environment still meets their needs. The deserts now separate them from the Sierra. The uplift of the California transverse ranges (see endpaper map) shut off the Sierran woodland from warmer southern California, restricting it to the cooler winter climate of the foothills surrounding the Central Valley.

In all of these regions the oak woodlands look much alike — a savanna-type growth of spaced trees and grass. The aspect is similar; the species of oaks are different. For in the last few million years of isolation, each region has been a proving ground for the evolution of its own species.

Unquestionably the most distinctive indicator of modern Sierra Nevada foothill woodland is the digger pine (*Pinus sabin-iana*). Sometimes called "the tree you can see right through," the digger has loose, long, pale green needles that cast a sparse shade compared to the ample shade of the tight dark green clusters of higher-mountain pines. The brownish trunk commonly forks and holds in its tops, forty to eighty feet above the ground, clusters of heavy cones six to twelve inches long and half as broad. The cones are full of sweet nuts but armed with fierce upcurved spines and generous resin.

In the few woodland areas where digger pine is missing, perhaps because of lower resistance to fire, oak associates persist. The blue oak (*Quercus douglasii*), a medium-sized deciduous tree of grayish trunk and bluish-green leaves, can take the drier, or xerophytic, soils. Interior live oaks (*Quercus wislizenii*), evergreen trees with dark green shiny leaves, grow to the ground, where they are not browsed, and cast a dense shade. Valley oaks (*Quercus lobata*) sometimes occur in moister sites. On steep rocky slopes, canyon oaks (*Quercus chrysolepis*) and California buckeyes (*Aesculus californica*) often join the "exquisite" tangles of poison oak (*Rhus diversiloba*), western clematis (*Clematis ligusticifolia*), and the blackberries (*Rubus*) that so impressed John Woodhouse Audubon.

. . .

Woodland often occurs on the moister north-facing slopes, with chaparral occupying the sunnier south-facing ones. But the hills are so many and the slope exposures so varied that every sort of habitat mixture emerges. One of the most favorable combinations for wildlife is the marginal zone, or ecotone, between foothill woodland and the yellow pine forests above. The best of both possible worlds seems to blend in a broad mixture of trees and shrubs, an ample ground cover, and a rich assemblage of animal life.

Here, on an April day, the strange courtship dance of the Siera Nevada salamander (*Ensatina eschscholtzi platensis*)[3] takes place among the leaf litter of the moist forest floor. Solitary the rest of the year, these wide-eyed gray and orange-spotted amphibians seek each other's company during the spring breeding period. For a brief while they travel in pairs and court.

The ceremony begins with the male creeping to the side of the female, his five-inch-long body and tail carried close to the ground. As he approaches her head, he reduces his pace to very slow motion, noses her neck, then rubs her face and throat with his. If she responds by tilting her head upward, he slides his body under the elevated head, keeping contact with her throat as he moves slowly past. He comes to a stop with his lower back under her chin and begins to massage her throat with a rotary movement of his hind quarters. If he has captured her interest, she leans her throat against his lower back and follows him as he creeps slowly forward, his back arched sharply upward, his tail trailing between her legs. This "tail walk" may go on for several hours over the forest floor.

Finally, in a spot of his choosing, the male stops, presses his vent against the substratum and begins a lateral rocking on his rear legs. The female keeps time with counterswaying. When the male crawls onward, the spermatophore (mass of spermatozoa mixed with gelatin) that he has deposited stays behind. The pair tail-walks forward till the female squats above the capsule of sperm cells. She pulls it into her vent and inner cloacal chamber with her cloacal lips, the male meanwhile stroking her back with his tail.

Weeks or months later she will lay a clutch of a dozen eggs in an underground rodent burrow or in the softly crumbling interior of a rotten log, fertilizing the eggs with the stored spermatozoa before they leave her body. During the long dry summer she will stand guard over them in their moist, well-insulated nest, often curling her constricted tail around their jelly clusters, keeping them moist with her own body fluids if desiccation threatens. When the first rains of autumn seep into her hideout, she and her newly hatched young will emerge, to go their separate ways for the active season.

The same rains bring other moist-skinned relatives, the arboreal salamanders (*Aneides lugubris*), climbing down from their summer holes in interior live oaks. All sizes, ages, and numbers sometimes use the same quarters. Up to thirty-five individuals have been found sharing one tree hole, scraping off fungi inside the knothole for dry-season diet, while their eggs hang like stalked grape clusters from the ceiling. The largest specimens total almost eight inches in length, smooth brown-skinned amphibians with sparse yellow dots.

Aneides is the agile climber of Sierran lungless salamanders (family Plethodontidae), using expanded toes and a prehensile tail as climbing aids. Like the Sierra Nevada salamander, and other lungless types, it breathes through its skin and throat. Mucous glands scattered throughout the thin skin keep the skin moist. This permits oxygen from the surrounding air to pass through skin pores in a liquid film into the blood vessel network just beneath the surface. A similar vascular network lines the mouth, and air is passed over this lining and absorbed by rhythmic movements of the salamander's throat.

All this necessitates a moist environment to enable breathing. *Aneides* can choose its habitat liberally in the rainy season, feeding on spiders, centipedes, false scorpions, termites, flies, and other insects. The heavy jaw muscles, especially well developed in males, enable it to seize prey as large as the pencil-thin California slender salamander (*Batrachoseps attenuatus*), which uses the same underbark runways. But with the advent of the dry season *Aneides,* in company with other salamanders, must seek a damp retreat.

It has, on occasion, more to fear than the dehydrating air of summer. The common kingsnake (*Lampropeltis getulus*), which roams the foothill woodlands, is a good climber and includes amphibians in its wide-ranging diet. This handsome black-and-white-banded snake, adapted to a variety of United States habitats, is probably most famous for its ability to kill and eat rattlesnakes. In the Sierran foothills it meets them at regular intervals, since the western rattlesnake (*Crotalus viridis*) frequents wooded grassy areas with rocky outcrops, chaparral, and streamside canyons.

Rattlesnakes occur in many plant belts of the Sierra Nevada to the 8000-foot level or even higher. Their abundance varies locally from none to plenty. Their enemies number more than might be suspected for a poisonous reptile. Many snakes besides kingsnakes are immune in large degree to rattlesnake venom. Striped racers (*Masticophis lateralis*) take a periodic toll of rattlesnakes in chaparral areas. Recent experiments indicate that a rattlesnake can sense the approach of possible enemies such as kingsnakes, racers, and whipsnakes by detecting certain odorous substances in the skin. These cause the rattler to retreat with its head and neck held close to the ground and showing no inclination to rattle or strike.

Foothill rattlers come out of hibernation when temperatures rise above 70° F., usually in mid-March, and are most abundant in the balmy months of April, May, and June. Summer heat drives them to hole up in burrows or rock crevices during the day and seek food at dusk and during the night. The temperature-sensitive structure contained in the pit below the eyes helps them locate the warm-blooded cottontail rabbits, ground squirrels, voles, and pocket mice, California quail and brown towhees which are their chief prey. Most foothill hikers never see a rattlesnake; the snakes usually vanish silently unless caught unawares. But, like the ticks of the chaparral, they are a potential hazard to respect.

Sometimes mistaken for a rattlesnake is the nonpoisonous Pacific gopher snake (*Pituophis melanoleucus catenifir*) of the foothill grasslands. The Pacific gopher snake's mottled tan and brown back pattern can superficially resemble a rattler's as it melts into summer grass. And when alarmed, a gopher snake may vibrate its tail, producing in dry grass a sound much like the feared rattle. Its ability to vibrate the epiglottis, so that air can be sucked through in a loud hiss, and to spread its head, adds further to the impression of a viper. These habits may be the basis of the erroneous story that rattlesnakes and gopher snakes occasionally interbreed to produce a dangerous hybrid, the hybrid species, the "bull rattler," having the option of poisoning or squeezing its prey to death. Actually the Pacific gopher snake kills by constriction only. Like its eastern United States counterpart the bullsnake, it climbs trees in search of young and the eggs of birds. And it is equally adept at digging — loosening dirt with its snout, then hooking out the soil in a loop of the neck. This technique gains entrance to plugged holes and runways of gophers, mice, ground squirrels, and other rodents that it hunts effectively.

While many snakes and lizards, and some birds and mammals, move freely between the two major foothill communities —

woodland and chaparral — the dominant woody plants of the two are very distinct. The densely aggregated masses of evergreen shrubs that make up chaparral form one of the unique vegetative habitats of the world. The word chaparral is a Spanish-Californian derivative of the Spanish *chaparro,* meaning scrub oak, an evergreen oak common in much California chaparral.

Sometimes known as elfin forest or Mediterranean scrub forest, chaparral grows primarily around the borders of the Mediterranean Sea, in central Chile, the southern tip of Africa, southwestern Australia, and parts of Mexico, in addition to California and Arizona in the United States. Along the Mediterranean chaparral is known as machis. In South Africa it is called macchia, or *fynbos,* an Afrikaans word for small bushy vegetation. Australians speak of it as mallee scrub. Everywhere it presents a nearly impenetrable shrub front five to eight feet high, with a few taller plants shooting up to heights of perhaps fifteen feet. The species of plants that compose it are distinct for each part of the world, but their growth aspects and their adaptations to their semiarid environments have much in common.

Sierran chaparral, though long since adapted to summer-dry climate, still carries links to the summer-rain chaparral of Arizona, its ancestral home region. A number of shrubs are common to the two areas, among them deerbrush (*Ceanothus integerrimus*), mountain mahogany (*Cercocarpus betuloides*), hollyleaf redberry (*Rhamnus crocea ilicifolia*), and gooseberry (*Ribes quercetorum*). In addition, such California chaparral species as fremontia (*Fremontodendron*) and tree poppy (*Dendromecon rigida*) occur elsewhere only as relicts in central Arizona chaparral.

In California, chaparral covers about one twelfth of the state, spread widely over the southern mountains, in arid sections of the Coast Ranges, and as a discontinuous band throughout the length of the western Sierra Nevada foothills. Sierran foothill chaparral is the dominant vegetation in its region. It forms the climax plant community that will replace itself over and over again under natural conditions, which include fire.

The shrubs are adapted in every conceivable way to the rigors of the long dry summers and withering heat. Their leaves are tough, waxy, and often small, reducing evaporation to a minimum. The larger leaves carry sunken stomata (pores) to further preserve moisture. Their roots, as in the widespread dominant, chamise, may extend far deeper into the coarse rocky soils than the plant's height above ground.

So tight a web do the stiff branches make that a man attempting to push his way through mature chaparral will wear himself out and within a few hundred yards tear any but the toughest clothing. This is why cowboys of the early West used to wear trouserlike leggings of leather over their blue jeans. These flared breeches were called chaps, an abbreviation of the Mexican-Spanish word *chapajeros,* meaning apparel for chaparral. Chaps provide equal protection against thickets and burrs and rope burns and are still a part of some brush riders' gear today.

Chaparral shrubs follow closely the seasonal pattern of their Mediterranean climate. Growth in chamise begins in January after winter rains have permeated the soils, accelerates in April and May, terminates in June. August and September are the chaparral's dormant "winter."

No plant demonstrates this seasonal adaptation more dramatically than the oddly picturesque California buckeye of the dry foothill slopes and canyons. The pale green compound leaves of this small deciduous tree unfurl in February, long before the blue oak buds show any sign of bursting. The buckeye is the first fresh green tree of spring in the foothills. By May its white flower spikes have come and gone. By late July the leaflets dangle withered and brown. Their drying retains water that would otherwise be lost through their pores. Pearlike fruits appear in August on branches that remain functionally leafless and crookedly silver for six months of the year.

Chaparral shows considerable diversity in the Sierran foothills. The dominant plants vary with the region and local conditions. One of the most common and widespread chaparral shrubs is chamise (*Adenostoma fasciculatum*), the *chamiso* of the early Spanish Californians. Pure stands of chamise cover miles of south-facing slopes with a uniform growth of woody bushes four to eight feet high, each clothed with fasciculate bunches of short green needlelike leaves. Much of the year the terminal growth carries the brown seedcases of last June's flowers, giving a characteristic green-brown tone to entire hillsides.

Mature chamise chaparral is notably meager in wildlife. Its thin leaves offer scanty shade on the bush and decompose slowly into a sparse, acid humus that repels most plant life except fungi. Recent studies have disclosed some details of the inhibiting process. The leaves, flowers, litter, and roots of chamise contain water-soluble and heat-labile saponins and unsaturated lactones. These accumulate in certain soils (mostly poor noncalcic stony and sandy types and shallow lithosols) to act as inhibitors of the germination and growth of grasses. The effect is so distinct that on steeper slopes chamise sometimes separates itself from adjacent grassland by a bare strip as much as nine feet wide.

When chamise grows on calcareous soils or on serpentine or on deeper, more fertile clays, its plant toxins seem to be canceled out — effectively absorbed or decomposed by a combination of microbiological and chemical activity that allows a subshrub and grass understory to appear.[4]

In addition to forming pure stands, chamise is a common member of the mixed chaparral community in the Sierran foothills. At least forty species of shrubs occur in many combinations from north to south, interlaced with vines like western clematis, wild cucumber (*Marah*), and poison oak. It is the mixed stands that support most chaparral wildlife. Here grow the ample berries of toyon (*Heteromeles arbutifolia*), California coffeeberry (*Rhamnus californica*), and the manzanitas (*Arctostaphylos*). Acorns from scrub oaks add to the insect crop and to seeds of the many species of *Ceanothus*, mountain mahogany, flowering ash (*Fraxinus dipetala*), and others. Chaparral thus supplied with food and cover, yet open enough to provide variable spaces for animal travel, contains a representative wildlife population.

. . .

One's best chance to observe the wildlife undetected comes on hikes along isolated dirt roads or the fire lanes cut through some chaparral. You never know what will cross the road just ahead of you and disappear into the sheltering brush, or what may be lying along the road's edge unmoving, like the striped racer that startled me one day. It could almost have passed for a garter snake — slim and black with an ivory stripe down each side — except for the long, tapering racer tail. I crept up on it cautiously, taking photographs at ten feet, seven, five, four. I began to wonder if it were alive; not a flicker of life showed. The body lay round and firm, its scales smooth and glistening and lacking the keels of the garter snake. The neck looked a bit flattened, the big eye stared. As I bent over the snake it rippled into the brush, out of sight in an instant. Striped racers are among the West's fastest snakes, estimated to attain speeds up to eight miles per hour. They can glide swiftly through the interlacing branches of chaparral, at home in any height of the shrub jungle.

Chaparral birds are, by nature of the habitat, difficult to see. Occasional small trees that protrude above the shrub mass serve as singing posts, but the singers are more often heard than seen. Unquestionably the most abundant bird in mature chaparral is the wrentit. It virtually typifies chaparral, since total distribution is only slightly more extensive than that of foothill chaparral itself. Found solely on the Pacific Coast of the United States, wrentits belong to a family of their own, the Chamaeidae, and are closely related to the dippers and wrens. Some authorities, however, regard them as isolated offshoots of the large Old World family of babblers.

Brown sparrow-sized birds with a white iris and long cocky tail, wrentits behave somewhat like wrens slipping through the brush. Their strong legs and maneuverable wings enable them to hop and flit from twig to twig "as fast as a man can run with no shrubs to block his way." [5] They rarely make flights of more than thirty feet, instead staying within the brush, where they maintain year-round territories and sing throughout the year. It is unusual for small perching birds to mate for life; banding experiments at Strawberry Canyon, Berkeley, indicate that wrentits are an exception.

The song is the only indication of the bird's presence that most chaparral observers get — the wrentit's secretiveness is legend. The bird's song rings out loud and clear, unmistakable once learned. The male starts with a series of slow staccato notes all on one pitch, then speeds them into a final trill. The female omits the speeded-up trill.

Wrentits make up one fourth to one third of the bird population in southern and coastal California chaparral areas where census counts have been taken. They appear equally abundant in Sierran foothill chaparral, but detailed studies remain to be made. Scrub jays, although not restricted to chaparral, are prominent in it. They control wrentit numbers somewhat by robbing nests and they add a touch of bright blue to a bird world dominated by browns and tans. The California thrasher, wrentit, bushtit, Bewick's wren, and brown towhee — which is partial to chaparral edges — are all drab brown in color.

The California quail blends camouflage and brightness; the male's brown back is complemented by a black and white face and throat pattern; the short black head plume, curving forward from the crown, bobs with each step. The quail, California's state bird, prefers somewhat broken chaparral with dense-foliaged trees nearby for night roosting and water within walking distance. It slips easily through the spaces on the elfin forest floor in its search for seeds and berries. All winter long, its three-syllabled call which translates perfectly as *Chi-ca'-go,* can be heard at intervals.

At nesting time the coveys break into pairs. These choose territories which the males guard from singing perches, sometimes uttering the explosive "All's well" signal every fifteen seconds or so. When nesting is finished, the heat of summer is usually in full swing. California quail then often migrate up to the 4000-foot level, where summer water and food are more abundant, sometimes overlapping the range of the mountain quail at this season. When the rains come, they return to the foothills.

Not all of them make it. The gray fox (*Urocyon cinereoar-*

genteus) keeps an eye out for quail, as well as for mice, brush
rabbits, and woodrats of the chaparral. And bobcats, coyotes,
and Cooper's hawks are all known to relish a plump, juicy quail.
The fox may sometimes be seen in the daytime following a
trail, sniffing a hole. It has been estimated that favored chaparral areas support as many as four gray foxes per square mile.
They are graceful creatures, the size of a small dog, steel-gray
with reddish-yellow flanks and black hairs along the top of the
back and tail. Retiring in the presence of other predators such
as raccoons, they are patient hunters. Their tree-climbing agility is unusual for members of the dog family. One that I knew
denned in an interior live oak knothole five feet above the
ground to produce its four pups. This fox ranges into the yellow pine forests of the Sierra Nevada but not into the high-
mountain realm of the red fox (*Vulpes fulva*).

Bobcats (*Lynx rufus*) are wider travelers, living in every
plant belt from valley to timberline. They sometimes crouch in
the mottled shadow of chaparral edges, eyes following any movement. The timid brush rabbit (*Sylvilagus bachmani*), which
seldom hops more than a few feet from its hiding place in a
dense thicket, may venture farther in search of tasty grasses.
The bobcat's stalk tests the rabbit's alertness. The lithe cat is
one of the major controllers of the chaparral's small-mammal
population. In addition to rabbits, it crops deer mice (*Peromyscus*), pocket mice (*Perognathus*), pocket gophers (*Thomomys*), California ground squirrels (*Citellus beecheyi*), and
woodrats (*Neotoma*).

Woodrats survive many enemies. Widely distributed throughout western North America from the Yukon to Guatemala, this
rat occupies every sort of habitat from mountains to deserts.
It superficially resembles the introduced Norway rat, but is a

much more appealing mammal. The fur is softer, the under-parts are white; and the tail is furry or hairy, not scaly as in the Norway rat.

The two Sierran species occur in widely separated plant belts. The larger bushytail woodrat (*Neotoma cinerea*) lives in rock crevices of the high country, from 6500 feet upward, and the dusky-footed woodrat (*N. fuscipes*) inhabits chaparral thickets and woodlands of the foothills. Both are known as "trade rats" or "pack rats" because of their habit of carrying off objects that they drop, or trade, for more attractive ones.

In the years before this habit was well documented, some curious incidents occurred in the wild. Walter Fry, one of the early naturalists at Sequoia National Park, tells of a camping trip he took in September 1899, with Professor W. F. Dean, to the Castle Rocks area of Sequoia National Park, altitude 8900 feet. They spread their blankets on the ground and, since the weather was quite cold, slept with most of their clothing on. Before retiring, Dean took from his pocket three goldpieces and a small amount of silver and placed them, along with a spectacles case holding his gold-rimmed glasses, in his hat at the side of the bed.

In the morning the money and spectacles were gone. In their place was a round ball of horse dung slightly larger than a walnut. Dean asked Fry what kind of trick he was playing on him. Fry was perplexed. Neither of them at that time knew anything about woodrats. After breakfast they threw a canvas over their camping gear and left to inspect the four hundred and eighty acres that Dean owned nearby.

As they returned at dusk, they saw a bushytail woodrat run from their camping supplies to a nearby rockpile, carrying a spoon in its mouth. Hastily they dismantled the rockpile. Beneath it, beside a soft grassy nest, they found not only the money and glasses but their two table knives, forks, and spoons.

"Never shall I forget the incident," wrote Fry, "which caused both of us some eleven hours of continuous worry and came mighty nigh to destroying what proved later a lifelong friendship." [6]

Fourteen years later, Fry watched the woodrat's trading technique at even closer hand. On this trip, in August 1913, he tented with a detachment of soldiers at Alta Meadow, 8600 feet high in Sequoia National Park. As Fry and Sergeant McCall lay on their cots, reading by a dim candle at about nine o'clock one evening, they noticed a bushytail woodrat slyly enter through the tent flap carrying a small bone in its mouth. It moved alongside a sack of potatoes, dropped the bone, and picked up a potato that was lying loose. Scrambling up over a pile of stovewood onto a bench, it found a small cake of soap. Dropping the potato, it took a bite of the soap, picked it up, and jumped to the tent floor near an eight-inch saw file. It examined the file thoroughly, then picked up its soap and ran to McCall's cot, where the sergeant's large corncob pipe was lying. Here it dropped the soap, sniffed into the pipe, sneezed twice, picked up the pipe, and moved over to some cavalry spurs. After scrutinizing the spurs, it picked up one of them and started dragging it toward the tent flap. With that the men drove the woodrat into the night.

Foothill woodrats build bulkier nests than their high-Sierran relatives. The house of the dusky-footed woodrat sometimes stands six feet high and almost as wide at the base. It is a rainproof shelter made of sticks, cow manure, tin cans, barbed wire, campers' silverware — anything the owner happens to carry home. Many other foothill animals share crevices in these quarters: fence swifts, arboreal salamanders, deer mice, triatoma bugs. A woodrat may own several houses, each containing nest chambers that connect with runways into nearby logs or ground cover to facilitate escape. The mounds frequently stand in the center of gooseberry thickets, which form an almost impregnable barrier to large predators.

The woodrat usually forages within twenty-five yards of his home, seeking berries, seeds, and grasses — any plant materials. Slightly over a foot long, this brownish-gray rodent with the clear white throat is of suitable meal size for most carnivores in the vicinity. If the striped skunk (*Mephitis mephitis*) doesn't surprise him at dusk, there is always the risk that the ringtail (*Bassariscus astutus*) will, toward midnight.

The ringtail is one of the more strictly nocturnal foothill mammals. On moonlight nights it carries its long, furry, black-and-white-banded tail arched high over its back when hunting among the boulders of brushy slopes. Its slim agile body, slightly larger than a gray squirrel's, merges into an inquiring pointed face. The large brown eyes, set off by nearly encircling white borders, peer with an acute curiosity.

In the chaparral and rocky slopes of the western and southwestern United States, where it dwells, the ringtail's distribution corresponds closely to that of its chief prey, woodrats and deer mice. In these areas it dens mainly in rock openings and hollow limbs of trees.

But it has always been quick to take advantage of the shelter of buildings. In the mining boom of more than a century ago, the animal was commonly called "miner's cat" because it moved into miners' cabins and kept them free of mice and pack rats. Visitors to the old movie house in Yosemite Valley in the 1930s recall the ringtails that stole the show chasing each other over the rafters. In the Sierra Nevada the ringtail follows favored habitats to 7000 feet, often utilizing mountain cabins for food and shelter.

The largest mammals in the foothill belt, the mountain lion and the mule deer, both range to timberline. In California's untrammeled past, another powerful animal occupied the foothill scene, one that perhaps exerted more influence on its wildlife than any species around today. The grizzly bear (*Ursus horribilis*) once made most of California its domain. It wore conspicuous trails in the chaparral; it sought out resting places beneath the interlocking branches; it ate berries of manzanita, poison oak, toyon, elderberry, coffeeberry, and acorns from nearby oaks. It dug out the rodents and brodiaea bulbs with its huge front claws, and gobbled up yellow jacket nests.

The grizzly vanished from California before its relationship to the land and wildlife could be ecologically assessed. But Tracy I. Storer and Lloyd P. Tevis, Jr., who surveyed all available historical literature in *California Grizzly*, expressed no doubt as to the big bear's role. "The grizzly must have been a dominant element in the original native biota of California — it was usually avoided by the Indians, and because of its size, prowess, and temperament it could preempt any available food." [7]

Its adaptability in diet was exceeded by no other local mammal. The grizzly was a big resourceful beast weighing as much as 1000 pounds or more, with tremendous daily food demands that left their mark on the coinhabitants of its home area. The only creature to whom the grizzly gave a wide berth was *el sorillo*, the skunk.

Before white men invaded California, there was space for Indians and grizzlies. When active hunting between 1849 and 1870 killed off the grizzlies in the valleys, the survivors took to the most rugged, isolated spots on the western Sierra Nevada slopes. A few scattered to the very crest of the range. The areas in which they held out longest were those where heavy and continuous chaparral kept out the sheepherder. The last California grizzly of certain record was shot in 1908, but there were fragmentary reports of the big grizzled beast with the shoulder hump in Sequoia National Park as late as 1924.

Grizzlies were common in the chaparral lands of northwestern Mexico and adjoining Arizona and New Mexico as late as 1892. By 1968 all had been extirpated except a small population that still persists in the upper Yaqui Basin of Sonora, Mexico. Grizzlies today occur primarily in the Rocky Mountains of the northern United States and Canada, and in Alaska.

Hunting in California is currently regulated by the California Fish and Game Commission. Despite some disagreement among game specialists, conservationists, and stockmen as to the numbers of mountain lions, deer, and tule elk which have a right to share the land, no species of large hunted mammal within the state stands in obvious and imminent danger of following the grizzly's path to extinction.[8]

. . .

The future of foothill animals depends on what happens to their habitat. Some foothill acreage lies within the jurisdiction of the United States Forest Service. Some is public domain land under the aegis of the Bureau of Land Management. Much is privately owned and used principally for raising cattle and sheep.

Chaparral has long been recognized by many soil conservationists as a valuable watershed cover that absorbs heavy rains and helps prevent mudslides, eroding gullies, and floods in the

valleys below. Its usefulness as a land sponge varies tremen-
dously with the age and shrub composition of the chaparral, the
amount and type of leaf litter and humus, the soil and the gradient of the slope. Many stockmen, however, rate all chaparral as
worthless. Mature dense chaparral affords almost no cattle feed
and consequently is being bulldozed, burned, and seeded to pasture in thousands of steadily increasing acres throughout the
foothill belt. Much of this habitat eradication has been subsi-
dized, from 1950 to the present, by the United States Department of Agriculture. The Department's Agricultural Stabiliza-
tion and Conservation Program operates on the premise that
our country needs more beef, hence more grazing lands, and
that other plants which compete with grass for water should be
eliminated.

Eliminating chaparral is not a simple procedure, for chaparral
is a rugged fire-adapted vegetation that evolved in the continued
presence of fire long before man's arrival on the scene. In unprotected situations few chaparral stems can be found which are
more than twenty-five years old: lightning fires throughout eons
have pruned the elfin forest and kept it young. Chaparral shrubs
adapt to fire in two readily observed ways. Some sprout from
buried root crowns after their tops are destroyed. Others produce heavy crops of seeds throughout their lives, seeds with hard
coats that require a fire's heat to crack them for good germination. Some plants use both means. During the first year after an
ordinary burn, the root sprouters such as chamise, scrub oak,
and mountain mahogany send up vigorous green shoots. The
fire-stimulated seeds of the manzanitas, ceanothus, and other
nonsprouters begin, more slowly, to grow. Grasses and invading
herbs — redstem filaree, miner's lettuce, golden brodiaea —
meanwhile move in and quickly cover much of the burned

ground with a profusion of seed and color. The seeds attract California quail, mourning doves, western meadowlarks, lark sparrows, and other adjacent-grassland birds. For three to five years this grassy herbaceous vegetation, with its bird and mammal life, dominates the stripped chaparral area. Deer browse on the new green shoots.

But by the fifth year the brush sprouts shoot up, close the canopy, shade out most of the grasses, and take over. Grassland birds disappear. Chaparral birds return from adjoining areas. Resident small mammals, which survived in rock crevices and burrows, increase to normal populations. The many-faceted song of the Bewick's wren once again rings out from a shrub cover that will become increasingly dense with each year — until the next fire — or until stockmen employ techniques to keep the region "permanently" in grass.[9]

Although foothill chaparral often looks monotonously alike to the cursory traveler, it holds many hidden diversities for the botanist. California is especially rich in species of plants that grow in only very limited areas. Geneticist G. Ledyard Stebbins of the University of California at Davis recently calculated that per unit of area the state has more than sixty times as many of these localized species, known as endemics, as northeastern North America. Only Spain, the Cape region of South Africa, and the Middle East can compare with California in this regard.

The Sierra Nevada has provided, over time, the variations of topography, temperature, rainfall, and soil that foster the development of restricted species. One of the more intriguing endemics grows in the central Sierran foothills near Ione. For about two miles the landscape along Highway 88 is dominated by a low-growing, heathlike shrub, Ione manzanita (*Arctostaphylos myrtifolia*). It occurs only here and on several "islands" like it a few miles north and south. The plant's tiny, elliptic, leathery leaves are brightened in January and February by clusters of pink and white bell-like flowers. The rest of the year its gnarled stems spread a brittle semiprostrate cloak of bronzed green over the earth.

Several other rare plants grow on the same ecological island. Woolyleaf ceanothus (*Ceanothus tomentosus*), a shrub with striking leaves dark green above and usually matted wool below, occupies some of the depressions. Its flowers of deep blue come out in April and May. Where the spaces between the Ione manzanita are a little wider and the gradient a little steeper than usual, the shrubby rockrose (*Helianthemum suffrutescens*) spreads its low, densely hairy branches and yellow flowers. One of the Sierra's two recorded species of rockrose, this species is confined to the Ione vicinity.

The rarest plant on the island, however, is an undistinguished-looking wild buckwheat that survives on the most barren, inhospitable hillsides where nothing else can grow. This species, *Eriogonum apricum,* was first discovered and described in the mid-1950s by John Thomas Howell of the California Academy of Sciences. G. Ledyard Stebbins says it "is so different from the 75 other species of Eriogonum in California that specialists who study the genus have been unable to determine its nearest relative." The plant is a low grower, with small roundish leaves that lie flat on the ground, and branching stems that support tiny whitish flowers in midsummer. A few years ago, on a field trip in the Ione hills, Stebbins could spread his arms over the only known specimens and proclaim to his colleagues, "I can cover with my arms all of the *Eriogonum apricum* in the world." Since then a few more patches have been found nearby.

At the periphery of the Ione manzanita island, the usual live oaks and taller gray manzanitas of the regular chaparral-woodland take over, and beyond them, the familiar blue oak woodland. But these common trees and shrubs are as completely barred from the Ione island as the islanders are from ordinary foothill terrain.

The reason seems to be principally soil — the unusual soil of the Ione island. Phenomenally acid, it carries a pH rating of 3 to 4, ranking at the far acid end of a scale where 7 is neutral and alkaline ranges to 14. In addition, it is extremely poor in minerals that most plants need for growth, hence in all ways a soil hostile to ordinary foothill plants. Composed of a hardpan clay of unique texture, it was deposited along the shores of the inland sea that covered the Central Valley of California some fifty million years ago. Perhaps Ione manzanitas once spread their low olive-green thickets abundantly along these same valley margins.

Fifty million years brought intensive geological and climatic changes, among them the reduction of the former seashore margins to occasional outpockets of clay. Today's Ione manzanita exists as a holdover from an environment once more common. Ecologically it is a relict species. Relicts usually persist as long as their habitats do. In Ione manzanita's case, this may not be as long as it might have been. The clay of the Ione island is of an excellent texture for ceramic products and is being commercially mined for this purpose at present.

Farther south, in the Sierran foothills east of Fresno, another rare plant holds out in a very limited range. This one, *Carpenteria californica,* is a good-sized bush that grows right in with mixed chaparral and scattered woodland trees on moderately steep foothill slopes. Carpenteria is thought to be a relict of former times when the climate was more moist than it is now. The gradual climatic desiccation apparently restricted the species to the few less harsh sites it occupies today, most of them along foothill tributaries of the San Joaquin River. Its entire world distribution encompasses a longitudinal range of about twenty miles and an altitudinal range of 1500 to 4000 feet. Within this zone, its occurrence is sporadic; locally it may be quite abundant, nearby entirely absent. The shrub is a spreading type, many-stemmed from the ground, ranging from six to twelve feet tall; frequently four or more individuals form a huge clump. Long evergreen leaves hide a rather unusual bark, smooth and of light buckskin color, and shed in paper-thin sheets. The flowers are particularly appealing, over two inches across, with usually six white petals surrounding a central core of more than one hundred rich golden stamens.

Carpenteria was for many years "the lost shrub" of California's botanical history. Originally collected by General John C. Frémont in 1846 in "the Sierra Nevada of California, probably on the headwaters of the San Joachin," its location remained a mystery for nearly thirty years. In 1876 Gustav Eisen exhibited specimens found in the foothills east of Fresno, and the limited range of the rare shrub soon became known.

A part of carpenteria's range lies within Sierra National Forest. Where the plant grows thickly, its blossoms form sparkling clusters over the mountainside at the end of May. They stand apart from the white spikes of California buckeyes and the flat-topped white heads of elderberry by their brighter, cleaner look, and often bloom at the same time as golden fremontias. Around and among them grow redbuds (*Cercis occidentalis*), choke cherries (*Prunus virginiana*), bladdernut (*Staphylea bolanderi*), hoptrees (*Ptelea crenulata*), gooseberry, manzanitas, yerba santa (*Eriodictyon*), ceanothus, Sierra plum (*Prunus subcordata*), poison oak, California laurel, and others. The usually common chamise is strangely absent.

Wild cucumbers twine the scattered live oaks. Occasional digger pines rise from a knoll. The views lead to blue mountains beyond. In the lushness of spring it would be difficult to find a more idyllic foothill setting. The chaparral is rich, some of it rare. And nearby are the moister, deeper soils where woodland trees grow in profusion; where ash-throated flycatchers and Bullock's orioles nest; where plain titmice whistle querulous tunes and Nuttall's woodpeckers hitch up the furrowed trunks toward a foothill sky.

3. Midmountain Forests

In the late 1800s, tourists and scientists traveled long distances to visit the newly publicized forests of the Sierra Nevada. Among them were such renowned botanists as the American Asa Gray and the Englishman Sir Joseph Hooker. Sitting around a mountain campfire one night with Gray and Hooker, John Muir asked Hooker, who had seen and studied most of the great forests of the world, if he knew any coniferous forest that rivaled the Sierra's. Hooker's reply was decisive. "No," he said. "In the beauty and grandeur of individual trees, and in number and variety of species, the forest of the Sierra surpasses all others." Nearly a century later his evaluation still stands.

The midmountain forests of the Sierra Nevada's western slope begin where the foothill woodlands end. From roughly 2500 to 6000 feet they cover the broadest timbered segment of the range, a region of mellow summer climate, moderate winters, and varied plant and animal life.

Dominating this forest belt is the western yellow pine, or ponderosa pine (*Pinus ponderosa*). Widely distributed throughout the western United States in several racial forms and subject to greater variations in temperature and precipitation than nearly any other North American tree, this versatile conifer reaches its prime growth in Sierran montane forests. Here the broad-plated yellowish-tan trunks of mature pines rise from sunlit forest floors brown with needles. In favored sites they attain diameters of eight feet and heights exceeding two hundred feet, soaring well above the California black oaks (*Quercus kelloggii*) and incense cedars (*Calocedrus decurrens*). The incense cedars, as well as the sugar pines (*Pinus lambertiana*), which grow in the middle and upper reaches of the zone, are almost exclusively Californian, with a slight overlap into Oregon's Cascade mountains; the white firs *(Abies concolor)*, common associates, occur widely throughout much of the West. All can form, as Hooker said, specimens of "beauty and grandeur."

The broad belt of yellow pine forest is dissected at frequent intervals by deep canyons. Cut by the ten master rivers and their tributaries, later plucked and quarried by glaciers, the canyons expose the granite core of the range, particularly in the central and southern sectors. Sometimes the granite forms massive monoliths, unbroken by any stress; sometimes it rises in vertically jointed blocks hundreds of feet high; sometimes it rounds off in domes that exfoliate loose layers of rock as an onion sheds its skin; sometimes it forms cliffs of small-jointed blocks.

Wherever exposed rocks of the canyon walls develop cracks into which water seeps, freezes, and expands, fragments break loose and go tumbling down to join the jumbles of rock below. This sloping rock mass at the base of cliffs, known as talus, shelters many animals — from insects to lizards and carnivores. Talus slopes occur commonly in the Sierra, from middle elevations to the bases of the highest cliffs.

On the older talus slopes and in adjacent canyons of the middle elevations grow the trees of the mixed evergreen forest community. Douglas firs (*Pseudotsuga menziesii*) send up tall spires softened with downsweeping streamers. California laurels (*Umbellularia californica*) hug the slopes, their long shiny leaves emitting the aroma of "bay" when bruised. The rare California nutmeg (*Torreya californica*) flanks some canyons with its small checkered trunks and dark green foliage. In summer the nutmegs dangle miniature avocadolike fruits over beds of old sharp-pointed needles. It was the resemblance of their wrinkled seed coat to the true nutmeg of the Molucca Islands that gave the Sierran tree its common name. It is actually a member of the yew family.

The most abundant tree of the canyon slopes is a species of several growth forms as well as many names. The canyon oak (*Quercus chrysolepis*) is equally known as goldcup or goldencup oak for the velvety golden cups that hold its acorns; canyon live oak because of its evergreen leaves; golden oak for the golden fuzz on the leaf undersides; maul oak because of its tough wood, so strong that pioneers used it for the heads of mauls, or hammers. In canyons of the Merced, Kings, Kern, and other rivers, canyon oak often grows straight and clean of branches for forty or more feet, sometimes reaching one hundred feet in total height — the deeper the canyon the taller the oak. But among the huge granite boulders of Yosemite Valley's north talus slopes it becomes a different tree. From a short thick base mighty branches, successively dividing, wind into a dome-shaped crown sometimes one hundred and twenty feet across, lower branches trailing to the ground or supported by gigantic rocky buttresses.

Whatever form the tree takes, tall or open-grown, its acorns and abundant leaf insects attract many birds and tree-climbing mammals to the canyon oak areas. Band-tailed pigeons swallow the acorns entire. Gray squirrels relish them. More than fifty kinds of fly and wasp larvae grow to adulthood in the multi-shaped galls on the tree's leaves and twigs.

The colorful nymphalid butterfly, the California sister (*Limenitis bredowii*), flies regularly about canyon oaks, host trees on which she lays eggs and where her caterpillars get their start. The sister's black wings, marked with two vertical white streamers and large orange tips, are as distinctive as her flight style. She alternates a few rapid wingbeats with a glide in which the wings are held just below the horizontal. Boisduval's hairstreak (*Habrodais grunus*) is another butterfly that prefers the canyon oak domain. A one-inch brownish creature unusual for its crepuscular or dim light habits, it sometimes flies in the semidarkness before dawn or hovers above the oaks well after the last rays of sunlight have deserted the canyon walls.

The deeper rock crevices hold ringtails and spotted skunks, which come out at night to forage. Brush heaps conceal western fence lizards (*Sceloporus*) doing their curious push-ups off and on during the day and alligator lizards (*Gerrhonotus*) climbing sinuously through the thickets, purple tongues flicking, in search of crickets, spiders, termites, ground beetles.

Sometimes the secretive Gilbert's skink (*Eumeces gilberti*) moves in from adjacent open forest floor to hunt for insects among the surface cover in late afternoon. This colorful lizard sports a brilliant blue tail and striped back in youth; both change to an overall copper color in the adult. If attacked the skink drops its tail and often escapes while the wriggling tail holds the surprised enemy's attention. A new tail soon grows, usually not quite as smooth in its body connection as the original, often a different color and of somewhat different structure, but functional in helping the lizard maintain proper balance in locomotion.

Many lizards possess this ability — known as autotomy, or self-cutting — to break off a tail at zones of weakness in several specialized tail vertebrae. Immediate blood-vessel pinchoff prevents significant bleeding. The severed tail writhes for two or three minutes, until the bare muscle at its base wears out and stops contracting.

Can a skink lose its tail more than once? Almost certainly yes. The regenerated tail itself can probably not break in two, since it usually grows back with nonsegmented muscles and a fibrocartilage rod that lack the capacity for self-cutting. But in side-blotched lizards (*Uta stansburiana*) that have been extensively studied, additional breaks always occurred between the regenerated portion and the body.

The usual food of the smooth-skinned six- to eight-inch-long Gilbert's skink is small insects, but it will tackle readily an antagonist as formidable as a three-inch scorpion. Anne Belisle of the Yosemite Field School once watched such an encounter. The skink, jaws open wide, rushed at the scorpion, seized the middle of its long abdomen, bit down hard, and shook its prey violently. Up swung the scorpion's tail with the stinger at its tip and delivered a solid strike on the side of the skink's head. The skink dropped the scorpion like a lead weight and rubbed its head slowly in the gravel. The scorpion moved dully off.

After a minute of head rubbing, the skink charged again and was again stung and repelled, but with less effect than the first time. On the third charge, the scorpion's stings were completely ineffectual and the skink bit and shook its victim until the body grew limp. Laying down the carcass, the lizard picked off and discarded the scorpion's crusty pedipalps, which bear the pincers, bit off the fore section of the scorpion's body and gulped it down. It then seized the front end of the abdomen and swallowed it whole by a series of muscular contractions preceded by shaking its reddish head from side to side. It kept on until the entire body, including the tail and stinger, was consumed. And after all was gone, the skink continued to open its mouth, contract its throat, and shut its mouth again and again, as though smacking its lips over the tasty morsel.

The talus slopes resound in spring with the songs of a variety of birds that use either the trees or the cliffs and air above them. There is the shrill chatter of white-throated swifts zigzagging high over the canyon; the slurred whistle of circling red-tailed hawks; from a rocky promontory the liquid cascade of the cañon wren "tripping down the scale." On the canyon floor, in the more open trees near water, male black-headed grosbeaks sing in mellow grosbeak style as they take their turn on the eggs. The canyon oaks usually harbor Hutton's vireos and the natty black-throated gray warbler, whose feeding grounds are the crown and upper foliage of the oak.

Sierran wood warblers, in the course of time and evolution, have "parceled off" their scenic summer mountain land between them so that each of the ten species has a separate foraging and nesting niche and competes little with the others. The black-capped Wilson's warbler forages in creek dogwood thickets of the lodgepole-fir belt. For the yellow warbler, "home" means streamside willows, alders, and cottonwoods, which it uses from nearly top to bottom. MacGillivray's warbler incubates her eggs in moist shady thickets of thimbleberry, bracken, or currant and forages close to the ground, slipping silently through the dense low cover.

She may sometimes find a Nashville (Calaveras) warbler as an associate ground-nester in slightly drier thickets, but the Nashville's foraging territory is well up in the black oaks and maples.

High in the dense canopies of Douglas fir, white and red fir, hermit warblers sing and feed, nesting slightly lower in thick branchwork. The more widespread Audubon's warbler forages and nests in nearly all of the conifers, from 3000 to 10,000 feet, hunting small insects in outer foliage and flycatching adroitly in short flights beyond the leafage. The yellow-breasted chat sum-- mers along scattered low western streamsides.

All of the warblers except the yellowthroat, resident locally on the lower western slope, migrate to warmer winter regions. Audubon's and some orange-crowned warblers winter in the Central Valley; the others move south to southern Arizona, Mexico, or Guatemala. By early May they are back in their Si- erran breeding niches. The buzzy song of the black-throated gray warbler floating out from the canyon oaks once again seems as much a part of talus slopes as the canyon oaks themselves.

. . .

The other prominent oak of the montane forests is the California black oak, the only oak in the Sierra with deciduous leaves resembling those of the abundant red and black oak types of eastern North America. The California black oak is a true associate of the ponderosa, or yellow, pine, contrasting its shiny sunlit foliage and broad graceful crown with the pine's tall nar- row spires on slopes and valleys throughout the yellow pine belt. In spring its new leaves glow chartreuse and radiant; in summer they offer welcome shade; October drops them, russet and golden, onto misty meadows or crunchy forest carpet.

Like the canyon oak, the black oak forms the focal point of a whole small subcommunity of animal life. The noisiest, most gregarious component is unquestionably the acorn (California) woodpecker, a bird closely linked to oaks in its entire Pacific

Coast range from Oregon to Mexico and found abundantly in foothills or yellow pine forests of the Sierra. Nasal, grating *ya-kup, ya-kup, ya-kup* calls pour out of the oaks where these flashy black and white woodpeckers with the harlequin head pattern are at work. The birds sometimes become so closely associated in communal living that two or more pairs cooperate in nest excavation, incubation, and feeding of the young. Acorns are their stock food, though they occasionally vary the diet with insects seized flycatcher style. Nesting holes are usually drilled in decayed parts of living oaks or in dead trees, or, where these are missing, in telephone poles or fence posts.

The acorn-storing habits of this woodpecker never cease to amaze ornithologists. During years of plenty, the bird tucks away endless numbers of acorns in holes individually drilled for each nut, in tree trunks, poles, fence posts, or wooden structures. The acorns are usually inserted point-first into these custom-made pits, then tamped in for a tight, flush fit with the surface. The holes almost never reach through the bark.

Some of the woodpecker storehouses or "cupboard trees" show riddled barks from three feet above the ground to forty feet up. Joseph Grinnell estimated 2360 holes in one forty-five-foot dead incense cedar in Yosemite Valley and 10,500 in a large living yellow pine. William Ritter, in his classic study *The California Woodpecker and I,* estimated that there were 31,800 holes in an old yellow pine log in the San Jacinto Mountains. Small wonder that the early Spanish Californians called the bird *el carpintero.*

The "carpenter's" apparent "foresight" in filling the cupboard for a rainy day takes a curious turn in his drillings in wooden cabins built of shingles. The pit in a shingle or siding is easily drilled, but when the acorn is hammered into place, it slips through the hole and drops out of sight. As long as the hole remains, the bird must fill it and so pushes through acorn after acorn. The pile on the floor inside builds higher and higher. Ritter reported finding over 62,000 acorns inside an old abandoned miner's house. Countless attics and walls of buildings hold bushels of acorns never retrieved. Further indication of the instinctive rather than reasoning nature of the acorn woodpecker's actions shows up in some of the other objects it sometimes stores — cherry pits, prune pits, bracts of pine cones, pieces of bark, pebbles, and rock fragments. These, in Ritter's words, "tend to dispel the conjecture of something superavian" in the carpenter's activities.

The bird's carving of nest holes produces home sites for other dwellers of the black oak subcommunity. A regular occupant of the holes is the Sierra Nevada's smallest owl, a round-headed, yellow-eyed hunter no bigger than a bluebird, who, unlike most owls, is active and abroad by day. The pygmy owl's mellow series of whistles all on one pitch, punctuated by regular pauses, may be heard in yellow pine forests up and down the length of the Sierra either by day or night. The clear song is disproportionately loud for a seven-inch ball of feathers.

Pygmies usually nest near meadows where their preferred food of mice and grasshoppers abounds. They are affectionate mates, snuggling shoulder to shoulder in courtship and greeting each other with soft fluttering trills at the nest hole. The male owl provides the lizards, snakes, voles, and other varied fare for his incubating partner and for the scraggly little owlets that appear in late May. While the owlets are growing, the male's talons often take a heavy toll of small songbirds near the nest. The small birds caught are plucked first, an unusual habit among owls, which customarily swallow feathers, hair, bones, and all and cough up the indigestible parts later as pellets. Charles Michael, who studied pygmies extensively in Yosemite in the 1920s, reported that pygmies produce no pellets.[1] He watched plucking many times and described a male pygmy bringing a limp solitary vireo to his mate. For ten minutes there was a rain of feathers down from her perch as the female held the vireo under her feet and plucked the feathers one by one. Then off she flew in a swift undulant manner to a black oak and disappeared into an old woodpecker hole with her burden. Through the opening echoed the squeals of ravenous young birds.

As the young owls mature, the male hunter reverts to the mammal-reptile diet that predominates most of the year and the female teaches her progeny to tear off bites from chipmunks or skinks held in her talons.

The western gray squirrels (Sciurus griseus) spend much time beneath the oaks in the autumn, bounding gracefully about, gathering and burying acorns. Two feet long, including the bushy gray tail, the squirrel pretty well confines its range to that of the oaks, leaving the higher coniferous forests to the chickaree, or Douglas squirrel (Tamiasciurus douglasi). Acorns are its staff of life and old woodpecker holes in oaks its usual brood den, although it frequently builds large nests of leaves, twigs, grasses, and needles far out on branches in either oaks or pines.

Like many rodents, its numbers have been subject to cyclic increase and decrease in population. An epidemic caused by the scab mite killed off 90 percent of the western gray squirrels in Sequoia and Yosemite National Parks in the early 1920s. While the grays were almost nonexistent, chickarees in large numbers moved down from the red fir forests above to fill the gap in Yosemite. As the grays came back, the chickarees decreased but did not disappear. The 1950 Field School wildlife census of Yosemite Valley listed 155 gray squirrels and 163 chickarees by rough count. Today both species occupy Yosemite Valley; gray squirrels are once again more numerous than chickarees and their population percentage is still increasing.

There is little apparent competition for food between them, the chickaree feeding largely on conifer cones and the gray on acorns. The gray squirrel theoretically could survive in the next higher mountain zone above the oaks and live on the pine nuts and fungi it sometimes eats. Mammalogist Lloyd Ingles has pointed out a curious behavior pattern that seems to limit the animal's effective spread. The gray buries every item of its cache singly in the ground, a nut here, a fungus there. When the winter snows come, it finds this hidden food by smell, digging a hole through the snow for each solitary tidbit. In the yellow pine belt where it lives, the snows are not too deep or persistent; in the fifteen-foot snows of the red fir forests the energy output to reach so little food would be too great.

The chickaree has a different behavior pattern. It buries its cones in large numbers at the same site, and when the snow becomes deep it has only one hole to dig to reach them all. Thus it thrives in the red fir community and, when vacancies appear, moves down into the yellow pine forests, where its inherited food-storing pattern operates equally well. The presence of the agile marten in the red fir forests also militates more heavily against the slower-moving western gray squirrel than the lively chickaree.

The only nocturnal member of the squirrel tribe in the Sierra Nevada appears equally at home in the black oaks and the red firs. The versatile northern flying squirrel (*Glaucomys sabri-*

nus) occupies old woodpecker holes or tree cavities in both zones, sleeping during the day curled up with the tail over its face. As darkness fills the forest, it sallies forth in search of food — whatever can be found in the way of berries, nuts, fruits, fungi, seeds, birds' eggs, buds, insects, flesh. More nimble in the treetops than any of the squirrels, it is also an extremely adept glider. Leaping outward from a high fir or pine, the squirrel extends the furred membrane that connects wrists and ankles, flattens the extended tail, and volplanes swiftly and silently downward at a fairly steep angle. Gauging the distance to the target carefully, it bends its body upward just before contact and lands head up with a light *plop* low on the trunk of another tree. Up the trunk it races, pelting the ground with a shower of bark, and on to more glides from the heights as it scours the woods for food.

Without actually flying at all these little glider pilots can cover distances of as much as one hundred fifty feet in a single leap; they can make sudden turns of 90 degrees; and can change either direction or landing speed by manipulation of the parachutelike membrane and rudderlike tail. They have been observed walking clotheslines like tightrope acrobats, hanging by one foot and pulling themselves erect and running in a split second. Such agility renders them immune from enemies except those like the large owls and barbed-wire fences.

Whether living in the lower black oaks or the higher red firs, the flying squirrel is active the year round, feeding on the black hair moss lichen (*Alectoria*) when it can get nothing else in winter. Probably as abundant as the diurnal squirrels, it passes unnoticed to most campers. Occasionally, light sleepers hear curious thuds or pelting sounds during the night and discover that their butter or bacon has been nibbled by "some creature larger than a mouse." Yosemite naturalist Robert McIntyre, camping in the Ten Lakes Basin, was once awakened by the noise of a whole family of flying squirrels trying to get the trout from a creel hanging above his sleeping bag. This squirrel, more than most, has a taste for meat or flesh. Observed at close range, it is a handsome animal. The fur, buffy gray above and whitish below, is soft and silky; the eyes, dark and lustrous, are large, as in most nocturnal creatures. The squirrel's low vibrant call note is sometimes heard in the darkening oaks at twilight.

. . .

Yosemite Valley's black oaks, one source of this colorful oak fauna, have drawn visitor comment for at least three decades on an ecological problem of wide-reaching implications in Sierran montane forests. Why is there a nearly total absence of young black oaks around many of the magnificent old ones? And why are there so few showy flowers and deciduous shrubs on much of the valley floor?

As far back as the late 1940s, Emil Ernst, veteran park forester, could lead visitors to three fenced-in study areas that offered an answer. For eleven years enclosure Number 1 produced an abundant summer concentration of showy native flowers within, but not outside, the wire. Inside the fenced area, seedlings of California black oak came up so thickly that many had to be pulled to prevent too dense a stand; not so outside. The second enclosure was well known for the marvelous display of evening primroses (Oenothera hookeri) in season. Before the fencing and the introduction of a few parent native plants, once luxuriant in parts of the valley, the site was barren. Plot Number 3 produced a large number of seedlings of black oak, flourishing in good density. The area outside held few or none.

The reason for Yosemite Valley's barrenness seemed clear to Ernst — too many mule deer! Deer were the only browsing and seasonally grazing big mammals in Yosemite Valley. The only showy native flowers able to maintain themselves were those unpalatable to or unavailable to deer.

Yosemite was not alone in its denudation problem. Increasing deer pressure in Sequoia National Park led to fencing of sample plots there in the mid-1930s. The protected areas soon showed the same startling contrast as in Yosemite, though the plants were different. Sequoia's Giant Forest, 2400 feet higher than Yosemite Valley, contains mixed conifer areas with an understory of snowbrush (*Ceanothus cordulatus*) — also commonly called snowbush and mountain whitethorn — bitter cherry (*Prunus emarginata*) and other shrubs in places. By 1940 the snowbrush and bitter cherry inside Sequoia's fenced plot grew vigorously, producing new sprouts five to six feet long. Outside, the same two species had been almost completely killed by deer.

Seven years later, a large part of the entire shrub cover surrounding the plot had been destroyed. Over many acres flattened dead stems were all that remained of a once extensive leafy understory. "Large numbers of fox sparrows, green-tailed towhees, chipmunks and other small wild creatures that had once found food and shelter in these brush patches had disappeared when the vegetation died. Inside the fence, shrubs and young trees flourished shoulder high." [2]

As the deer's favorite browse diminished, the health and vitality of the herd declined with it. The Giant Forest campgrounds became summer concentration camps for skinny, sluggish, spiritless deer, ill nourished on candy, cigarettes, bread, peanuts, and chewing gum fed to them by tourists.

Where good forage is plentiful, a deer usually nibbles a few mouthfuls, moves on to another green shoot, and on a few steps to another. The traveling minimizes both overbrowsing and the spread of disease. But deer at the Giant Forest, increased to numbers above the food supply, stayed in the same areas day after day, overbrowsing what little vegetation remained until the campground floors lay barren. By direct frequent contact with contaminated animals and forage, they picked up debilitating diseases and pests: an eye ailment caused by the parasitic nematode worm (*Thelazia californiensis*), which impaired the animal's vision and sometimes destroyed it temporarily; botfly larvae, which became imbedded in the deer's nasal cavities; liver flukes, tapeworms, and excessive wood ticks.

Carcasses of deer from the Giant Forest, analyzed by California Fish and Game pathologists in 1945, were declared unfit for human consumption. One doe contained a greasy dishrag in her pylorus. The combination of too many mouths and too little natural food was as hard on the deer as on the vegetation.

Seguoia National Park field naturalist Joseph S. Dixon made pioneer attempts at trapping and transplanting 17 deer in 1938 and 30 to 40 deer in 1943 to relieve browsing pressure on the Giant Forest. It was not until two basic studies of California deer appeared in 1951 and 1952, however, that the first solid assessment of the situation was at hand.

In *The Jawbone Deer Herd* and *A Survey of California Deer Herds,* two teams of biologists from the University of California at Berkeley (A. Starker Leopold, Thane Riney, Randal McCain, and Lloyd P. Tevis, Jr., of the Jawbone study and William M. Longhurst, A. Starker Leopold, and Raymond F. Dasmann of the *Survey*) analyzed the deer problem in the state, its history, its complexities, its possible solutions. *The Jawbone Deer Herd* was an intensive study of one local deer population on the western slope of the Sierra Nevada.

There was much to tell. History, so often a clue to present troubles, played its usual role in the deer story. Mule deer were apparently scarce in much of the high Sierra but common residents of the foothills when pioneers first came over the passes. The discovery of gold brought heavy traffic into the Mother Lode region of the western slope, and locally into the eastern foothills, and with it unlimited year-round hunting for deer meat and hides by the miners.

Game brought such high prices that many miners abandoned the diggings to make a living by market-hunting. Between 1850 and 1903 commercial deer-hunting camps operated in scattered areas up and down the Sierra, from south-central Hazel Green to Quincy in the north and Lundy on the east. Jerky, hides, and meat were shipped to San Francisco in vast amounts — 35,000 deer hides from a single Redding firm in 1880. Individual hunters conducted big-scale operations on their own, one hunter taking over 300 deer in the Mineral King area in the 1880s, another marketing 120 deer in 1873 in the Kaweah River winter range. One killed enough deer in eighteen months to make $5000 by selling to miners. John Woodhouse Audubon wrote in 1851 of miners killing thousands of black-tailed deer in the woody dells and gulches. Deer were carted off "by the wagonload" in many regions.

At the same time, the remaining deer began to find their lush Sierran pastures diminishing. The tremendous buildup of sheep, cattle, and horses in the state, 6,000,000 head of sheep by 1876, many of them migrating each summer to Sierran meadows, took a devastating toll of the succulent vegetation. By the 1880s and 1890s, mile upon mile of former deer feeding grounds had been overgrazed, trampled dry and barren by the milling flocks.

As though this were not enough, "deer suffered some of the hardest winters in California history between 1879 and 1907." [3] In the northern Sierra at Boca, Nevada County, more than thirty-two feet of snow fell in 1889–1890 in what is now deer winter range. Placer County's deer winter range was covered by forty-nine feet of snow at Towle. Singly or in combination, overhunting, overgrazing, and snowy winters in the last half of the nineteenth century reduced Sierran deer populations to a low ebb by 1900. Between 1900 and 1910 a deer was a rare sight in most parts of the range.

Meanwhile the conservation movement had been born and things were changing. Legislation in California recognized the dangerous deer decline. In 1883 a buck law was passed protecting does and fawns from hunting. In 1893 the open season on deer was reduced to six weeks. Nineteen hundred and one saw a bag limit restricting the kill to three bucks within two months; 1905 reduced the bag limit to two bucks. These well-intentioned but completely unenforceable laws finally became effective in 1907, when a hunting license was legally required. Revenue from licenses paid salaries of wardens who could enforce the game laws and deal with violators. The deer began to come back. They found habitat changes strongly in their favor. Yosemite and Sequoia National Parks, created earlier, had first become effective wildlife sanctuaries around 1905, excluding competitive livestock and lumbering. Sierran national forests became functional about the same time and initiated the recovery of their badly overgrazed ranges by gradually reducing livestock grazing. The rangers also helped in enforcing state game laws.

Logging and fires had opened up much of the virgin forest,

creating brush fields where forests had been — brush whose new green leaves supplied much of the deer's favorite forage. As settlements and roads continued to open up the mountains during the early 1900s, mule deer made use of the openings and thrived. The state put a bounty on mountain lions and employed lion hunters; significant numbers of the deer's largest predator were wiped out, even within Sequoia National Park. By 1940 most of the better deer ranges in the Sierra were fully stocked. Parts of Sequoia National Park and many other areas were desperately overstocked. The pendulum had swung from too few to too many of the big adaptable mammals in just thirty years.

The Jawbone Ridge study of the late 1940s probed to the root of the deer problem. The mule deer is the Sierra Nevada's only species of deer. It takes its name from the large mule-like ears, eight inches long and half as wide, which, as in all of its kind, flick periodically for sounds of danger. Bucks stand forty inches high at the shoulder and five and one-half feet long, on an average, weigh around one hundred seventy pounds, and are toned reddish brown in summer and grayish brown in winter. Does are a trifle smaller. The tail, white with varying amounts of black and usually held flat, the two- to five-inch metatarsal glands on the hind legs, and the dichotomously branched antlers of bucks distinguish the mule deer readily from the white-tailed deer, whose nearest distribution is southern Oregon.

Distinguishing the four kinds of mule deer in the Sierra — all subspecies of *Odocoileus hemionus* and capable of interbreeding — is a trickier matter. In the heart of their separate ranges, each deer has a tail pattern and metatarsal-gland length typical of its race; but along the margins where the subspecies overlap, variations are numerous and it takes a sharp eye to spot significant differences. Geography helps, since the Rocky Mountain mule deer and Inyo mule deer live primarily on the eastern side of the Sierra Nevada, north and south respectively. The Columbian black-tailed deer and the California mule deer occupy the western slope, the blacktail in the north and the mule deer in the south. All the mountain deer migrate seasonally from well-defined winter to summer feeding grounds and return to these same winter and summer ranges year after year.

The Jawbone herd (about 6000 animals in 1950) fans out in the summer over 267 square miles of forest edge on the northern border of Yosemite National Park, most densely concentrated at 6000 to 7500 feet or higher. With the onset of snow in October and November, the deer start their downward trek, following the same migration routes year after year, a distance of 10 to 40 miles to the winter range at 1300 to 4000 feet. On Jawbone Ridge and adjacent slopes between the Tuolumne and Clavey Rivers they spend the winter in a total area of about 37 square miles, one-seventh the space of their summer grounds. Even in summer the feeding range of an individual deer covers a diameter of no more than three quarters of a mile. In winter it may be less than 760 yards in diameter for a buck, 320 for a doe — and apparently the same individual home range year after year.

The feeding habits of animals that live in such small areas are bound to influence drastically the vegetation. Deer newly arrived in their winter feeding grounds eat the tender twigs of their favorite browse plants — buckbrush and deerbrush species of *Ceanothus* and western mountain mahogany. These plants all are high in protein, mountain mahogany averaging a hearty 14 percent in October. If the herd is too large it soon eliminates the succulent twigs, leaving only the tougher, less nutritious stubs and other less desirable forage species for midwinter's diet.

The browse plants most preferred by deer very often contain higher protein percentages than do less preferred types; but these favored species, as with all plants so far tested, reach their protein maximums in spring and minimums in winter. Since proteins cannot be stored in any appreciable amount in the body and are a needed element in the day-to-day diet, deer on an overcrowded winter range soon find themselves in a critical protein bind. The most nutritious browse goes first, and good food becomes increasingly difficult to locate. What is uncovered, often by digging through snow, is so low in protein that the digging uses up more energy than the browse yields.

When the protein level of a deer's daily two-and-one-half to three-pound browse intake drops below 7 or 8 percent, he loses weight rapidly and becomes less able to withstand the stresses of winter. Under such circumstances many deer die, often with stomachs stuffed full of low-grade plants incapable of supporting life. Losses among fawns are most severe; their small size handicaps them in reaching high up on overbrowsed shrubs for forage. Does that have put much energy into nursing fawns the previous summer and young deer whose food still goes largely into growth lack a reserve of fat, and are especially liable to succumbing by February or March; old deer with teeth unable to grind the progressively tougher fare suffer a similar fate.

The average annual loss by starvation in the Jawbone herd and the Yosemite region Clark herd is 20 percent or more. One deer out of five dies on its winter range from direct starvation or from causes related to malnutrition. Mild winters cut a smaller swathe, but rigorous winters, like that of 1948–1949, may wipe out 40 percent of a herd. Along with the victims dies some of their staff of life. Plants whose new growth is browsed severely lose vigor and productivity; if severe use continues year after year, they die. The Jawbone herd consumed up to 67 percent of much of its new plant growth. Such heavy browse losses mean even less nourishing food for the herd the following winter.

As goes the winter range, so go the deer. Yet the herd will migrate up to its summer meadows and browse fields, fatten on the lush green forage, produce fawns that increase its numbers by nearly a third, and return to the restricting winter quarters to lose the excess by starvation. This has been the pattern in much of the Sierra Nevada since the 1930s. And these winter herd losses still have not been enough to protect the summer ranges of the Giant Forest, Yosemite, Huntington Lake, Lake Alpine, and other areas from overbrowsing.

. . .

In primitive California, deer populations were probably relatively stable, kept down to the carrying capacity of their ranges by abundant predators, which included the grizzly bear. Though records are scarce, Longhurst, Leopold, and Dasmann believe that early California's situation may have been much like that observed by Leopold in the Gavilan wilderness of northwestern Mexico in 1949. High populations of both deer and deer predators were found there, including numerous mountain lions and wolves. Residents of the adjoining ranches, long familiar with the local situation, indicated that numbers of deer had not fluctuated greatly within their memory. It appeared that the deer population was determined there, as in California today, by the quality of the range — and that in the Gavilan predators removed no more than the annual surplus.

Sierra Nevada predators are too scarce today to remove (in the quick and relatively painless manner of their kind) the deer surplus that otherwise starves each winter. They take only a small fraction of it. Warred on since the earliest days of settlement — shot, trapped, poisoned — the bountiful numbers of carnivores which amazed the Spanish and American explorers have been reduced (where not extinct) to residual populations that maintain themselves but wield far less than their potential influence in the mountain ecosystem. There is little question that the slaughter of large predators has accelerated the increase of deer and permitted deer populations to build up to temporary levels above the optimum range carrying capacity, with resulting range damage.[4]

Of Sierran predators the coyote (*Canis latrans*) is the one that most frequently makes itself heard; its yaps and howls are regular night sounds in many parts of the range. Coyotes sometimes run down yearling or weakened deer, especially in winter. In Yosemite Valley one January day, Rangers Sedergren and Robinson noticed a small deer standing in the frigid waters of the Merced River a short distance from shore. The animal was visibly trembling, and gave every evidence of fright and fatigue from a chase. On the riverbank a coyote lay in wait. Deer often try to throw off pursuit by seeking refuge in a stream, where coyotes will not follow. But this stream was too wide, deep, surging, and cold to permit a crossing, and the deer was stranded. The rangers couldn't resist driving the coyote away to give the shivering deer a second chance.

Coyotes take fawns occasionally, as do black bears, golden eagles, and bobcats, but none of them regularly goes after healthy alert adults. That role falls to the mountain lion, or cougar (*Felis concolor*), the prime natural predator of deer. Six to eight feet long including the long black-tipped tail, and standing taller than a police dog, the big reddish-gray cat totals

165 pounds of sinewy power. It is a proficient hunter with a geographical range from British Columbia to Patagonia. Of the 600 estimated mountain lions in California, probably 150 live in the Sierra Nevada from the Feather River to the Kern. The bulk of these roam the 2000- to 6500-foot western belt, although some are known to cross the crest as high as 11,500 feet.

Elusive and seldom seen, even by people living in lion country, cougars seek out brush and timber on rocky, rugged terrain — concealment that helps them approach deer undetected. During a night's hunt they often cover great distances with their easy-striding walk, muscles flowing like rippling water. On horseback, Donald McLean, California Fish and Game manager, once followed fresh tracks in falling snow for five hours, until darkness turned him back. In that time the lion had covered almost twenty miles. The cougar's route meandered along the sides of a high ridge for about seven miles, turned off down a long spur ridge for another five miles, crossed a canyon to a different series of ridges, and followed these to their end. "The lion swung back and forth from one side of the ridge tops to the other exactly as would a good deer hunter working the same country," wrote McLean. "In this manner, one basin head after another could be scanned." Ridges frequently occupy a good part of a male cougar's one-hundred-mile or so circuitous beat. Females ordinarily travel in canyons and on shorter circuits, especially when the young are too small to go far.

The kittens may be born any month of the year, but most frequently birth occurs from April to August in the Sierra Nevada. The litter usually contains two or three, rarely more than four spotted, ring-tailed babies with eyes closed and with the usual appetite for milk. After ten days the eyes open on to their nest world in a thicket or rocky cavern. Long before the spots disappear at about eight months, the mother has been leading the young to her fresh kill to feed; and she has been teaching them to hunt. They learn on rabbits, mice, squirrels — anything that moves — and in later hungry times, fall back on these small mammals when no larger food is obtainable. It is a long jump from the awkward pounce of bumbling young lions to the skilled spring achieved by the maturing cougar from his second year onward.

The mule deer, the cougar's principal target, is no easy prey. In the tens of thousands of years that these two have lived in the Sierra, the long cocked ears and moist black nose of the deer have tested each breeze to detect the approach of the big cat. So effective is their defense that former state lion hunter Jay Bruce claims two out of three deer escape a mountain lion's charge. A successful stalk must be a work of art, a masterpiece of perfection, or the tawny cat with the flowing rhythm will go hungry.

Well done, it is a remarkable performance. At Pigeon Flat in the western foothills, a large cougar crawled on its belly for about two hundred yards stalking a lone doe that was browsing on buckbrush. The last shielding rock between them stood no higher than a large sombrero, yet the lion crawled thirty feet from a small ditch with this single rock as his sole cover. Behind it he crouched, still seventy-five feet from his prey, until the deer was off guard for an instant. Then the charge! In three and one-half bounds he closed the distance and struck the deer as she started her second jump, killing her quickly with a bite through the base of the skull. Don McLean read this story in the snow after coming onto the doe's still-warm body and interrupting the cougar's siesta.

Stanley Young quotes Daniel Singer, who watched a cougar stalk a doe through frost-tipped foot-high grass that harmonized perfectly with the cat's coat: "So light, silent and cautious was his every move that he might be said to drift light as a wisp of smoke toward his prey before making the death-dealing spring."

But thousands of cougar springs that could have kept the prolific mule deer from eating itself out of a range never got off the ground in the Sierra Nevada in this century. California, along with most states, has been slow to recognize the predator's place in the natural cycle of things, and paid bounties on 12,461 cougars between 1907 and 1963. An antibounty campaign initiated in the early 1960s by conservationist Margaret Owings brought a four-year moratorium on the state mountain lion bounty. In 1967 the bounty was permanently repealed by the Legislature. In 1970 on the recommendation of the California Department of Fish and Game, the cougar was given the status of a game mammal, to be hunted during a specified season with a bag limit on the take. A tag system will provide a record of the number of lions reported killed, including those shot by livestock growers, who are legally free to kill offending lions. It apparently will take another conservation campaign to put the mountain lion on the protected list.

There is no question that some cougars, at times, take livestock. There is also no question that this consideration has in the past outweighed all others and has been given precedence over the centuries-old ecological patterns built up between deer, lions, and the land.

Lowell Sumner, United States Park Service biologist, noted years ago at Sequoia National Park that "undamaged deer range definitely corresponds with the best populated lion range." [5] Sumner and the 1963 Leopold Committee report to the Secretary of the Interior both advocate the establishment of "buffer zones," in which all predators are protected, around national parks. This is a necessary step toward the Park Service objective of restoring park fauna and flora as closely as possible to natural environmental conditions that prevailed before the impact of European man.

Sumner started things rolling in this direction at Sequoia in 1955, when he was regional biologist. He selected a Giant Forest pilot unit of nearly seven square miles which showed the usual deer overbrowsing signs: snowbrush tightly hedged, mountain dogwood (*Cornus nuttallii*) sharply highlined four and one-half feet above ground, greenleaf manzanita devoid of outer leaves, littleleaf ceanothus (*Ceanothus parvifolius*) defoliated, lupine missing, grass in the wet meadows looking as though it had been mowed. From this area 175 deer were removed the first summer. By August that same year, the meadows again supported flowers and tall grass that nearly hid the deer, and a few lupine pushed up for the first time in years on previously bare forest floor. In 1956 an additional 199 deer were removed. The next year saw three small units added to the program and 62 deer taken from all four units of twelve square miles. In the following three years 430 more animals were eliminated.

It was not until 1961, six years after the start of the program and with 866 fewer deer, that significant improvements in the plant growth were evident. That summer, littleleaf ceanothus put out new leader growth eight to fourteen inches long; dogwood sprouted from the base, and by summer's end still retained leaves and stems on the sprouts; dogwood branches again began to hang down within reach of deer; the highline was fast disappearing. On north slopes, modest growths of hazelnut (*Corylus cornuta*) were getting established, and snowberry (*Symphoricarpos*) was seeding in. Lupine continued to finger out over the forest floor. By 1961 the Giant Forest summer range was well on the road to recovery.

To keep it headed that way, and to meet requests by sportsmen that *they* instead of park rangers be allowed to take the deer, special late-season, out-of-the-park hunts were established in 1964–1966. These were either-sex hunts, with a designated number of hunters and animals. The hunts were later than the usual hunting season in order to catch animals en route to their winter range. Rated as successful, these hunts are being continued and are designed to maintain deer populations that will allow both the winter and summer range to recover as rapidly as possible. When recovery is complete in future years, herd levels will be increased to the point where deer and range are in proper equilibrium. Annual hunts and increased populations of native predators will both be needed to help maintain a dynamic condition.

Yosemite National Park too has been attacking its deer surplus problem with removal of over one thousand animals from the park during 1963–1966. Park foresters have also set up six new rodent-proof, deer-proof fenced plots in which to study black oak reproduction and ecology.

The national forests are the sites of most public hunting. But the forests lack the total jurisdiction over their fauna which the national parks possess, and have been less able to step into a forthright range-recovery program. The United States Forest Service has the responsibility for protection, development, and management of wildlife habitat in Sierra Nevada national forests, but turns to the California Department of Fish and Game and the California Fish and Game Commission for management of the animals themselves.

It is Forest Service policy to manage public lands under the principle of multiple use. This involves setting land-use priorities for one or two primary uses such as timber-growing, recreation, or livestock grazing, then fitting in as many other uses as possible, without serious conflict with the higher priorities. (Many ecologists doubt that most wildlife can be "fitted in" with other priorities.) Deer are given priority on key deer range, which ordinarily means the most concentrated part of their winter range. On the balance of the range, timber-growing, livestock grazing, recreation, and other uses have priority, with provisions made for deer.

While the Forest Service claims that forage preferences of deer and cattle are, in general, different, the Jawbone Ridge report indicates distinct competition between the two for favorite herbs and browse in certain areas. The Forest Service feels that "if livestock numbers are regulated to the carrying capacity of their prime feeding areas, little conflict with deer occurs. If, however, either deer or livestock or both are too numerous, damage to range can be expected." [6]

Cattle graze on Sierran national forests in numbers determined by the Forest Service at fees that averaged $.61 per animal per month in 1968. Since the cost of grazing cattle on private lands averages around $2.50 per animal month according to a recent California survey, the difference in cost is, in essence, a subsidy that Uncle Sam pays the cattlemen. A 1968 ruling of the Secretary of Agriculture will, if not rescinded, raise the base fee to $1.23 in ten equal increases over the next ten years. This, along with the requirement that grazing permittees maintain range fences and water developments and meet higher herding, driving, and hauling costs, would make fees more equitable.

Deer are crowding their ranges on most national forests, and both deer and range would benefit by removals of surplus animals. The Forest Service would like to see the Department and the Fish and Game Commission left free to manage deer in accordance with their established deer-management policies.

The California Department of Fish and Game, with the example of every other state in the western United States before it, has mountains of data to support the stand that either-sex hunting and scientifically timed hunting seasons are needed to cull the surplus deer in the national forests. The Department can by law only recommend to the Fish and Game Commission that such hunts be held, and where and when. Sportsmen, landowners, and other interested parties also make recommendations, often against either-sex hunts or special hunts. The Commission, a group of five laymen appointed by the governor and confirmed by the senate, considers all recommendations and sets hunting regulations accordingly.

There has never been sufficient support to establish statewide regulated either-sex hunting; to set later hunting dates that would give deer time to leave the national parks for winter ranges in national forests; or to go along wholeheartedly with the recommendations of the Fish and Game management specialists who keep in touch with the deer-range problem and evaluate the year-to-year variables and degree of reduction needed.

If the Commission does propose an either-sex hunt or special hunt in a local area, a hearing must be held in the counties affected. In some counties the county board of supervisors has the right to veto the proposed hunt, and often does. One Sierran county turned down a 1967 special antlerless, either-sex hunt proposal: the hunt would have let sportsmen bag, out of the park, six hundred deer that were damaging Yosemite Park summer range. Instead they had to be eliminated by park rangers.

Some sportsmen's groups now recognize that every environment has its carrying capacity of deer, whether doe or buck, and back the Department of Fish and Game in its requests for either-sex hunts. Some are becoming interested in the whole intricate cycle of the range and what it can or could support, taking a hard look at both deer and cattle in the national forests.

But to other hunters and influential local citizens the doe is still sacred, and their own opinions about deer are regarded more highly than those of trained wildlife managers. These same men overlook the fact that a doe's teeth are just as destructive to plants as a buck's; that if you attempt to reduce the herd size by shooting only bucks, the protected does will fill out the range, produce more fawns, and compound the food problem. Thus a curious combination of legislative procedure, local ecological illiteracy, multiple use, and a buck law as outmoded as the horse and buggy has locked out of Sierra Nevada national forests the full-scale deer-management programs that their over-browsed and overgrazed ranges sorely need.

Aldo Leopold was not jesting when he remarked that a mountain must live in mortal fear of its deer.

4. Giant Sequoias

WHEN HUNTER A. T. DOWD, chasing a wounded grizzly bear, stumbled on to the huge trees of the North Calaveras Grove in 1852, he forgot all about the bear in his astonishment. He wondered if he were suffering from hallucinations; there couldn't be trees that big. The men back at camp ridiculed his "big trees" story. Only by the ruse of needing their backs to haul out a monstrous bear that he had shot did Dowd get them to the grove to prove his find.

There the trees stood, mostly in groups, immense brownish-red trunks rising with a clean nobility to rounded green crowns two hundred feet or more overhead. It took twenty men standing with outstretched arms barely touching to circle one.

Word of the "mammoth trees" in Sierran midmountain forests spread quickly to the nearby gold camps of Murphys and Angels and to the outside world. Murphys Camp immediately became famous as the nearest stopping place to the grove of big trees and saw a steady stream of tourists and scientists.

One of them, William Lobb, a British botanical collector, took seeds and specimens back to England in late 1853. From these botanist John Lindley named the tree in honor of the hero of Waterloo. Wrote Lindley, "We think that no one will differ from us in feeling that the most appropriate name to be proposed for the most gigantic tree which has been revealed to us by modern discovery is that of the greatest of modern heroes. Wellington stands as high above his contemporaries as the Californian tree above all the surrounding foresters. Let it then bear henceforward the name of *Wellingtonia gigantea.*" [1]

But *Wellingtonia* met an abrupt taxonomical wall the very next year. French botanist Decaisne pointed out that the genus *Sequoia* had been described seven years earlier by Hungarian Stephan Endlicher when he christened the coast redwood of the northern California Coast Ranges with the scientific name of *Sequoia sempervirens.* By nomenclature's sacred international rule of priority, if the big tree was a sufficiently close cousin of the coast redwood, its genus already had been determined as *Sequoia;* only its species was new to science.

So, to many botanists convinced of the close generic kinship, *Sequoia gigantea* the massive trees of the Sierra became. And so they remained by long usage, including that of the National Park Service, until recently. Since 1939 a new name, *Sequoiadendron giganteum,* has become generally accepted among botanists. Research indicates clear distinctions between *Sequoia sempervirens,* the coastal redwood, and *Sequoiadendron giganteum,* the Sierran big tree. Chromosome numbers differ; the formation and development of the embryo is different; and the two appear to have no immediate common ancestors.

To the tourist of the 1850s, "big tree" was the only name that was needed for the "biggest-around tree on earth"; "Sierran redwood," "sequoia," and "giant sequoia" were other naturals. Endlicher's source of the name *Sequoia* is not certainly known; but since he was a linguist as well as botanist, it is generally supposed that he gave the name in tribute to the Indian chief Sequoyah. This remarkable Cherokee invented an alphabet so simple and so effective that anyone in his tribe could become literate in Cherokee within a short time — one of the cultural achievements of the nineteenth century.

Dowd's discovery leading to scientific recognition of the big trees was not the first sight record; the Joseph Reddeford Walker party apparently saw them in 1833 in the Yosemite region; but Dowd was the first to publicize the tree's existence. During the succeeding thirty years after Dowd's find, one grove of giant sequoia after another was discovered in the isolated mountain forests between the deep river canyons of the central and southern Sierra. All were on the western slope in scattered locations from 4000 to 8000 feet. A total of 70 to 75 groves grew in a narrow broken band 250 miles long, from the middle fork of the American River south to Deer Creek. The largest groves and biggest trees were in the south. Within this Sierran province, in protected spots where the soil was deep, rich, and moist, where winter snows built ten- to fourteen-foot anklets around the broad tree bases, where temperatures sometimes fell to zero, lived the surviving giants of a once widespread tribe.

As the trees became known to admirers, they were eyed equally by exploiters. The 1880s rang with the crackling thunder of falling sequoias. In sharp response boomed back the battle cries of Visalia news editor George W. Stewart, John Muir, and the California Academy of Sciences' Gustav Eisen. They wrote, talked, and fought to preserve the trees and get them into safe hands. But protection took time.

Meanwhile loggers felled hundreds of giants in accessible areas despite the difficulty of the operation. A six-foot platform had to be erected to clear the flying buttresses. Standing on it, two men chopped out chips, so large that a boy could hardly hold one, until a ten-foot notch was cut. The fellers then carried a twenty-foot saw around to the opposite side of the tree and for days ground it in and out, greasing it to make it slip, and inserting huge wedges to prevent settling. At last the ponderous trunk leaned and pitched to earth with a roar that shook the forest. The trunk usually broke into transverse chunks on falling, making it an exceedingly wasteful lumber tree; but the great durability of the brittle wood promised long-lasting shingles, fence stakes, posts, and flumes.

Southern Miwok Indians, to whom the sequoia was sacred, tried to persuade lumbermen to spare the *wawona*, their name for "big tree," and warned them that *wawona* destroyers would be visited by bad luck.

But the loggers steamed on, blasting down by dynamite the trees that were impossible to saw. In Converse Basin only a single sequoia, the Boole tree, was left standing in what had been one of the finer southern groves. The ground beneath it lay strewn with thousands of logs never utilized because they proved too big or costly to handle or had smashed to bits in the fall. Mill crews invaded Big Stump Basin, Redwood Mountain Grove, and others.

It was probably the Kaweah Cooperative Colony of about fifty-five socialists who set up a utopia near the Giant Forest in 1885–1886 which ignited the fuse of events leading to federal action on the southern big trees. The colonists, some half of them from San Francisco, applied for quarter-sections of timberland in the area surrounding the Giant Forest. They built an eighteen-mile road in to their timber stands and planned an economy based on lumber sales. They renamed the largest local sequoia (General Sherman) the Karl Marx tree and other big trees for their various heroes.

In the office of the *Visalia Weekly Delta* thirty miles away, George W. Stewart and Frank Walker shifted into high gear to get the trees into a national park. Said Stewart later: "We wrote letters to every person in the United States, in and out of Congress, whom we knew to be in favor of forest conservation and to every magazine and newspaper we knew to favor the idea. Their name was not legion in those days. The response, with few exceptions, was cordial." [2]

The movement to save the big trees spread over the country. Washington was listening. In 1890, in two bills, Congress created Sequoia National Park to preserve thirty-two groves of big trees and General Grant National Park to save the General Grant Grove. (General Grant National Park was incorporated within Kings Canyon National Park in 1940.) The Giant Forest became a part of the park along with extensive high-Sierran wilderness. A year later the Giant Forest's socialist colony crumbled in dissension.

The Mariposa Grove of big trees had come under state protection along with Yosemite Valley in 1864; both became part of Yosemite National Park in 1906. The North Calaveras Grove was acquired by the state in 1931 with the help of the Save-the-Redwoods League and the Calaveras Grove Association, among others. In the early 1950s these same two groups, aided by John D. Rockefeller, Jr., the California War Memorial Park Association, the Sierra Club, and others, raised matching funds to add the South Calaveras Grove of big trees and prime sugar pines to the state park system.

For nearly a century, from 1864 to 1954, every grove had to be fought for, wrested from the ever-threatening saw. Today 93 percent of the world's native giant sequoia groves are in national or state parks, or in national forests;[3] the price of preserving

In early May the meadows of the western foothills
glow with wildflowers.

Tidytips and pale yellow butter-
and-eggs grow on middle ground,

meadowfoam in the wet places;

and monkey-flowers rim the creeks.

On the dry open slopes
white lupines,

California poppies,

and mariposa tulips bloom.

In the foothills the light shade cast by digger pines encourages grasses and blue brodiaeas on the open woodland floor. Brodiaeas' edible corms once were a major food of the California Indians.

The scientific name for fairy lanterns — *Calochortus albus* — meaning "beautiful white grass," apparently refers to the leaves, since they are members of the lily family.

Chinese houses (*Collinsia bicolor*) surround a cluster of poison oak.

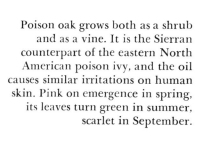

Poison oak grows both as a shrub and as a vine. It is the Sierran counterpart of the eastern North American poison ivy, and the oil causes similar irritations on human skin. Pink on emergence in spring, its leaves turn green in summer, scarlet in September.

By late May most foothill grasses have browned for the long dry summer. Digger pines, uniquely Californian, curve above evergreen live oaks and old stone fences.

The Sierra Nevada salamander finds shelter in damp earth or hollow logs.

The scrub jay is the jay of the Central Valley and western Sierra foothills.

As summer settles over the foothills, snow plants announce spring in the yellow pine and red fir forests 2000 to 5000 feet higher.

The meadow below Half Dome turns green in early June,
when springtime comes to Yosemite Valley.

what has been saved still is *constant vigilance*. Mount Stewart and Mount Eisen, two towering peaks of the Great Western Divide in the southern Sierra, Zumwalt Meadow, Muir Grove, and the Founders Group in the Giant Forest all stand as memorials to some of the men who made Sequoia National Park a reality.

Every sequoia grove diffuses a mood of its own, distinct from the others; in sheer forest depth none exceeds Sequoia National Park's Giant Forest. Here the groves go on for miles; hikers may wander, as Muir did, for days among the cinnamon columns, crunching the egg-shaped cones into the soft duff, shaking out the tiny seeds, tracing the reddish trunks up and up.

Reaching out at the base for a firm though shallow grip on the mountainside, the big trees climb with hardly a taper to the first clumps of green foliage 100 feet up. Above these, muscular branches push out and turn abruptly upward, hiding the burnished boles with scale-like leaf tufts until they emerge 200 to 275 feet high in round green crowns against the sky.

The size of the trees is incomprehensible at first view; people who live among sequoias say that they never really get used to them; photographers reach quickly for a wide-angle lens. The immensity is concealed by the harmonic proportions. From buttressed base to superstructure they look so functionally right that you hardly notice the twenty-foot width of the trunks or reflect that if one fluted base were moved into a city street it would block it from curb to curb. The neighboring conifers offer little help in eye comparison; sugar pines, magnificent large trees in their own right, seem moderate-sized alongside sequoias.

Which is the largest giant sequoia? There is no one answer. The greatest in girth is not the tallest, and exact dimensions are not always agreed upon. Rumors of a newly found, exceptional big tree crop up about twice a year, thus far unsubstantiated. The three most voluminous individual specimens are Sequoia National Park's General Sherman tree (272.4 feet high; 36.5 feet maximum basal diameter); Kings Canyon National Park's General Grant tree (267.4 feet high; 40.3 feet maximum basal diameter); and Sequoia National Forest's Boole tree (268 feet high; 35 feet maximum basal diameter).

The National Park Service considers General Sherman "the largest living thing in the world" on estimated total volume in the trunk alone of 50,010 cubic feet. The General bears a branch, growing out of the trunk 130 feet above the ground, which is itself larger and longer than most forest trees of the eastern United States, measuring 6.8 feet across and 140 feet in length. Yet General Sherman is only a nod bigger than three others less than a mile from it in the Giant Forest, one of which, the McKinley tree, is taller — 291 feet high. Some big trees have exceeded 300 feet in height, but 220 to 275 feet is a more common attainment. Several thousand of them have basal diameters greater than 15 feet and a good many from 20 to 30 feet. No living giant sequoia comes close to the record heights of 367 feet or more held by the coast redwood; and no coast redwood approaches the girth of the biggest giant sequoias.

It was once thought that size and age were correlated directly, that you could judge the age of a living tree by counting the growth rings of a fallen tree of equal size. Recent studies have revealed that it doesn't work this way. Environment is more important than age. A young sequoia that sprouts in a sunny area where there is plenty of soil moisture will quickly outgrow an older sequoia struggling in the shade with less favorable water supply.

The story of the famous Stump tree in the North Calaveras Grove shows how misleading size can be. In 1853 five men decided to cut down the largest standing big tree in the grove, partly to see how old it was. They had no saws large enough and it was impossible to chop it down, so they hit upon the idea of boring the tree down with two-inch augurs. There were no augurs long enough to reach across the trunk, but by welding iron bars to the augurs to extend their length they managed to bore completely through in one direction again and again, and to cross-bore in the same painstaking way. It took twenty days to sever completely the trunk from the stump; but still the tree stood. They inserted large wedges; the giant refused to fall. On the twenty-second day after work began, while the men were away at lunch, a sudden wind toppled the tree. Another version says that two pine trees were felled against the sequoia finally to push it down.

The tree measured 24.1 feet across at stump level, 30 feet across at the ground. In spite of its enormous size, one of the largest on record, and a height of 302 feet, its growth rings showed only 1320 years of age. Situated in a moist, favorable site in the grove, it had simply shot up in a hurry. The stump was smoothed and became famous as a dance floor accommodating thirty-two couples; it was later roofed over to become at different intervals a theater, a small hotel, and a newspaper office. Today it stands open to the sky.

One thousand three hundred and twenty years represent adulthood for the big tree but they are a long step from old age. Longevities of 1500, 2000, and 2500 years appear common. Experts of the past century have estimated the age of patriarchs like General Grant and General Sherman as between 3000 and 4000 years, and the Grizzly Giant in Yosemite's Mariposa Grove as perhaps the oldest of them all. Current researchers Richard Hartesveldt, Thomas Harvey, and Howard Shellhammer of San Jose State College suspect that the latter estimates are too high. Their studies indicate that these three trees, like the Stump tree, have grown very rapidly because they are in especially good sites, with ample soil moisture during the entire growing season. "These trees may be comparative youngsters." [4]

The usually helpful increment borer offers no certain solution to the age puzzle in living sequoias. The borer proved invaluable in determining the age of the more ancient but much smaller-trunked bristlecone pines by removing a core of countable tree rings from bark to center. But such instruments will penetrate only the outer two feet of a big tree, a rather inadequate sample of a 15-foot trunk. The San Jose State College team hopes eventually to present accurate age estimates built on a basal area regression curve from a 12- to 15-inch core. At present, the only authentic records come from logged trees, and ring counts of these verify the oldest known giant sequoias as about 3200 years old.

Is it possible for human beings who live sixty- to seventy-year cycles to comprehend such life spans? That fire-scarred giant at the meadow's edge was a sprouting seed on the moist bare earth when Rome was founded. In the first two hundred years of its youth, it sprang steadily upward, a conical shape clothed to the base in blue-green leaves. Beneath the ground its roots spread laterally at a six-foot depth, beginning the horizontal network that would reach out ultimately to two thirds of the tree's height.

By the birth of Christ seven centuries later, the rich red bark and upbending arms gleamed high above the meadow. Inside the trunk, rose-colored heartwood deeply impregnated with tan-

nin was forming, increasing as a thousand years passed so that by
the time of the discovery of America it filled most of the vast interior with a rot-resisting durable wood. Outside, the bark thick-
ened to a two-foot blanket of asbestoslike cinnamon fibers.

Throughout the fires and storms of centuries, through the rise
and fall of Rome, the Mayan empire, Spain, through Magna
Carta, the Renaissance, 1776, the birth of the United Nations,
this statesman has heralded each sunrise anew for nearly three
millennia.

· · ·

Dawn is a magical time in the groves. As the first rays of sun
strike the big-tree tops and lance down from one ruddy limb to
another, the birds take over the forest. From still dim recesses
ring out the robins' morning carols. The three-part song of the
western tanager lends a strident base to the rapid bubbling war-
bles of California purple finches. Wood pewees dart about,
snapping mandibles on tardy moths. A burst of melody hovers
over the meadow — the black-headed grosbeak's morning flight
song. On upturned fingerlike roots of fallen sequoias, Oregon
juncos pipe out a dry trill. The day's foodlift recommences in
the red-breasted nuthatch nesting hole in a white fir stump.
The *yank-yank-yank* notes of busy parents rebound from insect-
collecting forays up the higher trunks and branches of all the
taller trees that furnish their foraging niche.

Sometimes the deep *kuk kuk kuk* of the West's largest woodpecker resounds throughout the forest, as the big black bird,
nearly the size of a crow, wings its way to a favorite snag. Landing with flaming topknot erect, the male pileated woodpecker
turns his striped red, black, and white head to right and left and
goes to work. Tilting back his body, leaning on stiffened tail,

gripping tightly with the claws, he throws his heavy head and long sharp beak through an arc of eight to ten inches. As he bombards the trunk, striking first where wood is more decayed, his bill's hard glancing blows split off slivers a quarter-inch wide. Chips and flakes fly as the woods ring with the pummeling. The pileated woodpecker's Sierran niche includes dead trees of midmountain forests, where for rapid woodcutting it is unexcelled; it has been known to dig out a hole large enough for concealment within thirty minutes in a dead but firm sugar pine.

All woodpeckers possess extra-powerful neck muscles; the pileated can render a whack nearly equal to that of a person with an ordinary hammer. Its holes often measure six inches long, three inches wide, and three inches deep in firm wood, penetrating the deeper wood channels to reach the boring beetle larvae and carpenter ants that form its major diet.

Occasionally it eats wild berries. This can be awkward for such a heavy bird. Ranger-naturalist Allen Waldo observed a pileated feeding on ripe blue elderberries, bending the branches over in so great an arc that the the bird hung upside down as it cleaned off a berry clump at top speed. When eating was nearly finished, its feet suddenly slipped from the stem, dropping the woodpecker to the ground flat on its back. It recovered immediately and flew off.

In spite of its size and power, the bird has enemies. Among avian predators, both goshawks and Cooper's hawks inhabit its range. Lowell Sumner and Joseph Dixon tell the story[5] of a family of pileateds that experienced a near-tragic ending at the Parker Group of big trees in Sequoia National Park. A pair of these woodpeckers chiseled out a nest chamber at a height of twenty-four feet in a large fir stump above the camp kitchen of a troop of soldiers. The birds, wary at first, grew used to the troop's presence and became quite tame. The troop, in turn, became greatly attached to the birds and named them Cap and Phoebe.

Phoebe laid an egg a day from May 7 to 10. The parents shared daytime incubation, "but at night Phoebe always occupied the nest, while Cap roosted in the doorway with his head outward." After the eggs hatched, both parents went far afield seeking food for their young. On the evening of June 16, as Phoebe was flying toward the nest, a Cooper's hawk struck and killed her and carried her to a nearby tree.* Cap, who witnessed his mate's death, appeared to lapse into a state of shock. For a day and two nights he just sat in the door of his nest. By the morning of the 18th, the continuous chirping of his extremely hungry brood seemed to arouse him and sent him into the forest to quiet their appetites. From then on he was a diligent provider.

The task became more and more strenuous as the fuzzy fledglings grew large and waited, clamoring, at the nest door for him. On July 19, as Cap left the nest, "they all sailed out after him . . . and soon hit the ground with a thud." Cap collected them as best he could and led out into the forest, feeding on nearby stumps and logs, his brood scrambling and flapping along after him. For several days the procession remained around the camp, but finally drifted away.

A companion woodpecker with feeding habits different from those of the pileated is the smaller white-headed woodpecker. Hopping up the trunks of the conifers, it pries off thick bark scales to obtain insects living in the crevices. Its bill serves as a crowbar more than a hammer. Whiteheads sometimes tunnel

---

* Walter Fry, the original source of this story in a Sequoia Nature Guide Service leaflet of December 23, 1931, definitely named Cooper's hawk as the predator. A pileated would be a big prey item for a hawk its own size, as Cooper's is; the larger, quite similar goshawk must be considered a possibility.

nesting holes in spongy sequoia bark, which is thickest at the lower trunk levels that the birds prefer.

Midday hours in the groves are a mingling of hot sun in the clearings, cool shade under the trees. The lupines, the crimson snow plants, the dogwoods of the forest understory pass from dazzling radiance to somber eclipse as the shadows come and go.

In depressions in some of the sequoia buttresses where bits of bark have accumulated, chipmunks, juncos, and robins take "bark baths," wallowing in the fine cinnamon dust, flipping it over their fur and feathers. Dust baths of any sort are thought to help animals clean their skin of oil, to discourage parasites, and to yield a pleasant sensation. Sequoia bark dust, impregnated with tannin, probably acts very much like insect powder, as Fry suggested. Tannin's astringency renders it unpalatable to most insects and antiseptic to most fungus diseases. In the huge saw-dust piles along the Big Stump Trail, tannin is believed to be the ingredient that has inhibited plant growth on the piles for more than seventy-five years.

In July and August that lively little harvester of big-tree cones, the chickaree, goes into action, and any time of day a shower of two-inch bombs may thud to earth. This small, im-pish tree squirrel, sometimes called the Douglas squirrel, is the Pacific Coast relative of the North American red squirrel. It frolics up and down sequoia trunks, peels off soft spongy bark strips for its nest, leaps from high swaying branches of one tree to the next, explodes spontaneously in high-pitched squeals and scolds, and pops around trunks with its bushy short tail jerking and bright eyes bulging at totally unexpected times.

But when it decides to harvest cones, several hundred feet up and out on the tip of a branch, the chickaree does it as though winter were closing in the next day. Its ivory sickles often snip off more than twenty cones a minute. Working at peak activity, it can drop a fusillade of thirteen green sequoia "grenades" in ten seconds. When enough have accumulated on the ground, it comes down and stores them away, carrying one at a time to great caches in hollow logs, under prostrate trunks, in crevices or creeks. These moist, cool, and shady spots keep cones from opening for at least three years.

California ground and golden-mantled squirrels frequently run off with a share of the fallen harvest, but the chickaree tucks away most of it. Walter Fry watched one energetic chickaree cache more than thirty-eight barley sacks of cones in twelve days. From these, Fry extracted over twenty-six pounds of seeds.

It is generally considered to be the seeds that chickarees seek in sequoia cones. Observations by Hartesveldt, Harvey, and Shellhammer cast doubt on this. With pine cones, chickarees do discard the woody cone scales and eat the seeds. But the seeds of sequoia average 91,000 to the pound; the seeds of one cone weigh less than .06 ounce, only a fraction of which is embryo food. A large part of what chickarees eat is the fleshy sequoia cone bract, stripped while the cones are green and soft. Not all of the hidden cones are eaten during winter's scantier times. The chickaree's habit of storing big-tree cones alongside decaying logs at meadow edges has undoubtedly planted many trees over the centuries.

Sunset in the groves intensifies the burnt umber of the big-tree pillars, setting them off in bold relief against the lengthening shadows. This is the time when deer seek the meadows, when the last bird calls rend the stillness. As night's cool air rises into a darkening forest, chipmunks retire to their burrows and the nocturnal mammals emerge.

The coyote trots out on its beat. Raccoons (*Procyon lotor*) amble along the creeks and through the campgrounds. The black bear (*Ursus americanus*) prowls wherever a morsel seems promising, rising on hind legs at certain preferred trees to reach high up and sharpen its claws on the bark. The bear manicure tree in Sequoia National Park is one of its favorites. The naturalist Ernest Thompson Seton believed that such trees were used as "bear signboards," conveying through the bear's acute sense of smell pertinent facts about the tree's previous user — much the same as urinary signal posts of dogs, wolves, and coyotes. The trees may be a kind of "social register," telling a newcomer that his claw marks are the highest on the trunk or that a larger bear is boss of this domain.

All through the underbrush, in hollow logs, among rocks, in the myriad openings that tiny animals make use of, the most abundant mammals of the groves, the deer mice (*Peromyscus maniculatus*), scamper on their nightly hunt for seeds and berries. Almost every bird and mammal predator feeds on these little mice, yet they are one of the most successful animals in the Sierra, and in North America, if judged by numbers and wide range. Joseph Grinnell and Tracy Storer estimated that in Yosemite they nearly equaled in numbers all the other mammals of the area. Sumner and Dixon considered them the most widely distributed mammals in Sequoia and Kings Canyon National Park in the early 1950s. George Lawrence's recent live-trapping census of the mammals of Whitaker's Forest, in the same region, found them extremely abundant but cyclic. In many places where mammal surveys are made, deer mice are so numerous that it is necessary to trap them out before other species can be captured.

This elegant native is far different from the drab-colored, musky-smelling city-dwelling house mouse. The soft brownish-gray fur and pure white underparts of the deer mouse contrast cleanly. Its tail is well furred with dark hair above and white below. The large delicate ears and wide eyes surmount an inquiring face.

Recent findings indicate that deer mice in other forested regions of the United States perform a real service by feeding on larvae and pupae of insects detrimental to the trees. Whether similar ecological relationships exist in Sierran forests is yet to be determined, but the rodents are known to eat heavily of insects in the spring. In the summer and fall they turn to buds, nuts, berries, seeds — and meat, butter, or cheese when within reach in cabin or campsite. Throughout the long cold winters of the groves, the mice remain active underneath and above the snow, weaving a tracery of tiny footprints, living on large caches.

They climb trees readily, if slowly, and in emergencies jump into space from any height without hesitation. Sumner and Dixon watched deer mice fall thirty-eight feet and run away with no noticeable distress. "Since they are so light in relation to their surface, a fall usually has no serious consequences for them." [6]

All their defenses cannot, of course, ward off the longtail weasel, striped skunk, and innumerable other enemies. Among the crawling predators is a native member of the boa family, the "two-headed snake" with a blunt tail that closely resembles the head and sometimes even moves and strikes like a head. Known as the rubber boa (*Charina bottae*), it both looks and feels to the touch like brown rubber, and is, like all Sierran snakes save the rattlesnake, harmless to man. Sheltering by day in damp places under logs or rocks, often near streams, it produces in season up to eight young, born alive. Nightly at dusk its search for small mammals and lizards begins, a hunt that may require burrowing, swimming, or climbing to appease its hunger. A visitor who reported seeing "an eel" climbing a giant sequoia at twilight was among the few to watch a rubber boa in action. Although rated the most common snake in Yosemite's Mariposa Grove in a summer vertebrate survey, the boa, like most nocturnal creatures, is seldom seen by man.

Nocturnal life has its sway in the groves; again comes the dawn. Over the centuries the wheel goes round and round. Individual chipmunks tumbling in their bark dust baths are here, probably at most, three years and gone; the woodpeckers, four years; mule deer, five years; man, perhaps six decades. A 3000-year-old sequoia, the same solitary individual, lives on and on — through 1000 generations of chipmunks, 750 generations of woodpeckers, 600 generations of deer, 50 generations of man.

5. Fire Ecology

IN THE FORMER AFRICAN STATES of Ruanda and Urundi there was a legend of Batutsi tribal origin. The first Batutsi came from the sky. His father was Imana, God the Powerful. His mother was called Gasani. Though life in the sky was beautiful, Gasani had not been happy. She wanted children and begged Imana to help her.

So Imana took a piece of clay, moistened it with His tongue and shaped it to the form of a child. "Hide this in a pot of fresh milk for nine months," He told Gasani, "and promise to tell no one."

Gasani promised, nine months passed, and the clay child awakened and began to cry. It was a handsome boy. Then Imana made a brother and sister so the little boy wouldn't be lonely.

When Gasani's sister saw the beautiful children, she coaxed Gasani incessantly, trying to discover the secret. One day she tricked Gasani into drinking too much beer and Gasani whispered the story. Imana heard at once. Very angry, He seized the children of Gasani and dropped them through a big hole in the floor of Heaven onto the inhospitable earth.

For ten days they suffered, cold and hungry, until Imana relented. He shot a streak of lightning to start a fire in the grass.

The next day seeds and plants rained down — peas, corn, beans, sorghum, bananas — and began to sprout and grow in the fertile ash. Imana had helped His children.[1]

.   .   .

In legend and actuality nearly all primitive peoples have been associated with fire from their earliest days. Carbonized artifacts are linked with the oldest human remains. Australian aborigines of today still burn the isolated outback on animal hunts perfected in age-old tradition.

Man has probably used and "kept" fire for more than 500,000 years, though he seems to have learned to produce it only during the last 20,000. In the beginning his constant concern must have been to keep alight flames secured from lightning fires. His methods of fire "storage," the inevitable escape of sparks to the surrounding wilderness, and his use of fire in the hunt for plant and animal marked the initial stamp of his influence on the earth's landscape. Curiously, man's long walk with fire now seems to be circling back toward its starting place, for different reasons.

The American Indians probably knew how to make fire when they crossed the Bering Strait land bridge from Asia to Alaska somewhere around 15,000 years ago. From the California Indians to the Incas of Peru, they used the fire drill for producing fire.

Ishi, the last California Yahi Indian to emerge from the Stone Age culture of the northern Sierra–Mount Lassen border, lived as a modern for nearly five years. He had always carried his fire drill with him on wilderness travel, protecting the drill and tinder in rainy weather with a buckskin covering. Ishi demonstrated its use to many avid Sunday crowds at the University of

California Museum of Anthropology in San Francisco, where he lived those brief, intriguing years of 1911–1915.

Ishi's fire drill was typical of those used by other California Indians. It consisted of two pieces, an upper and a lower. The lower, called the hearth, was a flat slab of wood (usually willow or cedar) with one or more sockets gouged a quarter of an inch deep, notched at one side and with a shallow channel leading from each notch to the edge. The drill, or upper piece, was an ordinary round stick of a size that would fit the hearth socket and was arrow length, larger at one end, and preferably made of buckeye. Before drilling, Ishi spread dried moss, thistledown, or shreds of inner willow bark along the channel of the hearth and on the ground beside it. Then, squatting, pushing the hearth firmly against the ground with his toes, he placed the larger end of the drill in the socket, held the other end between the palms of his open hands, and began to rub back and forth in opposite directions.

Applying downward pressure simultaneously, he pushed the rotating stick into the socket, grinding off sawdust on the inner edges. As he twirled faster and faster, this fine wood powder began to pile up, turn black, and smoke; then, as it grew, to move out into the notch and down the channel. When a spark finally twinkled, it was in the notch, from whence it spread down the channel to the tinder on the ground, where Ishi fanned it gently into "his fire." [2]

Producing fire with a fire drill takes much skill, strength tempered with delicate control, and perseverance. So laborious and time-consuming a job was it that American Indians, as well as ancient cultures all over the world, went to considerable trouble to preserve fire rather than manufacture it. This was done by burning into a large log or into the roots of a bush or banking a

fire with ashes, so that a spark would be available upon their
return from a hunting or food-gathering trip. Tribes who knew
about it, such as the eastern, northern, and southern Sierran nations, sometimes carried a "slow match," a tightly rolled rope of
bark that would stay alight by burning very slowly at one end.

Early trappers and explorers in the American west were
amazed to discover that most Indians did not extinguish their
campfires. There were good Amerindian reasons for this. It
gave the Indians a chance to get fire easily if their slow match
went out, and they recognized no harm in igniting any vegetation that would burn. The burning of vegetation, either pur-
posely or accidentally, has long been recognized by anthropolo-
gists as a nearly universal custom among early humans. Omer
Stewart, University of Colorado anthropologist, claims to have
"evidence of almost every tribe in the western United States
using fire to modify its vegetational environment." He is convinced "that primitive man, with fire as a tool, has been the de-
ciding factor in determining the types of vegetation covering
about a fourth of the globe."

There seems little question that Indians across the United
States used fire as a land-management tool. Cabeza de Vaca, the
Spanish soldier who survived shipwreck near Galveston Island
in 1528 and lived for eight years among the Indians of the Gulf
Coast, told of the Indians firing the plains to destroy mosquitoes
and to compel deer and other animals to go for food where they
wished them to go. Fire was also used to encircle game and
stampede it within range of hunters.

In New England of the 1620s, "the savages are accustomed to
set fire to the country in all places where they are and to burn it
twice a year . . . The reason that moves them to do this is

because it would otherwise be so overgrown with under-weeds . . ." [3]

Explorers of the American prairie in the early 1800s reported that Indians fired grassland and forests to aid traveling and hunting and to improve pasture for wild game. One of them, Wells, concluded that the tallgrass prairies between the Mississippi River and the Appalachians were caused by repeated intentional burning-over by Indians.[4]

Here was a forerunner of the more recent work of Carl Sauer, University of California geographer, who has pointed out that much of the primeval scene discovered by European invaders of the New World had been "painted by primitive man," using fire over thousands of years to modify vegetation in various ways. Grasslands, the world over, are there because of fire. Remove fire, and woody shrubs or trees quickly take over, as grass-woodland managers in Texas, Arizona, California, and Africa have found to their dismay in recent decades.

Were the forests of the Sierra Nevada likewise painted? Anthropologist Alfred L. Kroeber gave a clear-cut answer in his classic *Handbook of the Indians of California*. The Indians of the northern Sierra, the Maidu,

like most of the Californians who inhabited timbered tracts . . . frequently burned over the country, often annually. It appears that forest fires have been far more destructive since American occupancy, owing to the accumulated underbrush igniting the large trees . . . The Indian was not attempting to protect the stand of large timber: he merely preferred an open country. This is shown by the fact that he also burned over unforested

tracts. Travel was better, view farther, ambuscades more
difficult, certain kinds of hunting more remunerative,
and a crop of grasses and herbs was of more food value
than most brush.

Galen Clark, who came to Yosemite in 1854 and served for
many years as official guardian of Yosemite Valley and the Big
Tree Grove, wrote of those early years:

> The Valley had then been exclusively under the care and
> management of the Indians, probably for many centuries.
> Their policy of management for their own protection
> and self-interests, as told by some of the survivors who
> were boys when the Valley was first visited by whites in
> 1851, was to annually start fires in the dry season of the
> year and let them spread over the whole valley to kill
> young trees just sprouted and keep the forest groves open
> and clear of all underbrush, so as to have no obscure
> thickets for a hiding place, or an ambush for any invad-
> ing hostile foes, and to have clear grounds for hunting
> and gathering acorns. When the fires did not thoroughly
> burn over the moist meadows, all the young willows and
> cottonwoods were pulled by hand.[5]

Richard Reynolds and others have corroborated the red man's
use of fire in Yosemite.

Miwok Indians in other yellow pine and foothill sections of
the central Sierra burned off dry brush in August to get a better
growth the following year and to prevent fires hot enough to
ignite the acorn oaks on which they depended. They set

meadow fires that attracted deer and then shot the curious, investigating animals with arrows from ambush. Miwoks also collected grasshoppers by building a large circular fire in a flat grassy spot and letting it burn slowly toward the center where a hole had been dug. "This took care of everything except ladling the hoppers out after they had been roasted." [6]

.   .   .

The California Indians probably molded the Sierra landscape with fire for more than 3000 years. For much, much longer, jagged forks of lightning have struck dry tinder ablaze and sent flames licking through the pine and fir forests. The Mediterranean climate of the Sierra Nevada's middle and lower western slopes and the arid climate of the eastern slope provide just the long, hot, almost dry summers that make the land extremely vulnerable to fire. Despite the lack of rain, thunderstorms build up at regular intervals to spark the earth.

Meteorological figures from the California Forest and Range Experiment Station show that in the area from Yosemite Park north to the Feather River, lightning caused well over 100 fires a year in the last decade. Some seasons saw up to 300 such fires, with at times as many as 300 lightning strikes bombarding the dry timber during one storm. Lightning fires are thus a natural climatic feature of the current Sierran environmental scene, and rate as an important landscape architect of the past — as far back as similar climate prevailed, throughout the eons of time when fire suppression and control measures of today were totally lacking in the summer-dry forests.

Ten times more critical, however, is lightning frequency in the Rocky Mountains, climatically endowed with almost daily summer thunderstorms that produce as many as 3000 lightning fires a year. Occasional fire periods, like the 1940 nightmare, registered 2000 fires in three days.

So vital a factor are lightning fires, not only in the Sierra and Rockies but throughout the United States, that the Forest Service, which by means of its lookouts and fire crews maintains a constant vigil in national forests, recently launched Project Skyfire. Skyfire is a study of meteorological problems associated with lightning-caused forest fires. As Project Director Keith Arnold analyzed it:

At this very moment some 1800 thunderstorms are in progress over the earth's surface. During the next 20 minutes these storms will produce 60,000 cloud-to-ground lightning discharges. Some of them will start fires. This sequence of events occurs 9000 times each summer in America's forests and grasslands. During the period 1942–62, the United States experienced more than 140,000 lightning-caused fires. Eighty-five percent of them occurred in the western United States, causing severe losses of timber, wildlife, watershed and recreation resources. We believe that the magnitude of the lightning fire problem calls for intensive research on lightning phenomena.

What can the Forest Service do about something as untamable as lightning? Skyfire's research program includes four study areas: (1) regional study of thunderstorms and resultant forest fires; (2) study of individual thunderstorms; (3) characteristics and effects of individual lightning discharges; and (4) weather modification.

Thunderstorm reports from fire lookouts in the northern

Rocky Mountains have already disclosed definite zones of high-lightning occurrence. So far these zones do not necessarily coincide with high-fire zones. Is lightning a more efficient fire starter in some areas than in others? If so, what combinations of topographical, meteorological, and fuel conditions account for this? With the new lightning sensors recently developed, technicians may eventually be able to detect which lightning discharges are fire starters.

Much is being learned about the character of lightning itself, with instruments even ingenious Ben Franklin could hardly have dreamed of. A bolt of lightning is actually made up of many currents traveling back and forth from cloud to earth, the current durations measured in microseconds — millionths of a second. This is "a short piece of time when you consider that a microsecond is to a second what one minute is to 23 months." [7] The current has been measured as high as 340,000 amperes and the voltage in hundreds of thousands of volts.

The old saying "Where there is thunder, there is lightning" hits home in this case. The primary generator of lightning's tremendous electrical discharge is the thundercloud. Within the thundercloud's updrafts and downdrafts, humid air condenses into raindrops, and these to ice crystals. Electrical charges build up until there are positive charges in the upper part of the cloud, negative charges in the lower, and positive charges on the surface of the earth. When these charges become so strong that the air can no longer keep them separate, lightning jumps the gap between opposite attracting charges. It may be from cloud to earth, from cloud to cloud, or within the same cloud, and its intensity depends on the size and intensity of the thundercloud itself. Generally, the larger the thunderclouds, the greater the lightning.

There is always a slow leakage of electricity from the earth because air is an imperfect nonconductor. As a thundercloud approaches a forest, this "leakage" takes a positive charge and reaches up toward the strong negative attraction at the cloud base. Within this contacting cloud mass, the tallest trees stand out as waving electric leaders of positive charge and will usually be the ones struck by lightning. Not always, however, since conductivity of the surface makes a difference, and there may be other reasons yet undeciphered.

It has been known since A. S. Kinney's experiments at the Massachusetts Agriculture Experiment Station in 1897 that plants vary in electrical potential from species to species, even from winter to summer in the same species, and that certain plant parts are better conductors of electricity than others. The cambium, or growing layer, is sometimes a good conductor, whereas the sap is not.

German investigators of the 1920s drew an interesting correlation between fatty oil in a tree's cells and its resistance to lightning. On the same plantation where beech trees were rarely struck by lightning, oak trees were frequently injured. Microscopic examination revealed that the wood cells of beech contained oil; those of the oak were almost free of it. They concluded that the richer the wood was in fatty oil, the more difficult it was for lightning to destroy it.

Lightning starts forest fires in one of two ways. A direct, intense hit splits most conifers wide open, blows them apart, and sets the remnants ablaze. More often, a strike runs down the trunk with lesser damage and lights fine fuels, dry needles, leaves, and brush near its base. Giant sequoias, extraordinary trees in most ways, show an extraordinary response to lightning. John Muir described it vividly in "Hunting Big Redwoods."

No ordinary bolt ever seriously hurts sequoias. In all my walks I have seen only one that was thus killed outright . . . I have seen silver firs, 200 feet high, split into long peeled rails and slivers down to the roots, leaving not even a stump . . . But the sequoia, instead of being split and slivered, usually has 40 or 50 feet of its brash knotty top smashed off in short chunks about the size of cord wood, the beautiful rosy-red ruins covering the ground in a circle a hundred feet wide or more . . . All the very old sequoias have lost their heads by lightning. "All things come to him who waits"; of all living things sequoia is perhaps the only one able to wait long enough to make sure of being struck by lightning.

Individual sequoia strikes have been observed by rangers in recent years. In a 1942 storm lightning struck the Grizzly Giant in Yosemite's Mariposa Grove six times, wreaking great havoc and piling branches many feet deep on the ground beneath.[8] Near the Telescope tree of the same grove can be read, even today, the story of one of the most titanic dramas that ever took place in these giant forests. Some sixty years ago, a low-hanging thunderhead moved up the east side of the basin, which shelters the grove, churning, swirling, and massing so low as to swallow the treetops.

Suddenly a blinding flash lit the forest. Spears of flame simultaneously struck each of a group of three big trees about one hundred feet above their bases, blasting twelve feet out of the center of their trunks and hurling huge pieces fifty feet away. The first tree, fourteen feet in diameter, was struck just beneath its lowest limb; the remaining snag was pushed twenty feet forward against the second tree, its trunk seared to the ground by the bolt, which ripped out huge slabs of bark and left a fire to crater its dead crown. The upper half of each of the three trees, suspended in midair for the microseconds of the flash, crashed to earth, smashing smaller trees. There the broken chunks lie today. True to species' durability, the second and third sequoias have sprouted new luxuriant foliage from their fragmented tops 150 feet up.

. . .

To the lightning fires and Indian fires of the past which helped shape Sierran forests of today must be added three more potent fire influences — miners, stockmen, and loggers. Before 1849, the ridges, canyons, meadows, and slopes of the Sierra were Indian country, with well-defined territories bounding each tribe. The discovery of gold in the western foothills changed all of this for ever. The inrush of immigrant miners precipitated one of the most frenzied digging sprees in human history, accompanied by cutting of timber for houses, stores, flumes, mining props, fuel, and the burning of slash and brush to bring gold-bearing rocks into better view and give easier access to working and living areas. With these changes came the quick demise of the Indian and the advent of the cow and sheep.

In the 1850s, 550,000 sheep plodded the trails to mine diggings throughout the foothills' Mother Lode belt. As a standard food item for work and exploring parties, they were highly popular, "furnishing their own transportation and needing no refrigeration." [9] When the first gold bloom had faded, men began eying more thoughtfully those lush green mountain pastures and these baa-a-ing dollars on the hoof.

The Civil War, which started in 1860, cut off the supply of cotton from the South and spurred a boom in wool and sheep prices. Sheep in California increased from 1,000,000 in 1860 to 6,000,000 by 1876, with equally impressive numbers of cattle and horses. From 1860 to nearly 1900, the Sierra Nevada became a "shepherd's empire," with cattlemen not far behind. The mountains were free for the taking, and the stockmen took them.

It was in the 1860s that the first great trail herds began their circular sweeps through the mountains. Starting in Kern County in the southwestern Sierra in the spring of the year, thousands upon thousands of sheep moved through Walker Pass to Inyo County, northward up the east side of the range, crossed back via Sonora Pass, and nibbled their way southward down the west slope of the mountains to winter lambing grounds in Kern County.

Up every thoroughfare into the mountain's heart moved imported Basque, French, and Portuguese herders with flocks of up to two thousand sheep apiece. Shrouded under a cloud of dust, the flocks came on "like a plague," cropping every green thing in their path. The tinkling of bells, the blatting of ewes, the barking of dogs, the bleating of lambs, the calls of herders became unwelcome familiar nightmares to ranchers along the way, many of whom guarded their own green holdings with shotguns.[10]

For the first few years the formerly unexploited middle and higher mountain meadows and forest undercover could take it, but by the 1870s ranges everywhere were overgrazed dustbowls, prompting Muir to write in 1873, "It is impossible to conceive of a devastation more universal than is produced among the plants of the Sierra by sheep . . . The grass is eaten close and trodden until it resembles a corral . . . Where the soil is not preserved by a strong, elastic sod, it is cut up and beaten to loose

dust and every herbaceous plant is killed." [11] After a hike
through the Tule River sequoia forests two years later, he wrote
in "Hunting Big Redwoods," "All the basin was swept by
swarms of hoofed locusts . . . until not a leaf within reach was
left on the thorniest chaparral beds, or even on the young conifers, which unless under stress of dire famine sheep never
touch."

Along with the sheep came the sheepmen's fires. In place of a
corral, many shepherds hemmed in their flocks for the night by
setting fires in fallen timber or living trees, at points that would
keep "wild beasts" off. At their camps one could hear great
pines fall in the night. The fires burned for days, sometimes
spreading over large areas.

It was a habit of many herders to set fire to the undergrowth
as they passed out of the mountain forests in the autumn en
route to the valleys below, in order to ensure an abundant
growth of tender sprouts on their return the following spring.
The next spring when flocks five times the size that the range
could support came eating their way back up the mountain,
they followed close behind the melting snow, reached the fire-
stimulated newly sprouting shoots before the plants had had
time to mature, cut the soil, exposed the plant roots, and nulli-
fied the effects that a pruning fire might have brought.

Muir pressed home a sizzling indictment of the incendiary
shepherds in a *Sacramento Record-Union* article of 1876. "Indians burn off underbrush to facilitate deer-hunting. Campers
of all kinds often permit fires to run, so also the millmen, but
the fires of 'sheepmen' probably form more than 90 percent of
all destructive fires that sweep the woods . . . Incredible numbers of sheep are driven to the mountains every summer . . .
and fires are set everywhere to burn off old logs and under-

brush. These fires are far more universal and destructive than would be guessed. They sweep through nearly the entire forest belt from one extremity to the other."

Two decades later Stanford botanist William Dudley echoed Muir's sentiments on fire-sheep damage after a horseback survey of the southern Sierra. Marsden Manson, an explorer of the sheep-denuded Pyrenees, Caucasus, and Atlas Mountains, was appalled to find the same sort of bare-earth erosion havoc on northern and central Sierran slopes, fires that followed shepherds like a rash, and in what had by then become Yosemite National Park, sheepmen openly threatening to burn the government out.

For over forty years sheepmen thought they owned the Sierra Nevada on a no-rent, free-feed, burn-as-you-please ticket. The fortunes that some of them reaped were immense, and their "rights" to the land were relinquished under the new park and forest reserve laws of 1890 and 1893 only when enforced by United States cavalry troops.

.   .   .

Compared to "mutton-chasing firebugs," as the shepherds were sometimes dubbed, loggers ran a scorching second. The prevalence of logging fires made the early lumbering period of 1850–1890 "far more destructive to the forest cover than logging has been at any time since." [12] By 1893, when the Sierra Forest Preserve was set aside by President Harrison to protect timber and watershed lands, tremendous wooded areas of the Sierra had been slashed and burned.

The Lake Tahoe region, the largest lumber-producing center in the state in 1875, was the scene of much flaming carnage, including a forest fire accidentally set by neophyte claim-staker

Mark Twain, a fire that he described graphically in *Roughing It:* "Within half an hour all before us was a tossing blinding tempest of flame. It went surging up adjacent ridges, surmounted them and disappeared in the cañons beyond . . . flamed out again directly, higher and still higher up the mountainside — threw out skirmishing parties of fire here and there, and sent them trailing their crimson spirals away among remote ramparts and ribs and gorges, till as far as the eye could reach the lofty mountainfronts were webbed . . . with a tangled network of red lava streams." [13]

Thus, by the time that the three national parks, one national monument, and nine national forests in the Sierra Nevada were set aside as protected areas in the 1890s and early 1900s, large sections of all of them (probably close to 100 percent) had gone through a bath of fire innumerable times.

The midmountain forests were "fire-type" forests, mixed stands of ponderosa pine, sugar pine, incense cedar, white fir, California black oak — species able to maintain themselves in the face of recurrent fires so long as the fires were not of too great intensity at any one time. Recurrent fires had been a part of their normal environmental fluctuation for millennia.

What were these fire-pruned forests like in the 1800s? No one knew them more extensively and intensively than John Muir. "The inviting openness of the Sierra woods is one of their most distinguishing characteristics. The trees of all of the species stand more or less apart in groves, or in small irregular groups, enabling one to find a way nearly everywhere, along sunny colonnades and through openings that have a smooth, park-like surface, strewn with brown needles and burrs . . . One would experience but little difficulty in riding on horseback through the successive belts all the way up to the storm-beaten fringes of the icy peaks." [14] Clarence King, a member of the first party to make a geological survey in California, wrote of the openness of the forests, of woods through which his horse could gallop freely.

With fire protection and suppression at the turn of the century, a new element quickly made itself apparent in the forest scene. It had been evident much sooner in Yosemite Valley, protected earlier (1864), where naturalists and residents noticed decided changes in the forest cover. A manuscript of Galen Clark's, written about 1907, described the evolution in detail:

A great change has taken place in Yosemite Valley since it was taken from the control of the native Indians who formerly lived there. In the early years, when first visited by white people, three-fourths of the valley was open ground — meadows with grasses waist high and flowering plants. On the dryer parts were scattered forest trees — pines, cedars, and oaks — too widely separated to be called groves of underbrush, leaving clear, open, extensive vision up and down and across the valley from wall to wall on either side. The Indians kept the valley clear of thickets of young trees and brushwood shrubbery, so they could not be waylaid, ambushed, or surprised by enemies from outside, and to not afford hiding places for bears (grizzlies then inhabited the valley) or undesirable predatory animals, and also to have clear ground for gathering acorns, which constituted one of their main articles of food. At the present time there is not more than one-fourth of the floor of the valley clear, open ground, as there was fifty years ago. Nearly all the open ground between the large scattering trees is now covered with a dense growth of young trees, which also extend out over hundreds of acres of the dryest portion of meadow land.[15]

The usual fate of mountain meadows that once were lakes and would eventually become forest unless deterred was overtaking the Incomparable Valley.

John Muir had spotted the trend and the accompanying dangers back in 1896. "Since the fires that formerly swept through the valley have been prevented, the underbrush requires much expensive attention . . . The underbrush and young trees will grow up as they are growing in Yosemite, and unless they are kept under control the danger from some chance fire, from lightning, if from no other source, will become greater from year to year. The larger trees will then be in danger. Forest management must be put on a rational, permanent scientific basis, as in every other civilized country."

But for more than seventy years since Muir's comment, the problems of young-tree congestion and fire hazard have been mounting ever more critically throughout the forests of the montane Sierra Nevada. As the Leopold Committee report to the Secretary of the Interior summed it up in 1963, "Much of the west slope is a dog-hair thicket of young pines, white fir, incense cedar and mature brush — a direct function of overprotection from natural ground fires. Within the . . . national parks . . . Yosemite, Sequoia and Kings Canyon — the thickets are even more impenetrable than elsewhere. Not only is this accumulation of fuel dangerous to the giant sequoias and other mature trees but the animal life is meager, wildflowers are sparse, and the vegetative tangle is depressing, not uplifting. Is it possible that the primitive open forest could be restored, at least on a local scale?"

Attempts to do just this have gotten under way in recent years in several different parts of the Sierra. Teaford Forest, near North Fork in the central range, has been the site of a pioneering experiment by Harold Biswell, professor of forestry at the University of California, who learned the uses of prescribed burning in the pine forests of Georgia from 1942 to 1947. Originally distrusting fire as the arch enemy of forests, Biswell came to see that under control it could be a vital tool in forest management, helping to prevent the very holocausts it might otherwise cause.

• • •

The southern United States was the place to go in those days to watch fire research in action. It was here from 1910 through the 1930s that the first insights into possible useful roles of fire in forest ecology blazed forth on a scientific basis. (Scientists have always required proof that early man knew what he was doing in his use of fire.)

The European school of forestry, which dominated the thinking and training of most American foresters in the early 1900s, viewed fires as the rare and destructive things they were in the forests of Europe and the spruce-fir forests of the northern United States. Against this armor of total fire abhorrence, a few independent-minded Southern foresters began to unloose a steady barrage of experimental evidence proving that in the South, at least, controlled fires could be an asset.

There was Roland Harper, who as early as 1913 pointed out that in the longleaf pine forests of Alabama it was a light fire sweeping through the grass and pine needles under the trees that bared the ground on which longleaf pine seeds germinated best. Without fires, most of the tree seeds lodged in the grass and pine litter, never reached soil at all, and the pine forest gradually died out.

There was S. W. Greene, who found by experiment in the 1920s that cattle gained weight faster in burned then in unburned pine woods because they had access to more leguminous forage.

There was Herbert L. Stoddard, Sr., whose classic volume on the habits of bobwhite quail in 1931 poked holes in the old idea that fire destroyed quails' food and shelter. Judiciously handled fire, by burning off dead grass such as broom sedge, favored the growth of legumes like partridge pea, a favorite food of quail. Fire stimulated important fruit-bearing shrubs such as huckleberry, blueberry, dewberry, ground oak, and others to bear heavily for two to four years. Where burns were mingled with "rough" (unburned vegetation), quail led "the best of all possible lives," with an abundance of fruits and insects near small brushy coverts for refuge. Both quail and wild turkeys were known to flock to light burns almost before they stopped smoking to take advantage of the sudden availability of food formerly hidden in the grass.

Over the decades the information backlog on controlled burning grew larger and larger in the South. It was discovered that in a roughly one-hundred-year period, southern pine forests were usually replaced by a hardwood climax* woodland, under fire exclusion. The interim saw brushy jungle-like stages when pine,

* Climax: A relatively stable, long-lived community that develops late in plant succession in the absence of disturbance. A loose term, variously interpreted, since forests seem never to reach absolute stability but always remain dynamic in some ways.

which could not reproduce in its own shade, died off and hardwoods, which could, took over. Where commercial pine was desired indefinitely, as in much of the South, burning at intervals proved an excellent way to forestall the usual forest succession. It killed the invading young hardwood trees, removed flammable tangles, and opened the forest floor for pine seedlings.

Pine forests that were allowed to "go natural" and fill up with brush and hardwood seedlings paid the price of almost total devastation when a forest fire struck, since the fuel buildup produced heat beyond the power of even many of the fire-resistant mature longleaf pines to survive. Occasional light burns acted as fire insurance. They encouraged longleaf pine seedlings by destroying brown-spot needle blight, which often attacks them, and by reducing the grass rough to expose seedlings to more sunlight. Fires took care of some of the necessary thinning of young stands of pine. In later years, controlled fires proved as beneficial in loblolly and shortleaf pine forests as in longleaf.

This was not so in the beautiful hardwood forests of the southern bottomlands. Among the willow oaks, overcup oaks, swamp chestnut oaks, hickories, and other species of mixed lowland timber, fire began a process that turned "healthy hardwoods into standing junk." [16] Research at the Southern Forest Experiment Station plots near Vance, Mississippi, showed that in hardwoods there was "no such thing as a harmless fire." All fires fried the saplings and wounded larger trees, initiating rot and eventual destruction. Maintaining low fire hazards in the surrounding pine forests could, however, provide a measure of insurance.

On the national wildlife refuges of the Southeast, fire rejuvenated rather than destroyed. The refuges' main objective was to create and maintain optimum habitat conditions for wildlife.

Prescribed burning proved an asset in doing the job. Marshes and adjacent pinelands burned in the fall provided fresh new marsh grass all winter for the huge wintering flocks of snow geese, blue geese, Canada geese, and ducks.

Without burning, the brackish Louisiana marshes filled up in a few years with the climax grass (*Spartina patens*), which was wiry and nearly valueless for wildfowl. Burning maintained good stands of the nutritious sedges, Olney's three-square and leafy three-square (*Scirpus*), the preferred foods of snow and blue geese as well as of muskrats.

It became clear, through experimentation in the South as well as in Arizona, Washington, Africa, and elsewhere in the first half of this century, that the value of controlled burning varied directly with the habitat, the purpose, the timing — as with any land-management tool — and that using it safely and effectively took technical skill and ecological "know-how." *

· · ·

When Harold Biswell began using it on the Teaford Forest of the Sierra Nevada in 1951, as part of long-term research on improving deer range and reducing the danger of wildfires in summer, he drew on this backlog of knowledge but had no certain way of knowing what he would find. The Teaford Forest was dominated by second-growth ponderosa pine, with sugar

---

* Since 1950 scientific interest in fire ecology the world over has mushroomed. The Tall Timbers Research Station near Tallahassee, Florida, initiated long-term studies on plant, animal, and genetic aspects of the ecology of fire on 2800 acres of land in 1959. In 1962 the station inaugurated an annual Fire Ecology Conference, bringing together the latest available intercontinental fire research, and publishing books of proceedings. Habitats worldwide — tundra, desert, northern coniferous forests, muskeg bog, savannas — are being fire-analyzed; foresters, range managers, and silviculturists increasingly are coming to the conclusion of ecologist Stephen Spurr that "frequent burning has been the rule for the vast majority of the forests of the world as far back as we have any evidence."

pine, California black oak, and incense cedar as secondary species. The young ponderosas grew thickly, their lower dead branches ghostly crescents, their crowns casting a shade too dense for grasses or herbs to prevail against over much of the forest floor. Red-trunked manzanitas curved toward the sun in openings that also harbored much dead brush — old gray manzanita clumps crumbling slowly, dry as tinder, dead deerbrush, dead buckbrush (*Ceanothus cuneatus*) — and new young shrubs of all these species popping up in too few places.

The fire hazard had to be removed and the area opened up to more sun and growth; the prescription, a combination of controlled burning and thinning. Thinning increased the distance between tinder trees and reduced the needle-fall, both lessening fire danger. It permitted more light to reach the forest floor, enough for sun-loving forbs here and shade-tolerant species there.

Prescribed burning removed some of the forest floor litter that had been smothering ground vegetation. It was done when the trees were dormant and the soil was still moist soon after a rain. The top pine needles dried quickly and would soon carry a surface ground fire along paths carefully fire-laned beforehand by the operators. Such fires usually removed about 75 percent of the needles and about 23 percent of the duff underneath, leaving sufficient soil protection against runoff and erosion and an ash that acted as a fertilizer on some plants.

Prescribed burning ignited the dead brush after the forest area around it had been safely burned. Its heat cracked the hard seed coats of manzanita, deerbrush, and buckbrush, fire-type shrubs that react by germinating. Burning stimulated the black oaks to sprout and prepared a receptive seedbed for their acorns.

The result of this combined burning-thinning treatment of fifteen years was an open, sun-dotted forest in which the fire hazard lay at a minimum, the ground cover supported ample grasses, legumes, bracken, and wildflowers. New green shrubs replaced old dried ones in the clearings, offering more and better forage for deer. There was more air space; there were more berries and seeds for "forest edge" wildlife. The project was paid what might be termed the supreme compliment of our times when the owner announced that the forest was now so appealing a piece of real estate that he was going to subdivide it.

Teaford Forest has not had to stand the test of a wildfire, but other prescribe-burned ponderosa pine forests have. On the Fort Apache Indian Reservation, Arizona, in June 1963, the Penrod Mountain fire, driven by thirty- to forty-mile-per-hour winds, swept northward along both sides of a road. The ponderosa forest on the left side of the road, a forty-year-old stand, had been prescribe-burned in 1956 and again in 1961. The fire crept through it on the ground, causing only minor hot spots. Over 90 percent of the dominant and codominant trees survived. On the right side of the road, the ponderosa forest had not been prescribe-burned. When the fire reached this self-made fuel depot, it leaped for the tree crowns immediately and continuously, and almost completely destroyed the forest.[17]

Harold Weaver, "dean" of nearly thirty years of prescribed burning in ponderosa pine forests of Arizona and Washington, has found that a single prescribed-burn reduces fuels by 50 percent and damage done by wildfires 90 percent.

• • •

Biswell's fire-conditioned eye meanwhile had settled on another trouble spot in the southern Sierra, this time on University of California owned Whitaker's Forest. Across Redwood Mountain from Whitaker's, a team led by Richard Hartesveldt of San Jose State College was digging into the same problem for the National Park Service. Both involved sequoias. Both began around 1964 or 1965. Hartesveldt slid into the project more or less by accident. His doctoral dissertation on the effects of human impact on sequoias in Yosemite's Mariposa Grove had found some indication of compacted or eroded soils around certain big-tree bases but little evidence of tree impairment. Staring him in the face everywhere he turned, however, were blatant symptoms of other more critical problems.

The big trees were being engulfed by a forest of white fir! In some places fir surrounded the big cinnamon trunks like bodyguards, cutting off the view completely. Elsewhere fir canopies cast deep shade over countless dead young sequoias that had lost the race for sun and soil moisture, a mortality of 86 percent over the past twenty-five years in the upper Mariposa Grove. One foot high to sixty feet high, in all sizes and ages, white fir was taking over. Beneath its dense stands lay a thick litter that sequoia seeds could not penetrate to reach soil. Sequoia reproduction had come to a virtual halt.

Equally serious, the accumulation of dead, combustible branches, brush, and debris of many years — and resinous fir thickets of all heights — set up a fire fuel supply that could trigger a holocaust.

How had this tinderbox situation come about? And others like it throughout the sequoia groves? The answer began to sound monotonously familiar: overprotection from fire — seventy plus years of it. The last good crop of young sequoias dated back seventy or eighty years to sudden opening of the forest by fire. In the absence of fire, forest succession since then had favored white fir, which could reproduce in its own shade. Sequoias could not. The big trees needed a forest-opening disturbance every now and then for survival. Strong evidence indicated that throughout the centuries this disturbance periodically had been fire.

Fire scars occur on virtually all sequoias exceeding five feet in diameter. In the process of healing, fire wounds become covered with a layer of woody growth that forms a permanent record of the fire. Correlating these healed "scars" with tree rings, it has been possible to date fires in the Mariposa Grove back to A.D. 450, and to show that between 1760 and 1900 Grove fires averaged one every seven or eight years.

Anyone walking through sequoia groves cannot avoid noticing the frequent char marks on the tree boles, occasional blackened snags and crowns, and the cavernous burns of individuals like Mariposa's Telescope and Haverford trees, which have been gutted by fires and burned through in several directions, left with only a few narrow strands of trunk to support several hundred tons of stem in midair but very much alive and flourishing.

Mature intact sequoias probably share few rivals as the most fire-resistant species on the earth today. It takes weeks of burning, fed by fallen branches or trees next to the trunk, for a fire to penetrate the thick unbroken bark. Even when this happens and its armor is pierced, the tree often meets future fires with a wood that chars more than it burns. However, recent National Park Service findings indicate that under certain conditions the tree is far from fireproof. Loosened sequoia bark, when dry and flaky, burns rather well; sequoia wood exposed in a fire scar also burns well when dry; and the dead branches in the upper part of the tree burn readily.[18]

Sequoias of the past lived with *recurrent* fires — fires that "cleaned up" the groves at chance intervals so that disastrous accumulations of debris never had time to pile up. John Muir spent several days in close quarters with a sequoia fire near the Kaweah River's middle fork in 1875, watching the flames creep and spread beneath the trees, with no danger of his being hemmed in.

"In the main forest belt of the Sierra," he wrote, "even when swift winds are blowing, fires seldom or never sweep over the trees in broad all-embracing sheets as they do in the dense Rocky Mountain woods and in those of the Cascade Mountains of Oregon and Washington. Here they creep from tree to tree with tranquil deliberation." [19]

Not anymore. California spends beyond $25 million a year on fire prevention and suppression, utilizing the finest skills of the craft, and doing a superb job, but when the "all-embracing sheet" fires hit, devastation is complete. Three percent of the state's forest fires do 95 percent of the damage. One 1959 Sierra Nevada fire that charred 50,000 acres in 36 hours, was estimated to cost as much as $66 million in timber and watershed alone.

. . .

The Redwood Mountain Grove project of the National Park Service and the Whitaker's Forest project of the University of California are both zeroing in on California's multiplying fire dangers. Their major objectives are similar: to develop management techniques that will reduce fire hazards in Sierra forests, and meanwhile maintain or re-create optimal conditions for native wildlife, enhance scenic and scientific values, and restore where feasible the open primeval forests.

The Park Service, committed by law to conserve sequoia

groves for the enjoyment of future generations, seeks the best way to encourage reproduction and growth of young sequoias. This means, at a minimum, removing some of the ground litter so that the tiny big-tree seeds can get a foothold in moist mineral soil and opening the canopy to make more sunlight and needed soil moisture available to seedling sequoas.

Some interesting preliminary results have emerged on the four park study areas that received various combinations of light broadcast burning, intense pile burning, white fir felling, and physical disturbance of the soil by removal of downed logs with brush-blade and cleat-tred bulldozers and rubber-tired pay-loaders. During the first summer after manipulation, 1966, in excess of two thousand sequoia seedlings sprouted in the treated areas; none in the controls. The means by which the substrate had been disturbed for seedbed preparation seemed immaterial at that time. What mattered, evidently was the contact of seed roots with moist mineral soil.

As the summer, an extremely dry one, wore on, the seedlings began to die. By October, only 30 percent remained alive; by the following July, 10 percent; by the following October, less than 2 percent. Most of the deaths were from dry roots. Meanwhile, a crop of more than five thousand new sequoia seedlings appeared the second summer in the treated areas, ten seedlings in control (untreated) areas. Like the earlier seedlings, each is being charted and watched individually to learn its fate.[20]

It is already apparent that to survive sequoias must walk a razor's edge of delicately balanced environmental conditions during the first critical years. Too much sun will scald and kill them; too little sun inhibits growth; too little water in the shallow root zone causes them to wither; too much disturbance from insects leads to their succumbing.

The latest evidence supports the fact that "the hotter the fire at soil level, the more apt the seedlings are to survive! The physical-chemical changes that take place make the soil more wettable and if direct sunlight doesn't deplete the moisture too rapidly, such soil may hold water in greater amounts — the opposite of what we have been told in the past. Further, the high temperatures may destroy spores of fungi which could be responsible for damping off and other diseases, and the hot fire eliminates much of the other competition during those early years of growth which are so delicate for the young sequoia seedling." [21]

The Whitaker's Forest study, in addition to burning and thinning, is also observing a cutover area on which deerbrush and California black oaks have been pioneer sprouters. The clearing is of an asymmetrical shape suggested by the landscape architect adviser so as to leave silhouettes of especially beautiful sequoias surrounding the opening.

Both projects are making careful before-and-after analyses of the plant and animal life to correlate habitat change with effects on individual species. The exact needs and role of sugar pine, incense cedar, and other species in the forest succession are under scrutiny.

As in much basic research, unexpected and surprising discoveries may emerge from these two somewhat comparable yet complementary studies by the mid-1970s, when they are scheduled to end. Whether their findings will, in part at least, make "prophets" out of foresters Biswell and Weaver and botanist Herbert Mason remains to be seen. It was in 1955 that Mason, in a discussion of how to save sugar pine, suggested: "In the long run the cheapest method will be to maintain a forest in low fire-hazard condition through controlled burning at intervals that will prevent the fire hazard from building up . . . Nature before us successfully managed the forest with her own system of controlled burning. As fire seems inevitable in our arid climate, would not the wisest course be to see that fire occurs only at such times and in such places as we choose?"

6. Red Firs and Lodgepoles

THE GLACIERS that capped the Sierra Nevada during Pleistocene times gouged out many U-shaped valleys on their downward flow, leaving piles of soil and rock along their sides and at their termini as they melted. On these lateral and terminal moraines, and in unglaciated deep soils throughout the 6000- to 9000-foot elevations of the Sierra, grow today's red fir forests.

In the northern Sierra, where the summit ridges are mostly under 9000 feet, red firs often are the trees of the highest elevations, wooding the crest with extensive almost-pure stands. In the south, where the divide is much higher and more rocky, the firs fill in the protected places well below the summits, often on plateaus where soil has accumulated and winds are not too strong. Throughout the length of the range, the red firs form a distinctive high-mountain community, a true climax forest in which young firs succeed the old. In many ways this forest is the Sierran equivalent of the taiga or circumpolar boreal forests. Many of its birds, mammals, and plants are similar to those of Canadian spruce forests, reflecting an ancestral relationship. Others are uniquely Sierran, the product of eons of isolation and evolution.

Among the singular species is the red fir (*Abies magnifica*) itself, which grows only in the Sierra Nevada, in the northern

California Coast Ranges, and the southern Cascades of Oregon. A virgin red fir forest has a mood all its own. The tall straight trunks rising one hundred fifty feet or more, massive as they reach four and five hundred years of age, are clothed in a deeply furrowed bark of the richest dark red. This mellow bark dominates the forest. Turning purplish red in the rain, chocolate-red in flat light, it sets off vividly the trees' close-fitting needles and the staghorn lichen (*Letharia vulpina*) that festoons trunks and limbs with luminous chartreuse.

A number of the firs are characteristically topless. The upper halves of dead trees sometimes come crashing down unpredictably, giving them the reputation among foresters as "widow-makers." On these stumps the bark clings for years. Throughout the forests where logs lie crisscross and splintered on the ground, their fast-rotting interiors powdery with decay, the rosy bark slabs persist in colorful intact chunks for decades.

In the densest stands of trees, the ground is thickly littered with fallen twigs and limbs, cone scales, needles, and humus. During the summer this collection sometimes becomes so compacted that it can be lifted from the soil in large mats. In these heavily shaded areas only a few plants will grow. Enough red fir seedlings survive to maintain the stand, and several species of gooseberry (*Ribes*) and snowberry (*Symphoricarpos*) exist.

Occasional wildflowers brighten the floor, snow plant (*Sarcodes sanguinea*) the most brilliant among them. Its stout fleshy stems, covered with reddish scales and crowded with bell-shaped crimson flowers, push through the humus just after the snow has melted. Sometimes there are two stems to a clump; occasionally as many as twenty-two. Lacking green leaves, the snow plant cannot manufacture its own food as plants with chlorophyll do. It feeds indirectly on decayed organic matter in the soil through the medium of a microscopic fungus that completely covers its roots. As summer wanes, its flowers produce small red marble-like capsules. By September the parent has one or more well-formed young plants underground at its base, ready to emerge next summer at the first sign of melt.

Other members of the heath family like the shady haunts: the waxy white-flowered shinleaf (*Pyrola secunda*) with green and white veined basal leaves, low twining pipsissewa (*Chimaphila umbellata*), and ghostly pinedrops (*Pterospora andromedea*). Minus chlorophyll, pinedrops lives as a parasite on fungi associated with the roots of nearby trees. Its flesh-colored gummy stems, one to three feet high, are partially covered by brownish scaly leaves and are topped with clusters of minute yellowish bells. Here and there rise brownish stems of another root parasite, the spotted coralroot (*Corallorhiza maculata*), carrying terminal clusters of quarter-inch flowers, each a miniature orchid, its lower lip white with purple spots. Even some green plants that seem self-sufficient — such as the shinleafs — are now known to be involved with or dependent on one or more types of fungi attached to their roots.

Of these shade-loving plants characteristic of the red fir and upper yellow pine forests, four types — the shinleaf, pipsissewa, coralroot, and pinedrops — range widely through boreal forests of the United States and Canada; shinleaf and pipsissewa occur also in Europe and Asia. Only the snow plant is of narrower western limits, confined to the Sierra and adjacent mountains of California and southern Oregon.

. . .

Many red fir forests have been opened by the fall of old trees, by fire, by logging — although their higher mountain inaccessibility spared most of them from the prolific lumbering of the late 1800s. Many fringe clearings and meadows.

In all of these more open and marginal areas, life in the red firs takes on decided volume and variety. Although the fir continues to dominate and to replace itself with thick stands of seedlings in the sunny glades, the other plants of the 6000- to 9000-foot belt become more evident. Lodgepole pines (*Pinus murrayana*), Jeffrey pines, and occasional but constant western white pines (*Pinus monticola*) intermingle.

Snowbrush, bush chinquapin (*Castanopsis sempervirens*), pinemat manzanita (*Arctostaphylos nevadensis*), and gooseberry add a shrub understory. And on the gravelly open soils grow patchy gardens of white hawkweeds (*Hieracium albiflorum*) on foot-high stalks; pussypaws (*Calyptridium umbellatum*) hugging the ground with rosy flowers and red spoonlike leaves; low blue lupines; golden-asters (*Chrysopsis breweri*) in solitary heads; and the almost prostrate shield leaf (*Streptanthus tortuosus*), displaying tiny magenta flowers above leaves that completely clasp the short stems.

The climate of these open gardens is as different from that of the dense forest as the two sides of a fir at forest edge. Hikers know this "bake or freeze" alternative. Sitting on the sunny open side of a mature red fir for twenty minutes heats you thoroughly. A 180-degree move around the trunk into complete shade provides nearly instant refrigeration. At first pleasantly cool, the air soon grows too cold for comfort, and within twenty minutes the sunny side of the tree is welcome once more.

In the frigidity of the shade the northern plants are at home; in the sunny places abound the plants more characteristic of the Sierra and other summer-dry Pacific slope mountains.

·   ·   ·

Among the conspicuous animals of the red fir forests are two scampering rat-sized rodents with black and white stripes on their backs and sides. The chipmunk (*Eutamias*) the smaller and more delicate of the two, has a pointed face with stripes on the head; the chunkier golden-mantled squirrel (*Citellus lateralis*), a ground squirrel, lacks stripes on its copper-colored head and neck. Both are as much a part of western mountains as the timber itself. In the Sierra Nevada the golden-mantle lives principally in the higher forests, but chipmunks of one kind or another occupy nearly every habitat up and down both sides of the range. The seven or eight chipmunk species look much alike except for the darkness of their color and the brightness of their stripes. Natural selection has obviously favored those patterns that blend with the environment. Chipmunks living in dense chaparral, where twig shadows are weak, have weak stripes; so do alpine chipmunks of the open talus slopes; the lodgepole chipmunks of the open red fir and lodgepole forests, where sunstruck twigs cast dark shadows, show well-demarcated light and dark stripes.

Depending for food variety on what the forest produces year after year, these spry little mammals are alert opportunists. Very fond of manzanita flowers, chipmunks in spring distend their stomachs with the sweet-smelling pink bells, leaving stumps littered with stripped flower stalks. Equally favored are manzanita seeds, which the chipmunks cram into cheek pouches until they seem ready to burst. Some seeds are carried into underground burrows; others are cached in small holes for later use but instead they often sprout in clumps after a fire.

In years of bumper crops of snowbrush, chipmunks rely on the seeds for nearly six weeks in late summer. They relish pine seeds, and some species climb high in trees to get them. Cherished delicacies are the spiny-skinned wild gooseberries, which they manage to harvest without swallowing spines or skin, and the tiny but sweet wild strawberries.

Burying whatever surplus seeds they can collect at harvest time in the fall, they eat some of these during the winter and seek the caches when emerging from hibernation the next spring. Failure of the autumnal seed supply means a serious spring food shortage. Since the animals are not leaf eaters, except as a last resort, new spring vegetation brings no bonanza to them until it flowers. They fill in their spring diet with surface fungi, with caterpillars dug out of leaf litter, and whatever other insects they can find. Rather fastidious eaters, they pounce on the big brown carpenter ants of decaying logs and always decapitate their victims first, then discard the heads.

The little rodents seldom miss an insect influx that means easy protein. In the years when aphids infest young fir needles, chipmunks often concentrate on aphids for an entire month, swallowing them whole and using them for over three fifths of their diet.

On the evenings when the forest comes alive with the wing-rattling of termites streaming from slits in damp logs and taking to the air in mating flights, as though by reflex chipmunks appear everywhere. Excitedly they run from hole to hole, grabbing the insects that pop out. Approximately one of every twenty emerging termites disappears down a chipmunk gullet.

Chipmunks and golden-mantled squirrels, although using similar holes and burrows under rocks and logs for shelter and nests, coexist without serious competition because of different food needs and different ways of obtaining food. The squirrels are heavy leaf and fruit eaters and restrict their feeding close to the ground.

When golden-mantles emerge from hibernation in the spring, they crop voraciously the green shoots of grasses and forbs, from tiny seedling height to maturity. They share the taste of chipmunks and black bears for manzanita flowers in season but depend largely on succulent leaves of green herbs until the plants begin to dry up in late summer. There's a kind of amazing precision in the way a golden-mantle squats on its haunches, holds a wild pennyroyal (*Monardella*) in its forepaws, and with quick bends of the coppery head nips off flower, leaves, and stem right to the ground like an automatic descending scythe.

When these squirrels turn to seeds, they eat primarily those they can get from the ground or from boulders or logs. Hence they harvest the ground-level nutlets of snowbrush and its mat-like relative, squaw carpet (*Ceanothus prostratus*), while the more agile chipmunks are climbing snowbrush branches and trees to garner seeds higher up.

In the autumn of good years, conifer seeds become an important food, often one third of the golden-mantle's diet. In bad years, when the forest floors are dusty and dry and most seeds have gone or have failed to set, only innumerable small pits in the ground give a clue to the one remaining source of rodent food. Every rodent around will have its stomach packed with truffles. These subterranean fungi thrive in the coniferous forests of the Sierra Nevada and southern Cascades in both quantity and variety. The color of the fungi may range from coal black, gray, brown, white, and orange to greenish or purplish; the consistency may vary from firm or soft to gelatinous. But in one form or another, the truffles are present in the soil, well adapted to the long dry season and able to attain maximum numbers in the warm autumn when other foods often are gone. In protein content they compare favorably with conifer seed —

roughly 24 percent for an average of three species of fungi compared to 21 percent for Jeffrey pine.

The ground squirrels apparently detect them by smell and dig them out. Many small mammals besides golden-mantles and chipmunks feast on the fungi — chickarees, California ground squirrels, gray squirrels, flying squirrels, woodrats, and deer mice, among others. During some years, when golden-mantles emerge from hibernation in advance of any new greenery, truffles left over from the previous fall provide their sole food for several weeks.

Ordinarily golden-mantles are not the insect eaters that chipmunks are, but an unusual insect outbreak can bring them running. The California tortoise-shell (*Nymphalis californica*) is a butterfly noted for sporadic population explosions in the higher forests of the Sierra. Some years its caterpillars completely defoliate snowbrush and other *Ceanothus* hosts. When this occurred in the northern Sierra in July of 1951, Lloyd P. Tevis, Jr., happened to be studying the chipmunks and golden-mantled squirrels of the infested area. What he saw was a concerted attack by the rodents on two stages of the butterfly's four-stage life cycle. After the spiny black and yellow caterpillars had gobbled up every leaf in sight on acres of snowbrush, they deserted the naked shrubs and migrated across the ground to nearby white firs. Here they pupated. En route on the ground, they were heavily attacked by golden-mantled squirrels, which fed on them to nearly two thirds of their diet.

Chipmunks, evidently repelled by the bristles of the caterpillars, ate few in that stage. But after the caterpillars turned into ashy-gray chrysalids hanging from the underside of fir boughs, chipmunks scampered nimbly over the branches to pick off and crunch the chrysalids for days. Some ate almost nothing else. Eventually the remaining butterflies hatched, swarmed over the forest, and drifted with the air currents up and over Lassen Peak to the north. Snowbrush regained its foliage within a month and the rodents returned to more routine fare.

Chipmunks, despite their small size, will defend a radius of fifty yards around their nest — a third larger than the golden-mantle's defended territory. Both rodents forage over a much wider distance. They need to know well every burrow and escape route within reach, for their enemies are many. Among the most difficult to elude are the weasels. These relentless hunters, slender and short-legged, can slip down rodent burrows with ease and speed. Two kinds of weasels of roughly similar habits live in the Sierra. The shorttail weasel, or ermine (*Mustela erminea*) — the smaller, shorter-tailed species of the high country — dens in rockslides and under tree roots. The much more common and slightly larger longtail weasel (*M. frenata*) inhabits all parts of the range, and much of North America as well.

Both weasels wear a summer coat of soft brown above and white below, and turn completely white in winter except for the black-tipped tail, which stays black the year round. Since they require about a third of their weight in meat every day, they use their sharp, inquisitive eyes and sensitive noses in ceaseless prowls for small prey. Chipmunks recognize them instantly as enemies and immediately inform every animal within hearing.

One quiet July morning in the red fir forest at Glacier Point in Yosemite National Park, a terrific commotion broke loose among the heavy population of chipmunks and golden-mantled squirrels. The rodents began darting to right and left as though life depended upon it. Some went into their burrows; others climbed stumps; every animal in sight took up a loud, continuous chatter that lasted for twenty minutes. Suddenly a weasel darted out from under a cabin, dashed to the left and to the right, then caught sight of three holes at the base of an old stump, smelled them, and disappeared into one. In a few seconds it reappeared with a young golden-mantle in its mouth. Repeating the performance, the weasel killed four of these ground squirrels within twenty minutes.

Death comes quickly to a victim — a bite through the base of the skull. And the operation has to be repeated many times by a tireless mother weasel during the five weeks that she assumes sole responsibility for her litter.

A female weasel that reared six young in a building in Sequoia National Park brought in a steady stream of small mammals during the 37 days that the youngsters were in the den: 78 mice, 27 pocket gophers, 2 moles, 34 chipmunks, 3 woodrats, and 4 ground squirrels.

Weasels, along with badgers and other carnivores, are among the controls that keep rodents from overrunning the woods and meadows. When weasels move into an area where fat, sluggish chipmunks are fed by campers, soon there are sounds of frantic chirping and scuffling in the woodpiles and under logs. Chipmunks pursued by weasels end in a few smothered squeaks. But in a week or so things quiet down. The weasels, having culled the surplus chipmunks, move into a nearby meadow to do the same for voles, often called meadow mice. The chipmunk population rebuilds, and eventually is ready for another influx of weasels.

Their streamlined build and speed notwithstanding, weasels are not foolproof hunters; they work hard for a living. A weasel observed chasing a shrieking golden-mantled squirrel down a road in Sequoia National Park caught hold of the squirrel by the back of the neck four times; each time the squirrel threw it off. The squirrel finally rushed blindly into a pool of water with the weasel right behind. The shock of cold water seemed to terminate the chase, since both animals scrambled separately and single-mindedly to get ashore and go their own ways.

Another golden-mantle eluded a pursuing weasel by dashing behind a bushy lodgepole pine and running four feet up into dense growth. The weasel, following chiefly by scent and about as fast as a man could run, missed the scent and continued straight ahead into the squirrel's empty burrow.

Always a formidable enemy, weasels are especially fearless in defense of their young. A miner who owned a cabin in the red firs of the northern Sierra told me of hearing a plop in his rain barrel one day and of stepping outside to investigate. A young weasel was struggling in the water. On the edge of the barrel pranced the mother and another youngster. He moved closer to lift the weasel out, when to his amazement the mother started for him threateningly, and kept coming. Taken aback, he stopped. She turned away from him, dashed to the far side of the barrel's edge, leaned way down in and managed to grasp the struggling weasel by the nape of the neck, then carried it a few feet with her teeth in its fur before she set it down on safe ground.

The weasel tribe is as well represented in the trees of the red fir belt as on the ground. Two of the finest arboreal artists of coniferous forests anywhere, the marten and the fisher, live in these woods. Of the two, the marten (*Martes americana*) is by far the more common. But a glimpse of its slim brown body running nimbly through the trees is rare enough to excite any naturalist anytime.

In summer martens prefer to hunt on the ground among the

talus slopes of the high Sierra. A rich crop of animals lives in these rockslides — pikas, bushytail woodrats, marmots, deer mice, with chipmunks, voles, and golden-mantled squirrels nearby, and ample berries — all welcome to a marten's palate. At this season, martens will sometimes come into fishermen's camps at night and steal trout off a line, or in broad daylight rob a lunchbox left unprotected. They occasionally pounce on grasshoppers that are soaking up the warmth of the granite rocks in the chill of evening.

When the first snows of the long winter fall on the high country, martens retreat to the red fir forests. The winter storms that carry moisture from the ocean up the Sierra's western slope drop the heaviest total precipitation on the upper yellow pine belt; the greatest snowfall settles among the red firs. In the record year of 1906–1907, seventy-three and one-half feet fell at the 8000-foot level of Tamarack in the central Sierra. Even in lesser years the snowpack ranks among the highest in the United States.

In these snowbound forests the marten struggles to subsist for eight or nine months. Its golden-brown fur reaches prime pelage as temperatures drop. The patches of yellowish orange on throat and chest stand out against a darker foxlike head, dark brown bushy tail and feet. Its footpads grow a dense coating of hair that insulates them from snow and ice. Averaging two feet in total length, the animal is light, weighing only about three pounds, and it can bound over slightly crusty snow without leaving a track. In the trees it looks somewhat like and moves like a squirrel, but is faster and can leap wider gaps.

During the winter martens live principally on chickarees, flying squirrels, blue grouse, and woodpeckers. All of these take much searching to find and nimble footwork to catch. Hunting territories apparently aid in the search. Each marten seems to have several such territories which it alternates, with absences from each circuit lasting weeks at a time. On these rather well-defined "runs," an animal may travel as much as ten to fifteen miles in one night, following a very erratic pattern, going in circles, zigzagging, backtracking, but making general progress along a definite course. Sometimes other martens follow over the "trails" within a few hours; the well-developed anal gland probably serves as a trail marker. Some trappers have been convinced that martens at times travel in small winter packs. The rugged, inaccessible winter terrain and the animal's primarily nocturnal habit make this difficult to check, since tracks are sometimes uncertain.

Martens are usually solitary when seen; they have been watched numbers of times chasing chickarees and capturing ground squirrels in daylight. When hunting arboreal squirrels, they may travel through the trees for miles without descending to the snow. They are thought to rob woodpecker holes of birds or eggs at night by reaching in with a forefoot. This is the position in which martens often were caught in traps in the Sierra during the first half of the century. The season was closed in 1952 to permit their much diminished numbers to increase, but they are still a rare sight in the range.

Rarer yet is the fisher (*Martes pennanti*). Once present in numbers throughout northern forests and down the higher mountain chains from the Appalachians to the Pacific, fishers have dwindled to remnants in most parts of their former range. Their beautiful fur, known to the trade as North American sable — even more costly than the marten's Hudson Bay sable — has been sought out by trappers since the mid-1800s. Now fully protected in the Sierra, the fisher's sparse but stable population between Yosemite and Sequoia National Park may be able to increase — if perennial threats of a trans-Sierran road can be averted.

When seen at a distance in the forest, the animal looks like a dark oversized weasel. Slung low, like all the weasel tribe, with brownish-black fur, black feet, and a grizzled head, the fisher averages about a foot longer and three times heavier than a marten and grows to a three-foot length and ten pounds. Its weight seems to add power and agility rather than bulk, for whereas a marten can overtake the fastest tree squirrels in full flight, the fisher can catch not only squirrels but martens.

The fisher's name is misleading: in the Sierra and most other areas the animal rarely goes after fish. The closest it comes to water is in following small creeks to seek out the aplodontia, or mountain beaver. Its usual haunts are the remote red fir and upper yellow pine forests, where it lives a solitary existence most of the year and travels at regular intervals over extensive territorial routes, principally at night.

When observed in the daytime, ordinarily it is pursuing chickarees or gray squirrels through the trees or stalking mice, rabbits, chipmunks, ground squirrels, or marmots on the ground. Its swiftness is extraordinary.

The trapper-naturalist W. H. Parkinson[1] tells of a November day in the red firs and lodgepoles of the southern Sierra when he and his wife saw a fisher jump gracefully and slowly across an opening. It seemed in no hurry and stopped to walk around a log, then disappeared into the forest. When they reached the place where it had vanished they saw their terrier, a great bear dog, look silently up into a lodgepole. Forty feet above sat the fisher.

When it saw them, it started down, headfirst like a chickaree.

Within fifteen feet of the ground, the fisher stopped and began scolding the dog "just as a big gray squirrel would do," hanging head downward, holding on with its hind legs and pounding on the trunk first with one forefoot and then with the other. All the while it gave out a kind of growl that terminated in a snarl or hiss, teeth white against the dark head.

To see what it would do next, Parkinson fired a bullet into the bark near it. The fisher leaped for the ground, landing fifteen feet from the tree and clear past the dog. The dog soon overtook it. For about three seconds there was "a blur of white dog and dark fisher." When the blur cleared, the fisher was fifty feet up a nearby fir; the game but dazed dog was bleeding with a dozen wounds from nose to tail. For the next quarter of a mile, the Parkinsons "were treated to a rare spectacle." The fisher traveled through the treetops nearly as fast as they could run, leaping from a branch of one tree to a branch of another with "the ease and assurance of a bird." When it finally reached an extra-large red fir with a heavy crown, it climbed into the top and vanished. There they left it.

Fishers seem to be the only predators to have mastered the art of killing porcupines. Oregon recently introduced two-dozen Canadian fishers as a means of porcupine control. A quick flip of the porcupine onto its back and a bite in the unprotected underparts can finish it off, but few animals are fast enough to accomplish this. Even the fisher often pays a price in quills but, oddly, the quills do not seem to fester or harm it as they do most victims.

The quills or hollow spines are sound reasons why the ambling, long-haired porcupine (*Erethizon dorsatum*) is left pretty much alone. One encounter discourages most aggression. When attacked, a porcupine drops its head between its legs, turns its rear to the enemy, and erects long sharp spines all over the back and tail. If approached too closely, it slaps violently with the tail, driving dozens of quills home. The quills, loosely attached and sharp-tipped, break off readily at the base when they enter flesh. Their back-slanting barbs continue to work in deeper and may eventually pierce a vital organ. Quills that have become loosened in a fight sometimes drop off the tail as it is flipped about, giving the mistaken impression that the animal throws its quills.

There is no question that spines penetrate deeply into the porcupine way of life. The lone baby, born in late spring, has a well-developed coat of hair and some spines at birth. The spines do not harden until later, however; actually they are modified hairs.

Generally considered a northern mammal because of its wide occurrence in northern and mountainous forests, the porcupine is really South American in origin. A few million years ago, when a land connection pushed up between North and South America after eons of separation, the porcupine was one of the South American fauna to attempt the crossing and to pass through the Costa Rican filter. Along with it came the capybara, armadillo, giant sloth, and many others. Not all of them made it — or for long. The porcupine survived and spread to become the only species of a South American-type rodent in the United States and Canada; its closest relatives are the capybara, guinea pig, and chinchilla.

Vegetarians by nature, porcupines eat herbs and shrubs in summer, the tender inner bark of young conifers at any season. In most areas they play the role of natural forest-pruners, killing off by girdling some of the young trees that would otherwise succumb in the competitive thinning of a maturing forest.

Their craving for salt and minerals drives them to gnaw deer antlers, ax handles, shovel handles, outhouse seats, saddles, any perspiration-touched gear around camps. Sometimes their choice of targets is bewildering. One summer in the Gold Lake country, I set out a salt block to attract porcupines for photography. Awakened about midnight by a loud gnawing, I grabbed the camera and stole quietly outside. The beam of the flashlight shone on a porcupine gnawing an empty brown cardboard carton, half eaten. Alongside, untouched, stood the white salt block.

After a summer night of feeding on the ground, porcupines pick their way slowly and deliberately to a fir or pine. Silhouetted against a dawn sky, they climb like bushy-haired mops to daytime roosts in the dense foliage above. Efficient climbers, they spend much of their time in trees, although some make dens in rocks. In the snowy Sierran winters, a porcupine sometimes lives in one tree for months at a time, sheltered from icy blasts by heavy foliage and its own hairy coat, resting in the crotch and eating everything within reach, preferably from a sitting position. Pine needles, buds, cambium layer, mistletoe all go into its grist mill; onto the snow below drop hundreds of one-inch pellets, each a compact oval of "pressed sawdust."

. . .

Not all animals of the red fir forests are as active during the long winters as porcupines, weasels, martens, and fishers. Even the mustelids (weasel family) curtail hunting during storms, holing up till the blizzards have spent their fury.

Other animals survive the winter by going underground into snug nests in burrows or dens or behind fallen tree roots. These hibernators handle their winter needs in several distinctive ways. Golden-mantled squirrels fatten up by heavy eating in the autumn and retreat to their underground nests with the first snows. Here they curl up and fall into a deep sleep, or torpor. The heartbeat slows to a few beats per minute; breathing ebbs to a barely perceptible rate; body temperature drops to within a few degrees of the ambient temperature. Periodically, every sixteen days or so, they rouse and regain normal body temperature, move about briefly, urinate but do not eat, and then sink back into the torpid state.

Chipmunks deal with the winters quite differently. Instead of putting on a heavy layer of body fat, they store a quantity of seeds in their underground nest and nibble on these at intervals. The cold and snow that drives them to shelter in a sluggish condition seldom completely inactivates them. Being "stubborn homeotherms," most Sierran chipmunks maintain a warm body temperature in the face of widely ranging environmental conditions. In many areas they come out when the ground is open in winter, inactive and lethargic in behavior and with slightly depressed temperatures, but move around, basking in the sun if there is any, and then return to light sleep on top of their seed pile.

Another shallow sleeper is the black bear. After adding a 30 percent weight increase of fat in autumn, it retires to a den in a hollow tree or cave. Here, with no food stored in advance, the bear lives on its fat, stays lightly awake much of the winter in a kind of "carnivorean lethargy," and comes out occasionally. Photographers who have quietly lowered cameras into the opening of an inhabited den, hoping to photograph a sleeping bear, have been surprised more than once with slashed, bleeding hands.

It has been presumed that a combination of cold temperature

and a lack of food causes animals to hibernate. Hibernation and prolonged sleep are efficient means of reducing metabolic rates so that a small amount of food energy goes far. If food is available, bears sometimes remain active at lower elevations in Sierran winters. In 1936, a year of unusually heavy snowfall and very low temperatures, six bears were observed in Yosemite Valley all winter. They spent considerable time around the incinerator, where scraps of food could be had.

Golden-mantled squirrels hibernate for different lengths of time at different elevations, the longer periods occurring higher up — an apparently clear adaptation to low temperatures and restricted food. However, their desert relative, the Mohave ground squirrel (*Citellus mohavensis*), has been discovered to maintain the same seasonal cycle when it is held at room temperature in a laboratory as when it lives in the field. This provides support for the idea of a biological clock somewhere in hibernators and estivators that runs their cycle on an inherent rhythm in a way we have yet to understand.

. . .

This inherent rhythm, unique to each species, is very evident among the animals of the mountain meadows. Thousands of meadows, varying from small seepages to spacious ranches, intersperse the midmountain and higher mountain forests. Each, in an unmatched setting of its own, is a serene open place where morning dew hangs heavy on the grass and sedge, midday sun dazzles, evening's coolness brings the deer. But each is much more than grass, wet soil, wildflowers, deer at twilight. Each is an interlaced community of plants and animals whose lives affect each other intimately the year through, often in ways that barely show above the surface.

Most obvious of the meadow mammals is the Sierra pocket gopher (*Thomomys monticola*), chiefly in evidence by the large mounds of fresh dirt that it pushes out of its underground burrows and the earthen plug with which these are sealed. In its extensive underground tunnel system, the pocket gopher lives solitarily for most of the year, feeding on the bulbs, tubers, and roots of plants that it runs into as it digs. Sometimes it ventures a few feet from a temporarily open door to snatch a favorite plant before backing quickly into its den, but mostly it stays out of sight.

Superbly equipped for digging with powerful shoulder muscles and long sharp claws on the forefeet, the pocket gopher also has small eyes and ears that do not get clogged with dirt and sensitive vibrissae, or whiskers, that help find the way through dark tunnels. When burrowing becomes too difficult, the tough incisors bite through chunks of earth or roots that bar the path, and a membrane behind the incisors keeps dirt out of the mouth.

The pocket gopher's most striking adaptation to the fossorial, or burrowing, life is a physiological one. Animals that live in narrow places need small hips so that they can turn around in the burrow. But if the hips are too small, the pelvic opening will not be wide enough to permit passage of the young at birth. The pocket gopher solves this neatly. Its pelvis is small, with right and left halves fused at the central pubic symphysis. In pregnant gophers an ovarian hormone dissolves the pubic symphysis, changing the pelvic opening from an O shape to a U shape, through which the large-headed young pass safely.

The California mole (*Scapanus latimanus*), an insectivorous small-hipped fellow tenant of the meadow underground, handles the same problem quite differently. In moles the reproductive tracts lie in front of the pubic bones, allowing the young to be born without having to go through the slim pelvic opening.

Pocket gophers establish definite territories in their meadows, in the shape of tunnels that radiate from a nest site. One acre of dry favorable ground frequently will support ten individuals and their home ranges. The animals' burrow systems must be large enough to provide for their food needs. Their systems may lie close together but evidently without intercepting; it is thought that they hear each other digging and thus avoid encroaching on each other's range.

When winter comes to the meadow, Sierra pocket gophers lay out new burrow systems between the snow and the ground. Animals with the best-located summer ranges move into the snow just above the old tubes; others move in from adjacent areas of frozen soil. They construct well-insulated, ball-shaped nests of shredded grass in the snow and radiate snow tunnels from the nests. Safely hidden by the snow, they feed on green stems of grasses and sedges, caches of snowbrush leaves, occasionally bark of shrubs, as well as corms and tubers.

With the melting of snow, the pocket gophers return to their underground burrows, which always need renovating and cleaning after a winter of vacancy. They push the earth that has settled and clogged their old burrows into the snow tunnels just above, packing them tightly. When the snow melts, these earth cores, some forty feet long, lie exposed like giant worms winding over the spring meadows.

Pocket gophers affect the life of mountain meadows in a good many ways. Their practice of plugging all entrances to the burrow maintains underground chambers with a temperature and humidity ideal for many other creatures. In weather extremes, toads, salamanders, snakes, mice, beetles, pseudoscorpions, and other arthropods frequently move in. Pocket gophers' continual burrowing exerts a significant plowing influence on the meadow. If each animal brings up about one hundred pounds of earth per week, as Lloyd Ingles found in a southern Sierran meadow, this amounts to tons per year that filter into the sod and enrich the soil. Subsoil brought to the surface weathers into topsoil much more rapidly than when belowground. The burrow systems have other favorable effects on the meadow. The heavy surface runoff each spring sinks into them, helping to reduce snowmelt floods down the mountains and to ensure a steady flow of springs later. The well-drained soil over the burrows dries out sooner each summer and supports grasses and forbs instead of sedges. Even the piles of pellets left in the "privies" near the snow nests undoubtedly add fertilizer.

On the Hoopa Reservation in northern California, pocket gophers served as agents of reforestation. Where overgrazing by cattle removed grassy turf from a range, allowing bulbs to invade, pocket gophers moved in after the bulbs and added their mounds and burrows. The bare earth that they tunneled up furnished the only successful seedbeds for a bumper crop of red firs the following year. Now a red fir forest is well under way.

The most numerous mammals of the meadow are unquestionably the mountain and longtail voles, or meadow mice (*Microtus montanus* and *M. longicaudus*). About half the size of pocket gophers, they live in the damper places among the deep grasses and sedges, active day and night, winter and summer. Like pocket gophers they construct underground tunnels and in winter continue life beneath the snow; but much of their summer activity goes on aboveground in the runways they cut through vegetation close to the surface. In dense grass these paths can be seen only by getting down to mouse level. Strewn

Chaparral covers a large portion of the western Sierra Nevada foothills with a variety of tough, woody shrubs (background). Blue oak woodland (foreground) often overlaps chaparral borders.

The western yellow-bellied racer (*Coluber constrictor*), above, and the striped racer are fast-moving foothill snakes. The striped racer sometimes kills rattlesnakes, and is often called "the chaparral snake" of California.

The gray fox and California quail occupy much the same range in valley and foothills, but the fox moves higher to the 5000-foot level as well.

The ringtail, related to the raccoon and coatimundi, is an agile climber of rockpiles and ledges in chaparral country. At times it emits a piercing scream, an explosive bark, or a plaintive long high-pitched call.

Bobcats (left) hunt from valley to high Sierra in any patch of brush large enough to house mice or rabbits.

The most common shrub in Sierran foothill chaparral is chamise (left), a drab green plant with needlelike leaves. In June white flower clusters cover its branches. One of the rarest shrubs is carpenteria (right). Its habitat (below) lies in a narrow foothill area east of Fresno.

Midmountain yellow pine forests cover the broadest belt of the Sierra, from 2500 to 6000 feet, encompassing the greatest variety of plant and animal life in the range.

Among the trees are Douglas firs.

incense cedars,

big-leaved maples near streams,

California black oaks,

and, in special groves, giant sequoias. This one, the General Grant tree, is slightly over 40 feet in basal diameter — the broadest sequoia known.

Two groups of prominent shrubs climb zonally up the Sierra, producing different species at different elevations. More than two thirds of the known species of manzanita (above) and ceanothus (below) in the world are native to California.

Along the streams grow California azaleas (*Rhododendron occidentale*).

Western gray squirrels live among the black oaks.

The musical calls of the black-crested, royal-blue Steller's jay are heard from the yellow pine forests up through the higher red firs.

with green fecal pellets and rich nitrogenous urine, the runways are well fertilized. They wind through the varied herbaceous plants on whose stems and leaves the voles feed.

In years when these voles erupt in the cyclic population explosions typical of rodents, the little brown creatures occupy every available space in the meadow, and sometimes nearly strip it of vegetation. At these times the endless runways are more evident than usual and the voles often scurry about in full sight in daylight. If captured in the field and placed in individual cages for study during such an epidemic, the voles invariably die within a few days, even with natural food and water fully available. If caged with several other mice, a seemingly fat, healthy vole often dies within twenty-four hours. An autopsy usually shows a full stomach and no apparent parasites or injuries. Yosemite Valley's vole eruption of 1957 revealed a number of just such fatalities.

The reasons for these puzzling deaths are apparently complex. Intensive field studies of lemmings, voles, and rabbits have been under way for years in an effort to understand the ramifications of the entire cycle. It has been shown conclusively that animals living in extremely dense populations suffer from internal stresses brought on by the crowding. The stress is tied somehow to hormonal imbalance, and the adrenal-pituitary complex plays a critical role in eventual death.

Following a meadow vole population explosion, there is always a sharp die-off and a period when numbers are low before they gradually build up again. This gives vegetation a chance to recover; meadow sod benefits from the honeycombing burrows of the epidemic years that let in air and water.

Among the willow, alders, and creek dogwood (*Cornus stolonifera*) in the wetter parts of Sierran meadows lives a curious, much larger rodent that is fairly common locally but shy and seldom seen. The aplodontia, or mountain beaver (*Aplodontia rufa*), about fifteen inches long and almost tailless, looks more like an oversized pocket gopher than a beaver. It has all the trademarks of a burrower — long, sharp front claws, small eyes and ears, long vibrissae, thick short brown fur.

Actually only very distantly related to true beavers, it is a relict rodent, the single species remaining in one of the most primitive living rodent families. Once widespread throughout the West, its range is now restricted to the Pacific Coast, where, as in the Sierra, it thrives near small streams or in wet meadows, always under dense plant cover. Here it digs underground tunnels as much as ten inches wide and three or four feet deep. Kept scrupulously clean, they are often damp, with water trickling through; in some places they drain the willows sufficiently to allow grasses to grow and other plants eventually to invade the meadow.

Like the mountain vole, the aplodontia cuts runways through the grass to reach its food supply. Often these surface tunnels run fifty yards or more to clusters of shooting star (*Dodecatheon*), wild vetch (*Vicia*), yellow monkey-flower (*Mimulus guttatus*), and columbine (*Aquilegia truncata*). It clips off many kinds of plants near the burrows for food and climbs shrubs and small trees to prune and dine on both leaves and bark. Piles of these cuttings are often left to dry outside the burrow and are taken into the tunnel when "cured."

Day and night appear to be all the same to the aplodontia. It follows a rest and activity cycle of its own rhythm. After feeding for about thirty minutes, it retires to the nest for a three- to four-hour nap. Upon emerging, it proceeds to its fecal pile. As it passes each of the half-inch-long hard pellets, the animal takes the pellet into its mouth and tosses it onto the pile. Now and then it chews and eats a pellet, a habit common to some other rodents and some shrews — possibly a means of conserving minerals, vitamins, or other needed elements. The usual half-hour feeding period then commences, followed by the next sleep, the next defecation, and so on — six to seven alternating periods of rest and activity over a twenty-four-hour "day."

Winter snows probably interrupt this cycle only slightly. The animal caches some food in its burrows, climbs trees and shrubs for new supplies as needed, and burrows through the snow to strip young red firs and lodgepoles of needles and bark, thus somewhat discouraging meadow invasion.

In the same thickets and meadows where the aplodontia plods its cycle, tiny voracious insectivores whirl through their lives at a fast and furious pace. Six or more species of shrews live in various habitats of the Sierra, small slim creatures with long pointed noses, highly sensitive vibrissae, and minute eyes hidden in velvety fur that brushes either way. Darting along their paths under logs or grass cover, they quiver noses nervously and emit occasional high-pitched squeaks as they hunt earthworms, insects, and animal flesh mainly by scent or touch.

There is good reason for their nervous restlessless. As the smallest living mammals they have the highest metabolic rates — the "living speed" of mammals goes up as size goes down. To support this high rate of living and compensate for the heat that their small bodies lose rapidly, shrews must eat their weight equivalent each day. This means eating every two or three hours.

The dusky shrew (*Sorex obscurus*) of the red fir forest meadows follows a built-in behavior pattern that accomplishes this feat with a minimum of effort over a twenty-four-hour day in

summer. Three times during the day the shrew feeds most heavily. The first peak comes in the coldest hours of early morning,
when insects and spiders have crawled down sedges and willows
into the meadow litter and are sluggish and readily picked off.

Later in the morning, when these insects and arachnids warm
up and crawl back up the sedges and grasses, many fall victim to
the shrew. In the afternoon, when insects are lively and hard to
catch, the tiny mammal works least. Then, and at other intervals, it breaks its almost endless motion with short naps thirty to
seventy seconds long. During these it stops, rests its nose on the
ground, closes its eyes, and apparently sleeps lightly, at times
twitching its vibrissae and turning completely around while
napping.

As the sun sets and a cool evening breeze begins to blow down
the mountain, the wetwood termites emerge from rotten logs to
fly to new locations. This signals the third feeding peak. The
dusky shrew snaps up half a dozen termites on the spot and im-
mobilizes fifty or sixty more for future use. Whether its saliva
contains a poison that partially paralyzes the victims, as in some
shrews, is not known.

Lloyd Ingles, whose Huntington Lake research uncovered
this shrew cycle, found that dusky shrews kept in captivity followed the same activity rhythm as those in the wild, in spite of
the food constantly available. This would indicate that the
shrew's pattern of behavior is inherent, "the result of ages of
selection which have fitted the animal to its environment." [2]

The dusky shrew does not hibernate. How it manages to find
enough food to stoke its fast-burning body during the one winter in its life is still a mystery. Major staples undoubtedly are
the eggs, larvae, and pupae of insects that winter at the same
ground levels as the shrew. Cannibalism may be part of the an-

swer, one high-strung little body refueling the other, although Ingles doubts that this happens in nature, having found many dead shrews without a mark on them.

Out of eleven dusky shrews that started the winter on one and one-fourth acres of overlapping home ranges at Huntington Lake, only two — a male and a female — were left by spring. Presumably these, the parents of the next generation, were the ones that most successfully defended their expanding territories as food ran lower and lower, until only they remained. "Theirs were the genes that determined next year's crop of young shrews. Year after year, century after century, the shrews best adapted to win this annual territorial competition give rise to the next generation." [3]

. . .

Spring snowmelt exposes the meadows weeks before it clears the pack from the adjacent forests. By mid-May in most years, new green spears of sedges and grasses push through the water and soggy muck. The brownish shrub mat reveals faint red buds and the dash of an occasional gopher from one dry clump to the next. Corn lilies (*Veratrum californicum*), two to four inches high, burst their protecting leaf sheaths. Quaking aspens (*Populus tremuloides*) on the meadow edge dangle catkins with crimson anthers; mountain chickadees glean food from cracks in the white barks. The sights and sounds of returning birds fill forests and clearings.

In the open meadow Brewer's blackbirds waddle once again among the six-inch-high grass as robins cock for worms on the higher spots. In a saturated corner, a trim brown sparrow with finely streaked buffy breast pours out a vigorous three-part song. Delivered over and over — alternately from a clump of young lodgepoles, a stump, and a twenty-five-foot lodgepole forming a rough triangle — it clearly denotes the territorial boundaries of the Lincoln's sparrow. A month later, the bird will be as shy and secretive as a mouse, slipping through the grass to its nest.

Spring brings the clear whistles of white-crowned sparrows back to the higher willows and the flash of black cap on yellow as Wilson's warblers flick through the moist thickets. As the snow-melt mosquitoes swarm and fade, and the meadows warm and dry, insects that escaped the ground hunts of moles and shrews are fed by meadow birds to their nestlings and are hawked by western wood pewees and Audubon's warblers at the meadow's edge.

Even these routine hunts hold occasional perils. Elisabeth Crenshaw and her daughters, while hiking near Long Meadow in Yosemite National Park some years ago, were startled to see a young Audubon's warbler flying back and forth in the grass as if it were tied to a string. It had swallowed a stalk of grass, probably while swooping after an insect, and was firmly anchored. They caught the bird, freed its wings and body from the entangling grasses, and gently and steadily began to pull the stalk from its throat. When they finally got it out, the warbler sat blinking in the hand for a moment, then flew into a lodgepole.

At twilight, bats take up the insect hunt, feeding until night temperatures quiet their prey in the upper and lower strata of forest and meadow. The leathery membrane that connects the bat's elongated hand bone to its legs and tail makes it our only mammal capable of wing strokes dexterous enough to capture the fastest-moving insects in flight. The bat locates them by echo responses of their bodies to the high-pitched sounds it emits.

Three kinds of bats, all rather widely distributed, fly commonly about clearings or among trees of the red fir belt in the Sierra. Two of them, the little brown myotis (*Myotis lucifugus*) and big brown bat (*Eptesicus fuscus*), are gregarious, spending the day in large numbers in caves or hollow trees and hanging upside-down by their hind claws in typical bat style. The long-eared myotis (*Myotis evotis*) is solitary, as is the uniquely American but less common silver-haired bat (*Lasionycteris noctivagans*), which roosts in trees by day. The silver-hair's habit of flying low over lakeshores or streams resembles the way in which bats generally drink, by skimming pools and scooping water into their open mouths while in flight. Now and then one gets caught by a trout.

Other predators lie in wait for the careless small mammal or bird of the meadow, day or night. Weasel families, a mother and half a dozen nearly grown young, sometimes fan out over a small area of the meadow, spread about a foot apart, and advance slowly, looking for voles. They find shrews less palatable because of the musky offensive odor given off by powerful scent glands in the skin, but rarely overlook a juicy pocket gopher.

. . .

Coyotes make the rounds of gopher diggings, standing for minutes at a time with head poised at a likely burrow entrance. A quick pounce, coming down with both front feet and mouth, sometimes produces a warm brown carcass. Pocket gophers are most vulnerable when they open the burrow to push out fresh earth; this movement may attract red-tailed hawks or goshawks. Badgers occasionally dig them out. With all their enemies, it is not surprising that pocket gophers rarely live more than three years and that there is a complete turnover in a mountain meadow gopher population every four or five years. Juveniles, on leaving home, may stumble into a beautifully laid-out tunnel system, freshly vacant, and take over.

Two large resident owls help create the vacancies. The great horned owl, a forest dweller by day, often begins its nightly food roundup with a vigil in an open tree at the meadow's edge. Noiselessly it drops onto small moving forms, powerful talons snuffing out life. Voles, pocket gophers, woodrats, rabbits, grouse, squirrels all fall victims — even malodorous shrews and skunks, which the owl, having a poor sense of smell, eats uninhibitedly. From foothill woodlands to the higher forests, this aggressive hunter culls nightly the surplus and the careless from bird and small-mammal populations.

The more rare great gray owl is a bird of diurnal habits. Found across the American and Eurasian arctic, it occurs sparingly in the Sierra, recent records entirely from the Yosemite region. At Peregoy Meadows and Crane Flat in the red fir–lodgepole forests, these big owls sit on small pines or firs along the meadow fringe early or late in the day, their bodies bent sharply forward as they watch for rodents. The great puffy round head with yellow eyes and lined facial disk seems immense; and the dusky heavily feathered body and long tail, huge. Indeed, in overall size, this is North America's largest owl. But the body beneath the fluffy feathers is slight; in weight the great horned owl outstrips it easily. In disposition, also, these two owls differ. The great gray has a gentler mien, lacking the erectable feather tufts (or "horns") and the ferocious glare of the other; it sometimes allows human approach to within ten or twelve feet when absorbed in catching and eating gophers.

Other owls in the surrounding forests combine to turn Peregoy Meadows into a second Madera Canyon, Arizona's famous owling spot, for some months of the year. The mellow whistles of saw-whet and pygmy owls, the flammulated's hoot, the barking of the spotted, the great horned's hoot, and the deep booming *whoo* of the great gray are all possible when conditions are right.

Summer daytime birds bring the colors and sounds familiar to campers and hikers of the red fir–lodgepole forests — the red-headed yellow and black male western tanager, Steller's jay flying in at the first rustle of a sandwich bag, Oregon juncos searching the ground for seeds or crumbs. The *pip-pip-pip* and ringing *hic-three-beers* of the olive-sided flycatcher are often the first sounds to greet the dawn from a red fir spire. I once counted eighty-five *pip-pip-pip* series in eight minutes between 6:00 and 6:08 A.M. The nasal call of the western wood pewee is just as early and nearly as frequent, often accompanied by the robin's cheery carol. Hermit thrushes send full, clear cadences into the cool air, each opening with a flutelike note that is held a moment. The ruby-crowned kinglet's song plays up and down the scale. The low thumping of the male blue grouse booms through the woods — seven deep notes in about four seconds, a pause of forty seconds, and another seven thumps, like someone pounding far away in an undeterminable direction.

Scattered among the forests are rocky promontories and boulder-strewn acres where Jeffrey pines (*Pinus jeffreyi*) rise as the dominant trees, often intermixed with small or extensive stands of high-mountain chaparral. Yosemite's famous wind-blown pine on Sentinel Dome is a Jeffrey.

Jeffreys resemble yellow pines sufficiently to have once been considered a variety of the more widespread species, and in Sierran regions where their ranges overlap, they hybridize. But on the dry rocky slopes from 6000 to 9000 feet, the beehive-shaped cones of the Jeffrey identify the tree beyond question. Six to ten inches long, larger and more rounded than the yellow, Jeffrey cones have prickles that point downward and are not felt when the cone is held in the hand.

The Jeffreys of these open slopes are often massive trees with reddish-brown bark, trunks clear of branches for a third of their height, then shaded by several large horizontal limbs and topped by smaller branches curving into flattened or rounded crowns. The crowns are a favorite singing perch of Townsend's solitaires, especially where they overlook great dropoffs. Here, in June, these slim gray thrushes pour out a torrent of liquid notes, beginning with robinlike phrases that flow together in a continuous, breathless warble, inevitably ending with clear bell tones of penetrating depth. At peak ardor the bird sings for four out of five minutes.

As late as mid-October, the solitaire's arresting song, minus its earlier fervor, floats out over the granite exfoliations of the rocky domes. With the winter snows the bird retreats to lower canyons, but moves back up in early spring just as soon as it can find food, even if a twelve-foot snowpack is still on the ground. Despite its tree-top singing perch, the solitaire is a ground- or bank-nester.

A number of ground or near-ground nesting birds find cover and food in the brushy shelter of mountain chaparral patches amid scattered Jeffrey pines. Here abound berries of greenleaf and pinemat manzanitas, snowbrush, serviceberry, bitter cherry, tobacco brush (*Ceanothus velutinus*); the acorns of huckleberry oak (*Quercus vaccinifolia*); the chestnutlike burs of bush chinquapin; seeds of wildflowers and grasses.

Chinquapin's golden fuzzy leaves and the silvery-green leaves of snowbrush often hide green-tailed towhee and fox sparrow nests. The loud bright songs of these finches liven the brush and open woods in June.

About this time the blue grouse, the Sierra's only forest grouse, leaves the trees to nest in the ground cover of the broken forest-chaparral areas. The female's grayish-brown mottled plumage conceals her perfectly on the nest. When she abandons it finally, at her deliberate walk, she does so with the chicks in tow, teaching them to feed on seeds and berries, to freeze or run for cover, to jump into the air after gnats and flies, and later grasshoppers and other large insects.

As summer wanes, males in small bands move higher up the mountains, followed by the hens and young. Winter snows drive them into the protected branches of dense conifers, where they feed on needle tips, well insulated from the cold by close-set body plumage and feathered legs. Summer finds them back on the brushy open-forested slopes.

On these same slopes mountain quail build needle-lined nests on the ground under brush and fill them with ten to twelve buff-colored eggs in late May or June. If all goes well, the downy broods in due course scurry from cover to cover after their plumed parents, directed by various low clucking and whining notes that lead them to run and hide rather than fly. Sometimes the eggs serve a different purpose.

Charles M. Wentz of the Yosemite Field School heard a mountain quail distress call one June day in Yosemite Valley. Investigating, he found a Sierra mountain kingsnake (*Lampropeltis zonata multicincta*) at the quail's nest, in which lay three eggs. Picking up the beautiful red, black, and white banded snake, he carried it fifty yards down the road and much below road level and let it go. The snake traveled rapidly right back to the nest. Recapturing it, Wentz took it three times as far

down the road and released it at the river's edge. Immediately
the snake crawled up the bank and, in spite of his attempts to
head it in another direction, persisted in returning to the nest.
A third time Wentz tried, making a journey of a quarter of a
mile down the road and one hundred feet up the mountainside
before turning it loose. The snake headed right back down the
mountainside and, following a route that was less direct than
previous ones, eventually reached the nest. This time its perse-
verence gained a dinner.

In addition to snakes and carnivores, which are always on the
lookout for nests, some rodents show an occasional taste for eggs
and young. California ground squirrels, although primarily
vegetarians, have been observed sucking mountain quail eggs
and carrying off the young chicks; at times they eat small animals that have been run over by automobiles or kill and carry
off golden-mantled squirrels.

Cannibalism used to be a problem among certain game birds
held in captivity, until it was discovered that this meat hunger
was caused in part by a salt deficiency. Meat eating in rodents
may be a symptom of the salt hunger common to deer, cattle,
porcupines, and probably other vegetarian species of the salt-
poor high Sierra. High-mountain birds, such as Cassin's finch,
sometimes eat mud at mineral springs and, along with red cross-
bills and pine grosbeaks, pick up "bits of something" from
campfire ashes and rock salt spread on the ground. Minerals
lacking in the soft water are in short supply and evidently are
acquired by the wildlife in whatever form they can be found.

The red fir–lodgepole pine forests of the Sierra Nevada share
a good many birds with the lodgepole–subalpine fir–Engelmann
spruce forests of the Rocky Mountains: Steller's jays, western

tanagers, olive-sided flycatchers, western wood pewees, mountain chickadees, hermit thrushes, Townsend's solitaires, Audubon's warblers, to name a few. The wetter summers in the Rockies affect the decay rate of forest humus more than they influence the bird life. By mid-August of most years, Sierran forests are so dry that the surest place to find birds is near springs or creeks or lakes, where they come to drink and bathe.

One August in the Gold Lake district of the northern Sierra, a partner and I maintained a dawn-to-dusk vigil at a creek fed by a spring in an open red fir forest, with a small meadow nearby. It was barely light when we arrived at the pool and took stations behind young red firs. The chill of night lay heavy and wet.

At 5:13 A.M., the first calls of wood pewees and olive-sided flycatchers rang through the woods, a half minute apart. The gray and white shape of a porcupine ambled across a clearing and clambered, scraping and scratching, up a western white pine to the first side limb twenty feet up, where it sat back on its haunches.

At 5:17, an Oregon junco visited the pool; at 5:25, a brown creeper crept out on the lower log, hopped down, and drank; at 5:30, a young Audubon's warbler took the first bath of the day. In the next fifteen minutes, it was followed by bathing hermit warblers, Nashville warblers, mountain chickadees, and an orange-crowned warbler in for a quick sip. This was the start of a parade that continued with varying intensity all day. At one moment the water lay empty; the next it was a-splash with birds; the next its encircling firs were crowded with preening, feather-shaking, disheveled creatures.

At one time, in the water or above, were two hermit warblers, two mountain chickadees, a Wilson's warbler, two red-breasted nuthatches, two Nashville warblers, and an Audubon's warbler. Most drank first, then bathed; some, like the tanager, only bathed; chickadees, Audubon's warblers, and juncos mixed it either way and often, the three steadiest users by far. Some of the scarcer visitors — Lincoln's, white-crowned, and chipping sparrows, and the white-headed woodpecker — left after a single drink, as did the painted lady butterfly (*Vanessa cardui*) and pine siskin.

Occasionally the air was alive with song — the lively, strident warble of a male Cassin's finch, the *chick-adee-dee* notes and gurgles of the mountain chickadees, the *mew* of a green-tailed towhee, the distant *pip-pip-pip* of the olive-sided flycatcher. Again all was quiet save for the buzz of bumblebees, the movement of flies, a golden-mantle nipping seeds from a pennyroyal (*Monardella odoratissima*), the click of a junco.

As evening approached and the three steadies — mountain chickadees, juncos, and Audubon's warblers — finished a very active bathing and drinking bout at 6:45, they left the pool clear. From a near fir out hopped an evening grosbeak, looking large and lordly compared to the smaller birds; it drank four times with pauses, then left in direct, propelling flight.

By 7:15, the damp cold waves of night were no longer intermittent, the pennyroyals quivered in the currents. Pewees and the olive-sided still called; an Audubon's warbler hawked an insect two feet from my ear.

By 7:30, visibility was becoming poor at the pool. There was quiet over all except for the distant roar in the treetops and the trickling of water. Suddenly a junco chucked, sounding very loud, and dipped its bill in the water.

By 7:40, all was still. At the creek pennyroyals, an underwing moth moved in and out of the flowers that the bumblebees had taken care of by day; the bees were now five black sleeping forms on the leaves.

. . .

Lodgepole pines sometimes play a successional role in red fir forests by pioneering into meadows, where their roots are more water-tolerant than the fir's. The lodgepole's sun-loving and shade-tolerant seedlings may be succeeded by shade-loving firs or hemlocks, but they often succeed themselves. Throughout much of western North America's mountain region, lodgepoles form extensive pure forests of their own.

In the Rockies the stands often consist of pole-sized trees growing close together, sometimes the result of fire, which opens tightly sealed cones and causes young trees to sprout in profusion. But in the higher reaches of the Sierra, lodgepoles grow tall and husky, with trunks four feet across on mature specimens. From scattered tongues that extend down into cold or wet pockets of the yellow pine belt, the trees reach nearly to timberline. They ring lakes, border streams, spread over moist slopes, surround and invade meadows from small ones to the largest.

In the light shade of the scaly thin-barked older trees, their silver branches densely clothed with short green needles, rise young lodgepoles of all sizes and shapes, some bent by snow. Patches of corn lilies and shooting stars lie tucked away in wet glades; among grasses by fallen logs sway purple asters, white bistorts (*Polygonum bistortoides*), blue lupines, larkspur, and yellow senecios in season. In June there are usually Williamson's sapsuckers and mountain chickadees nesting in nearby stump holes and pine grosbeaks whistling from the treetops.

For as long as man has known them, the lodgepole forests of

the Sierra Nevada, especially in the drainages of the upper Tuolumne and Merced Rivers, have been subject to periodic outbreaks of a tiny insect that turns them temporarily into ghost forests. During epidemics and for years afterward, thousands of defoliated trees stand bleak and gray, their hollowed-out needles lying in piles on the ground.

The cause of this shedding is a quarter-inch mottled gray moth, the lodgepole needle miner (*Coleotechnites milleri*), which follows a two-year life cycle intimately linked to the lodgepole. Appearing in late July of alternate years, the moths lay barely visible yellow eggs on the twigs, in old excavated needles, bud scales, and needle sheaths of mostly older lodgepoles. The eggs hatch in late summer into quarter-inch-long pinkish caterpillars that bore into the tips of needles and feed there until winter. As the caterpillars grow larger during the two springs and summers of their twenty-one-month span, they move from one needle to another, mining out the tender inner contents, turning the needles from green to yellow to brown. Each caterpillar destroys from three to five needles in its lifetime. Although small as individuals, their total numbers are enormous during an epidemic. By the time that the caterpillars pupate and emerge as adult moths in the second summer there may be as many as 500 moths flitting about a single lodgepole branch.

Adults mate and lay eggs, and the cycle continues. Five successive two-year generations of needle miners can cause as much as 90 percent needle loss in infested forests. Heavily defoliated lodgepoles die within a few years; trees weakened by the needle miner sometimes succumb secondarily to mountain pine beetles (*Dendroctonus*), although the exact relationship here is far from clear.

Three times in this century, needle miners have struck the

Tuolumne Basin in upper Yosemite National Park. An outbreak occurred in 1911–1921, another in 1931–1941; the latest started in 1947 around Tenaya Lake, spread to Tuolumne Meadows and surrounding areas, and subsided in 1965. Each time the miners left forests of bleached snags in their wake. And each time thousands of young lodgepoles surged up in the new openings to replace the dead trees.

As the needle miner cycle waned, yielding to natural controls, the forests slowly regrew as pure lodgepole stands. Within fifty years or more they would be fit targets for new needle miner invasions. In hastening the death of mature lodgepoles, needle miners trigger their replacement by younger ones; this ensures both the continuity of lodgepole forests and a food supply for future generations of needle miners.

The older epidemics in Yosemite ran their course. The most recent one aroused a strong controversy. As the needle miner reached increasingly into the heavily used recreation areas around Tuolumne Meadows, the National Park Service, guided by entomologists of the United States Forest Service's Pacific Southwest Forest and Range Experiment Station, embarked on a campaign to control it. Following initial life-history studies, parasites, viruses, and other natural controls received some attention, but the work soon centered primarily on insecticides.

The Forest Service researchers concentrated on how to preserve the standing lodgepoles. Abortive aerial spraying was tried in 1949 and 1953. The 1953 flight dropped 11,000 gallons of DDT on the area; only afterward did the Forest Service discover that the DDT had little or no effect on needle miners. Its effects on the other wildlife can, from recent snowballing evidence, be partially surmised. Insoluble in water, this chlorinated hydrocarbon travels wherever air and water take it and persists almost indefinitely. Swallowed or inhaled by animals, it accumulates in their fatty tissues, and even small amounts are capable of bringing about critical body changes. In some birds it upsets intricate hormone-enzyme relationships, causing them to lay thin-shelled eggs so deficient in calcium that they crack and fall apart almost at once. In others it causes infertile eggs. It has recently been found in fish and frogs of remote high-Sierran lakes. Increasing knowledge of DDT's spread and detrimental effects is leading toward its eventual ban.

Several years' further study led the Forest Service to its next lethal weapon, malathion. Belonging to a different group of insecticides — the organic phosphates — malathion is a fast-acting killer, deadly on impact, potent in even minute amounts, but, unlike DDT, short-lived.

In 1959, 1961, and 1963, park officials sprayed more than 12,000 acres in the Tuolumne Meadows region by helicopter, applying one pound of malathion in ten gallons of diesel oil per acre. About 16 percent of the area was re-treated. The spray was timed to make contact with the needle miners when 25 percent of the adult moths had emerged. The Forest Service estimated effectiveness of the 1963 spraying as ranging from a 46 percent needle miner mortality at Tuolumne Meadows Campground to 87 percent at Glen Aulin; the campground was sprayed early to avoid later contamination of campers.

The spraying drew strong protests from the Sierra Club. In an exchange of letters with the Park Service, former Executive Director David Brower wrote:

> . . . the 1916 act is a congressional mandate to the National Park Service for the conservation of scenery and wildlife and for that reason we are continually perplexed

by the non-ecological reasoning behind the needle miner control program. The lodgepole pine forms the base of an intricate wildlife pyramid. In addition to bark beetles and needle miners, wood-boring beetles, ants, woodpeckers, chickadees, chipmunks, hawks and owls are part of the pyramid. All are dependent upon a continual crop of dead and dying lodgepole pine. It is ecological nonsense to suppose that a spray program directed at the base of such a wildlife pyramid does not "entail harm to living natural resources." [4]

Conrad Wirth, former Director of the National Park Service, responded:

. . . the National Park Service Act of 1916 directs us to conserve the scenic as well as the scientific values within the National Parks for the enjoyment of present and future generations. This charge poses a serious conflict, since both values cannot concurrently be preserved in the face of the needle miner epidemic. While we agree with you that perpetuation of natural ecology is basic to National Park management, we must also recognize that quality of human experience for many park visitors is dependent largely upon scenic values. We must give reasonable consideration to these values. This we have done. We wish to stress again that this program covers only 4600 acres [in 1963] in public use areas and along roadsides, representing five percent of the total infestation.[5]

In the sprayed areas, and in unsprayed areas used as controls, before-and-after biological investigations were neither extensive enough nor long-term enough to present a full-fledged picture of the malathion and oil effects. They gave a mere indication. Chicken eggs in various stages of incubation were exposed in and under trees and in clearings. Their resulting hatchability varied considerably. The two- to five-day-old eggs in treetops and on upper limbs suffered heavy mortality. Many embryos died, showing massive hemorrhages, cyanosis, and edema. Most chicks that did hatch were crippled by a stiffening of the hock joint which left them unable to walk; control groups showed no such deformity. The Fish and Wildlife Service report concluded that spraying in July could definitely influence the nesting success of wild birds.

Adult birds and mammals seemed less vulnerable than the young on a direct contact basis. A few birds were observed spending unusual amounts of time ruffling and preening their feathers for several days after the spraying as though the feathers had become soiled. Some of this was undoubtedly the effect of the diesel oil, far too much of which was used, in the judgment of certain entomologists.

It is at the insect level that malathion strikes hardest; this is both its strength and grave danger. As the helicopter delivering the 1963 application began its seven passes over the area containing test tree Number 1, spray droplets hit the ground immediately and were still dripping from the foliage into a small stream six hours later. Dead and dying insects began falling to earth almost at once. Within eight hours a total of 719 insects and spiders tumbled into two drop cloths; during the next twenty-seven hours the cloths collected 208 more, then a diminishing few each day thereafter.

The first day's dead insects contained 550 ppm (parts per million) of malathion; those dead a day later, 52.5 ppm; residues

of 8 ppm remained on forest litter up to a month after the spray
— and all were hazards of unknown dimension to the insectivorous wildlife. In addition, insect eaters faced an immediate
food shortage, for other insects died along with the needle
miners. Members of 6 families of bees and wasps, 18 families of
flies, 4 families of beetles, 5 families of true bugs, and 4 families
of lesser-known orders were among the poisoned. This loss of
insect food may explain why bird numbers on treated areas
dropped 50 percent six weeks after the 1961 application and 35
percent in the summer following the 1963 spraying.[6]

Among the insects killed by malathion were many of the
needle miner's forty or more natural enemies, most of them tiny
parasitic wasps. A few of these micro-wasps attack no other prey
and are so intimately associated with the needle miner that their
own life cycles synchronize perfectly with the two-year cycle of
their host.

. . .

It was while studying these parasitic wasps in 1961 that entomologist Alan Telford and colleagues from the University of
California Division of Biological Control became aware that
they had been overlooking a very important needle miner
enemy — the mountain chickadee. To determine just how se-
lective a predator the chickadee was, and to establish its relationships with the lodgepole needle miner, they set up two study
plots in Inyo National Forest south of Tuolumne Meadows.
One of the plots was located well within a stand of infested
lodgepoles, the other in a nearly identical, noninfested lodgepole area.

The first winter's observations placed the chickadee firmly in
the category of a potent biological control. Traveling in bands

of 25 to 100 individuals, mountain chickadees foraged heavily on needle miners in the infested forest near Sentinel Meadow. The larvae accounted for nearly 90 percent of their diet. Deftly breaking the convex surface of the needles near the base of the larval mines, the birds peeled back narrow flaps of tissue to expose the larvae, often finding and eating six within ten seconds. One chickadee stomach contained more than 275 caterpillars; ten stomachs held 639 among them. Researchers estimated that the feeding of mountain chickadees reduced this epidemic overwintering population of lodgepole needle miner by about 30 percent during the winter of 1961–1962. In the nesting season that followed, the parent birds searched nearby aspens for larger, juicier worms to feed their young but continued to eat needle miner larvae themselves.

At least nine species of birds in the area fed on needle miners. Cassin's finches snipped off the end of infested needles to get at the larvae. Pine siskins and some migratory birds levied heavily.

This preliminary study convinced the Division of Biological Control of the need for longer-term research on the natural enemies of forest insect pests. The natural enemies may act in very different ways — shrews feeding on sawfly cocoons; woodpeckers on bark beetles; chickadees on needle miners, bark beetles, and mealybugs; untold others forming links as yet unknown in the forest food chain.

Almost overlooked in the past has been the role of insectivorous birds between outbreaks when insect numbers are at low ebb. Perhaps, suggests Donald Dahlsten of the Division of Biological Control, birds play an important part at that time in keeping pest numbers below the threshold of explosion.

If current studies bear this out, Sierran foresters may soon be putting up nesting boxes to encourage hole-nesting species. European scientists have attained up to twenty-five breeding pairs per acre through intelligent use of boxes. Where this was done over a thirty-three-year period at Stekby on the Elbe, the nest box area received little damage from its population of pine loopers, which were contained at a low level, whereas the control area without nest boxes suffered several looper outbreaks. In a similar experiment now being tried with mountain chickadees in four regions in California, first-year occupancy of the nest boxes averaged a "phenomenal" 46 percent.

Chickadees and parasitic wasps have lived with needle miners in the lodgepole pine forests for a very long time. If their numbers could be increased as a result of investigations in progress, they could be even more effective biological controls, perhaps restraining miners to levels that the National Park Service could live with. In the absence of as high a degree of control as these, the most valid ecological yardstick for management within the national parks would seem to be the Leopold Committee report to the Secretary of the Interior: "Some management methods now in use by the National Park Service seem to us potentially dangerous. For example, we wish to raise a serious question about the mass application of insecticides in the control of forest insects. Such applications may (or may not) be justified in commercial timber stands, but in a national park the ecologic impact can have unanticipated effects on the biotic community that might defeat the over-all management objective."

7. Tree Line and Beyond

ALONG THE SUMMIT of the Sierra Nevada extends an area nearly two hundred miles long and twenty miles wide known to thousands of hikers and backpackers as the high Sierra. Lying above the level of continuous forest, this spectacular belt stretches from Pyramid Peak near Lake Tahoe to Cottonwood Pass south of Mount Whitney, including all of the central and southern high country from approximately 8000 feet to the tops of the loftiest peaks. From Yosemite south it is a roadless realm, accessible in summer by trails. Plainly written on this wild, rugged landscape is the history of recent intense glaciation. The angular peaks sculptured by rock-plucking glaciers, the massive granite slabs planed and polished to mirror brilliance, the erratic boulders weighing thousands of pounds stranded where only moving ice could have left them — all speak of an age when rivers of ice overpowered the land.

During the Pleistocene three glacial periods separated by long warm intervals occurred in the Sierra. Unlike the one huge ice cap that covered much of northeastern North America, the Sierran glaciers were discontinuous. Some parts of the range had none; in northern areas only small ice patches nestled in basins or cirques of the taller peaks. But from Donner Pass south to the upper Kern River, ice fields varying from a few to many square miles sent trunk glaciers flowing down valleys to east and west. Formed in the high mountains when more snow fell annually than could melt or evaporate, and compacted year after year into ice, the glaciers eventually became heavy enough to move slowly downslope, usually following pre-existing stream valleys. As they moved, they plucked rocks from weak joints in the sides and floor of their path, scratching and scouring surfaces with them.

Over time, this action rounded V-shaped river valleys into U-shaped glacial valleys. Rivers and creeks pouring into the valleys from the side sometimes had their entrance channels carried away by the glaciers, which left them hanging high above the deepened gorge. When the ice later melted, the rivers descended in cascades or plunged over the brink as in the leaping waterfalls of Yosemite Valley.

The three glaciers that carved out Yosemite Valley flowed at one stage for thirty-six miles, reaching slightly below El Portal in the Merced River canyon. The first stage, 3000 feet thick opposite Glacier Point, submerged all but the tops of Half Dome, El Capitan, and a few other peaks. It deposited at the base of Sentinel Dome, 3000 feet above the valley floor, huge boulders of a different type of granite from that on which they now rest. Their point of origin was miles away, across a chasm that only an ice river 3000 feet deep and nearly a mile wide could have bridged. The last glacier left a terminal moraine across the valley near El Capitan. As the ice melted, this moraine dammed the valley to form Lake Yosemite. The lake gradually filled to become the meadow and open forest that it was when white men first saw it.

In modified form the glacier story was repeated in the San Joaquin, Kings, Kaweah, Kern, and other rivers of western and

eastern slopes. Everywhere glaciers carved and smoothed surfaces, swept away soil, enlarged stream channels, dug lake basins,
left their bold imprint on the land. Then, as the climate
warmed a few degrees and brought the Ice Age to a close around
10,000 years ago, the glaciers melted away, filling thousands of
tarns with their waters, the rivers with turbulent roar.

Today's high Sierra retains only miniature versions of the
powerful ice forces that shaped it. The sixty "glacierets" present on Mount Lyell, the Palisades, and on other high peaks
are products of a recent cooler period about 4000 years ago.
Though all of them are less than one and one-half miles long,
these small glaciers that cling to shady high-mountain cirques
exhibit all the characteristics of greater ones — crevasses, berg-
schrunds, glacial tables, moraines. Their bases pour out a steady
stream of "glacial milk," the meltwater whitened by finely
ground rock flour. In late summer when the snow is soft and the
crevasses gape two hundred yards long by four feet wide, with no
bottom in sight, and serrated icicles hang like long spears thirty
feet into the bluish-white depths, these glaciers seem frigidly
arctic in their setting among 13,000- and 14,000-foot peaks.

Although most of the high-country rock base is granite —
much of it a white granite that reflects intense light — the
whiteness is broken by green splashes of mountain meadows and
trees, the blue of lakes, and by black volcanic crags and red-
brown or purple metamorphic peaks. Red mountains such as
Dana and Gibbs carry metamorphic versions of summits originally formed under the sea through which the ancient Sierra
arose, and contain marine fossils to prove it.

From 10,000 feet to the crests of higher peaks cling the hardy
low flowers of the range's highest plant community — alpine
fell-fields. Below them, interspersed wherever trees can get a

footing, stand the subalpine forests from 9000 feet to timber-line. Subalpine trees are not many in kind: conditions of the heights are too rigorous for more than a handful of species.

In lower subalpine areas, mountain hemlocks (*Tsuga merten-siana*) associate with red firs, lodgepole pines, and western white pines in tall, beautiful forests. Here the hemlocks achieve heights up to one hundred feet, narrowly conical trees with soft bluish-green needles that look starlike in sprays; the terminal shoots of young trees perennially droop a little. Sometimes living where snow lingers well into the summer in north- or east-facing canyons, hemlocks form almost pure open groves — cool retreats vibrant with mature reddish-purple barks and saplings snow-bent to the ground but straightening resiliently when freed.

Brushing shoulders with them, or standing alone on rocky overlooks, western white pines lift characteristically swirling upper branches and needles that at times shimmer like silver. So distinctive is the sound in the wind of this and the other Sierran pines that John Muir claimed he could tell where he was by pine music alone if he were set down blindfolded anywhere in the mountains. Climbing this tree to listen closely to the needles, he found that they gave out a well-tempered, winglike hum, about 250 vibrations per minute, each needle in the cluster of five remarkably free from clicking against the others except in storms. The finest pine music, said Muir.

Closely attuned to the granite domes are the cinnamon-brown-trunked, shreddy-barked Sierra or western junipers (*Juniperus occidentalis*). Climbing over windswept ridges, pushing roots into every soil-collecting crevice, they are often almost the sole species spaced over miles of solid rock. Blasted by gales, weighted by snow, scored by lightning, junipers twist and turn in all the picturesque shapes of trees subject to the elements. Where they bend with the wind, their bleached windward trunks provide a buffer for the low green growth in the lee. In the shelter of boulders trunks rise to boulder height, then spread a tough horizontal mat of scaly green leaves sometimes twenty feet across, sloping like a roof to deflect the wind up and over. Other junipers stay erect, with rounded or flattened crowns.

The tendency of some individual trees to assume low matted forms on approaching timberline while others remain upright has been noted for a long time. The rigors of subalpine environment obviously do not force all trees into the same habit of growth. Lodgepole pines, for example, remain tall at tree heights normal for them practically to the tree's upper limits. Recent studies just east of the Sierra Nevada crest indicate that the most important factors determining tree growth are inherited differences.

Working at Slate Creek Valley, the timberline station of the Carnegie Institution of Washington, plant biologist Jens Clausen classified over 36,000 individual trees according to their growth form and the altitude at which they reached tree line. Clausen found three major conifers struggling up the moraines, talus, screes, and gravel beds of this glacial hanging valley from 10,000 to 12,000 feet. The climate in which they live is among the most severe in the temperate zone. It has ten-month-long winters; spring, summer, and fall telescope into two months from mid-July to mid-September; frost can occur any night of the year.

At the bottom of the valley, mountain hemlock, lodgepole pine, and whitebark pine (*Pinus albicaulis*) all attain full forest size. Lodgepole grows predominantly with a single trunk, whitebark primarily with more trunks, hemlock with either one or more. As the conifers climb, they reach a belt 200 to 300 feet below their own specific tree lines and here they assume one or more of three different growth forms: tall trees, low mats called elfinwood, or intermediate forms composed of several short erect trunks on a mat base. This is the border zone between subalpine and alpine, a kind of no man's land where conditions of the austere heights above begin to be felt. Into this testing arena the three trees drop seeds containing their genetic potential. Their chances for survival higher up depend on producing genetic combinations or mutations for plant forms that can exist under alpine conditions. Alpine conditions eliminate tall and intermediate trees and select for flat-growing mats.

Whitebark pine, with all the requisite genes, attains the highest tree line within the valley — 10,800 feet on south-facing slopes — and has evolved an elfinwood race that climbs at knee-high level up 12,000 feet. On east slopes mountain hemlock shows a parallel evolution. With tree line at 10,250 feet, its gnarly matted alpine forms range a thousand feet higher. Only lodgepole persists as a tall tree to its timberline at 10,500 feet on south slopes. But it, too, is in the process of evolving an alpine mat form, as pockets of elfinwood clearly indicate.

Mountaintops provide tremendous laboratories for evolution. The changes in genes, or mutations, that are evolution's working tool, are caused in part by oxygen deficiency, extremes of heat or cold, and radiation. All of these prevail with great force high in the mountains.

· · ·

In the southern part of the high Sierra, thriving in the most inhospitable places on rocky benches, grows the only other major subalpine tree, the foxtail pine (*Pinus balfouriana*).

From Mount Whitney, where they share timberline with lodge-poles, to Onion Valley, foxtails form groves that usually stand apart from other trees. They meet the demanding climate with thickset reddish-brown trunks that taper to a bleached tip, the foliage often borne asymmetrically, the branches clothed densely at the end somewhat like a fox's tail.

In the rocky substratum where foxtail roots anchor around large boulders, and in similar rockslides throughout timberline areas, live two of the high Sierra's most common mammals — the yellowbelly marmot and the pika.

A fat grizzled yellowbelly marmot (*Marmota flaviventris*) stretched out on a boulder, basking in the sun, is a familiar sight to hikers. Approaching it closely is another matter, for its sharp whistle of alarm is followed by a quick disappearance into an impenetrable pile of rocks. If the presence of blackish half-inch-long droppings reveals that this is a regular lookout, a quiet wait at a distance will usually be repaid by a black face with a white forehead patch peering cautiously out of a dark opening. When all is well, the basking resumes, alternating during the summer months with foraging trips to nearby meadows.

Feeding on tender green vegetation, the big rodent puts on a thick layer of fat to carry it through a long winter of hibernation. Unlike its fabled eastern North American relative, the woodchuck or groundhog, it does not usually emerge until April or May, when lean and hungry for fresh green shoots.

The smaller pika (*Ochotona princeps*) is less often seen but commonly heard in its rockslide niche throughout the high country. Nasal bleats ring out any time of day, warning other pikas to keep out of the territory; the pika marks its territorial boundaries with secretions from eye and cheek glands. Just before dusk the calls are especially frequent when these little gray "rock rabbits" perch on their favorite lookout posts, usually backward-slanting rocks with overhead protection, and sound off. As many as six animals per acre may claim home ranges along the margins of talus slopes. Sitting hunched up with the back higher than the head, and feet tucked under the body, they look like tailless bundles of fur. With each bleat the whole seven-inch body jerks forward and the round ears twitch upward. Although squat in appearance, reminiscent of a small guinea pig, the pika is very agile. The hairy soles with bare toe pads give superb traction on the rocks over which it bounds; in an emergency, the pika can spring ten feet.

It is as haymakers that pikas are best known. Near the jumbled rocks where they live are always small meadows or soil patches that hold clumps of wildflowers, grasses, sedges, or shrubs. During the brief summer season the pika feeds on these and harvests enough of them to last through the long winter. It works energetically at the task, cutting off stems and branches near the ground, loading them into bundles, and carrying them in its mouth to a sun-drenched shelter near its den. Each animal builds its own haypile, adds new cuttings daily, and allows the hay to cure slowly; a female and her young sometimes make a group cache. In special bursts of enthusiasm, an animal may bring in fifteen loads of hay in an hour, adjusting the plants on the pile with its teeth. The front feet, used for washing and grooming the fur, never gather or manipulate the food. Dried feces of neighboring marmots sometimes add variety to the food pile.

When winter snows cover the rockslides, pikas retreat to the seclusion of their dens, remaining active, moving short distances under the rocks to eat from their haypiles, which continue to be as natural in color and as fragrant as well-cured hay. Occasionally in winter the animals may be heard calling from under the snow.

The pikas' link to snow and cold is an ancient one, for they are among the creatures known as glacial relics. Widely distributed during the Ice Age, they now occur only where the climate is still similar to Ice Age type, hence are scattered disjunctively in the far North and on mountains in North America and Eurasia. The largest alpine areas in the world today occur on the Tibetan plateau and in the adjacent Himalayas; here live forms of pikas, pipits, rosy finches, horned larks, marmots, and sheep related to those found in mountains of the western hemisphere. Much evidence indicates that alpine species originated on the Tibetan plateau and later spread into the higher mountains of Europe and North America. The first pikas in North America probably crossed over the Bering land bridge in Miocene times and expanded south through the Cascades, Sierra Nevada, and Rocky Mountains as far as northern New Mexico — all areas where they occur at the present time.[1]

Also known as conies or rock rabbits, pikas show their relationship to rabbits in their rabbitlike hop, rabbitlike nose and teeth. Rabbits have four upper cutting teeth, instead of two as in rodents, and a lower jaw so narrow that the teeth can meet on only one side of the face at a time. Pikas and rabbits chew with a sideways motion, alternately chewing on the two sides.

Two rabbits are occasionally seen in the high country. The snowshoe hare or rabbit (*Lepus americanus*), ranging south from the northern boreal forests, is partial to forest and streamside thickets of the northern Sierra.* The whitetail jackrabbit

---

* Technically, the snowshoe, whitetail jackrabbit, and blacktail jackrabbit are all hares. Hares have precocial young, born fully furred and with eyes open; rabbits have altricial young, born naked with eyes closed. In common usage, hares are often called rabbits.

(*Lepus townsendi*) occurs over open alpine flats and sparsely wooded terrain up to 12,000 feet, as well as in sagebrush areas east of the mountains. As rabbits go, it is enormous, one and one-half times the size of the common blacktail jackrabbit (*Lepus californicus*) of the foothills, with tail and feet always white and with a warm protective coat that turns white in winter.

The whitetail's favorite daytime resting hollows ("forms") are among boulders or under matted whitebark pines at timberline; here their droppings accumulate. Primarily nocturnal, they are only occasionally seen by summer hikers. Winter records on any high-altitude species are scarce, but Orland Bartholomew, who spent most of the winter of 1929 above 9500 feet in the southern Sierra, observed whitetail jackrabbits haunting the windswept crests to the very summit of Mount Langley.

It was a year of normal snowfall. At a time when the snow-pack averaged four feet or less, he found southern exposures of canyons bare, and Mount Tyndall and Mount Whitney with naked summits and little snow on their slopes. Many streams were flowing; most lakes were frozen. In addition to the white-tail jackrabbits that were out foraging on the high slopes, mountain chickadees were "cheery companions to the last stick of timber"; Clark's nutcrackers and chickarees foraged below 10,000 feet; pikas and weasels were about; and martens raided foodbags at night, "in one case pilfering a whole pound of precious butter." [2]

Whitetail jackrabbits, being animals of the open spaces, have less to fear from martens than from the red fox. Despite their speed, they sometimes fall victims. Lowell Sumner and Joseph Dixon reported seeing fresh tracks in the snow at the head of the Kern River that told a clear story of ambush. One of a pair of foxes had lain in wait behind a pile of boulders while the other fox rushed the whitetail and drove it toward the partner. The tracks of foxes and rabbit crisscrossed round and round the boulders to a bloodstain where rabbit tracks ended. After the kill, the foxes sat in the snow for a while, then went over the ridge carrying the rabbit.

There is no dearth of food for vegetarians like the pika, yellowbelly marmot, and the whitetail jackrabbit in the high Sierra. Interspersed among the bare granite summits are timberline meadows and alpine fell-fields that carry a lush succession of shorthair sedges (*Carex*) and wildflowers in the brief summer. On moist slopes, among dry gravels, or tucked away in damp crevices grow colorful gardens, less showy in dry years, luxuriant following abundant winter snows. Some hold individual flowers that are large and striking; others tiny "belly plants" that require a chipmunk-eye-level view for full appreciation. Most plants are perennials, blooming year after year from the same sturdy roots; the growing season is too short to allow time for more than a few quick-cycling annuals to produce the seeds for perpetuating themselves.

All are adapted in one way or another to the elemental forces of alpine climate. The habitat in which they live is really a high-mountain desert. The solar radiation is intense, dehydration severe; the only water source is from melting snow and occasional summer rains; in many areas soil is completely lacking; where soil exists, it is thin, predominantly disintegrated granite, and sheds water quickly; much of the soil is unstable, subject to avalanches, rockslides, and the constant effects of freezing and thawing.

There is the nearly omnipresent wind that attains velocities up to fifty miles per hour, sucks up precious moisture, and batters and sandblasts. There are the daily temperature extremes, averaging 22°–62° F. on the summit of Mount Whitney in September, dropping to −2° F. in Gaylor Lakes timberline basin in winter.

Sierran alpine plants meet these forces with the same adaptations as alpine plants everywhere. Some grow as low mats or cushion plants, countering the wind by hugging the ground, countering the cold of night by trapping daytime heat within the close-knit foliage. Interiors of cushion plants have been measured to be as much as twenty degrees warmer than the outside air. All resist evaporation in one way or another — with leathery leaves, waxy leaves, leaves reduced in size, densely glandular, sticky or covered by a fuzz of hairs.

Some, like the rare snow willow (*Salix nivalis*), poke their one- to four-inch-high stems primarily through the old metamorphic or unaltered volcanic soils that occupy scattered strips in the Sierra. Others frequent granitic soils. A good many plants show no soil preference.

When the Sierra was overrun by glaciers in Pleistocene times, scattered alpine areas escaped the ice. Mount Darwin, the Dana Plateau, Koip Peak, and Mount Whitney, among others, kept their heads above it and still show an ancient preglacial surface. These areas are believed to have served as refuges, or refugia, for plants during the glacial stages. Later they served as bases from which recolonization took place. Today most of the more than two hundred species in the Sierran alpine flora live where they do irrespective of glaciated or unglaciated surfaces.

Among them are plants with affinities to far-flung places — the yellow hawksbeard (*Crepis nana*) of Asiatic origin, the snow willow of the American arctic, several phlox, gentian, and waterleaf of the Rocky Mountains, even John Muir's favorite creeping white heather (*Cassiope mertensiana*), which is found also in the Canadian rockies north to Alaska. "White heather grows where angels have trod," says an old Scottish fable; when several acres of north slope on the highest of the Echo Peaks is covered with the plant's white bells in mid-July, the fable is easy to believe.

The alpine Sierra holds a number of species that are entirely or nearly its own. Among the endemics is lovely sky pilot (*Polemonium eximium*), raising clusters of light blue phloxlike flowers on dry rocky ridges near the highest passes from 12,000 feet to the very summits. Appearing when the snow melts, it flowers quickly and is at its peak usually for only a day.

Among chaotic masses of granite blocks, especially in the southern Sierra, grow gardens of Sierra primrose (*Primula suffrutescens*), their royal purple flowers rising from rosettes of spoon-shaped leaves.

Under overhanging rocks bob the yellow-centered bluish flowers of alpine stickseed (*Hackelia sharsmithii*), reminiscent of forget-me-nots. Here and there can be seen the yellowish heads of many species of *Senecio,* reminding some people of goldenrods; the nodding purple blossoms of the alpine shooting star (*Dodecatheon alpinum*); the cream-colored flowers of alpine columbine (*Aquilegia pubescens*); the rosy bells of mountain heather (*Phyllodoce breweri*); the small yellow drabas on dry gravel (*Draba sierrae* and *D. lemmonii*); the pinkish blossoms of the dwarf bitterroot (*Lewisia pygmaea*); and several kinds of spring beauty (*Claytonia*), which in the West all are mountaintop dwellers.

As robust as any high Sierran herb is the yellow composite *Hulsea algida,* growing on nearly every high peak and pass from Yosemite to Mount Whitney, where it extends up to 14,000 feet.

Standing ten inches tall, the plant often has fourteen heads in flower simultaneously. Glandular-sticky all over, except for the rays, it gives off a pleasant scent of balsam when touched and is the favorite alpine food of bighorn sheep, which eat all parts of it, including the roots.

. . .

The only birds that nest in the alpine zone of the Sierra Nevada are the gray-crowned rosy finches. Chocolate-brown with pinkish wash on wings and rump and a light gray head patch, these sprightly finches spend most of the year above timberline. The size of house sparrows, they move about in large flocks that swoop down with twittering noises to alpine turf, harvest the sedge and grass seeds, then with a few throaty chirps burst into undulating flight that takes them off among the peaks. Strong fliers, they handle the winds with great skill, riding them on rather long pointed wings until the precise instant for a sudden turn and landing.

Along the edges of alpine lakes they hunt for mayfly larvae or for caddisflies freshly emerging from chrysalids. Winter or summer, they salvage seeds of plants and glean snowfields and glaciers for the thousands of insects that each year furnish a kind of manna from heaven. Whether these beetles, flies, butterflies, and others fly up or are caught in updrafts and blown up, they eventually reach the heights. The frigid air soon numbs their flight muscles and drops the paralyzed creatures as dark sprinklings on the snow.

During the ten years that Charles (Bert) Harwell, former park naturalist at Yosemite, was one of a team measuring glacier melt, he found that the surface of the Mount Lyell glacier lowered about four feet a year. The melt of 1933 exposed a deep-frozen mountain sheep. The quantities of frozen, embedded seeds, spiders, pollen, and insects that melt out of four feet of ice each year must be enormous, a permanent food supply for rosy finches, there for the finding and supplemented by the yearly windfall.

Harwell, on his October trips, discovered that rosy finches by no means had the alpine heights to themselves. There were dippers feeding with them at glacier fronts, golden eagles soaring above, and sparrow hawks catching grasshoppers on the tops of peaks. He saw small flocks of piñon jays flying over glaciers and water pipits wagging tails on the ice. The pipits, obviously migrating, are not known to nest in the high Sierra, although they nest in similar habitats on the northern tundra and south on the higher mountains to Oregon and Colorado. Lost in the past, or perhaps only undiscovered, lie the contingencies of historical geography that brought pipits, ptarmigan, and several forms of rosy finches to nest in the alpine zone of the Rocky Mountains, whereas of these only the gray-crowned rosy finch nests in the alpine Sierra Nevada. Birds of the crags, rosy finches leave them only briefly during severe winter storms to descend lower, primarily on the east side of the range. The winds that sweep arctic summits bare expose their food at any season.

Harwell found eared grebes in alpine lakes and sharp-shinned hawks often about. While he was at 12,400 feet on the Kuna glacier one day, a noisy, intense twittering caught his attention. "Here came a mad band of some fifty rosy finches chasing a sharp-shinned hawk off their mountain. The hawk made no attempt to do anything but escape." [3] The arch-enemy of the rosy finch, however, is not a hawk but the most conspicuous bird in the high country — Clark's nutcracker. During the breeding season, rosy finches build nests in caves or crevices on the faces of cliffs or under rocks of the talus slopes below, preferring cool shaded places. The cliff nests are virtually inaccessible to anything but birds. The big gray, black, and white nutcracker forages regularly along the craggy cliffs, examining every hole and ledge, eats eggs when it finds them, or carries out and devours fledglings.

Young rosy finches leave the nest when they can barely navigate and hide, well camouflaged, among adjacent boulders until able to fly well. During this interval, they are vulnerable to both the nutcrackers and weasels, which search the jumbled rockpiles persistently. There are other temporary hazards. The early California ornithologist William Dawson discovered one precocious young finch that had fluttered into a bergschrund — the crevasse at the head of a glacier — and was chirping cheerfully thirty feet down in the icy chasm as his mother fed him.

Clark's nutcracker winters regularly at lower altitudes, often nesting in the pinyon-juniper forests of the eastern slope in March, when the land is still covered with snow, and feeding largely on pinyon nuts, fruits, and berries. In June parents and young move up to the high country, where their raucous calls roll out from the tops of lodgepoles and whitebark pines as one of the familiar sounds of timberline. The nuts of the whitebark form a staple part of the bird's diet. The long sharp bill works like a pickax in splitting open cones to extract seeds; at times it is used as a crowbar, prying out seeds while one foot steadies the cone on the branch. Whitebark nuts are large and sweet, a dark chestnut-brown, and unlike most pine seeds are wingless. What the wind cannot do in distributing the seeds the nutcracker does. In its harvest, it occasionally flings seeds about the parent tree, drops others accidentally at a distance, and is believed to pass some through its digestive tract and void them as fertile embryos many chasms and ridges away from their source.

Nutcrackers are not as tame in the Sierra as they are at Crater Lake, Oregon, where they come down to feed at tourists' feet. William E. Colby has written that in the years when sheepmen pastured their flocks at Tuolumne Meadows the big birds fed on scraps and became as tame around camp as pets. When the sheepmen left the park for good, the nutcrackers reverted to their former wild unapproachable state. Omnivorous like their relatives the crows and jays, nutcrackers hunt carrion and any small prey — grasshoppers, beetles, grubs, even moths and butterflies.

Butterflies of the high Sierra include some wide-ranging cosmopolitan species such as the painted lady, mourningcloak (*Nymphalis antiopa*), and California tortoise-shell. But a number of them are rare types whose nearest relatives can be found only on other isolated mountaintops or in the arctic tundra.

Climbing a western mountain has often been compared to traveling north from the Great Plains; each increase of 1000 feet in elevation brings the approximate ecological equivalent of terrain lying 300 miles northward; far enough up or far enough north, you reach tree line and beyond. The rugged environments at sea level in the Arctic and on mountaintops farther south are similar enough to require the same sorts of biotic adaptations for survival, and they share a glacial history. As the Pleistocene glaciers retreated, butterfly species that were cold-adapted followed them northward and to the mountaintops, producing the discontinuous distribution of today.

Some types, such as the Ivallda arctics (*Oeneis ivallda*), erratic fliers of Sierran summits, have come to resemble exactly the texture and color of the particular rocks on which they alight. Near the crest of the range, where jumbles of metamorphic mountains tinted in subdued browns and reds contrast with peaks of pale gray granite, Ivallda arctics fly among the boulders, often leaning with the wind on landing, their mottled wings blending into patches of lichen. Gray forms occur on granite, brown forms on metamorphic rock, their caterpillars feeding on grasses.

The subalpine meadows are hosts to a variety of butterfly species. The "most intense bit of color on the wing" is probably the lustrous copper (*Lycaena cupreus*), a fiery orange-red flier with dark edgings. Most characteristic are the gray blues (*Agriades glandon*) that sometimes swarm about shooting stars and settle among the grasses and sedges as soon as the sun drops behind the western peaks. The host plants on which eggs are laid and caterpillars feed are unknown for both of these butterflies, and for a good many other Sierran species.

One known host is that of Behr's sulfur (*Colias behrii*), the only greenish butterfly in the Sierra. For a number of years around the turn of the century John Baptiste Lembert, pioneer homesteader in Tuolumne Meadows, held a monopoly on this butterfly. Only he and the Indians knew where to find it in this subalpine country at 8600-foot elevation, then highly inaccessible except by long and arduous treks. The butterfly, being rare, was much in demand, and Lembert supplied it in quantity to universities and museums.

When the Tioga Road opened the area in 1915, naturalists soon discovered the secret of this smoky-edged sulfur's haunts. Its larvae feed exclusively on the Sierra bilberry (*Vaccinium nivictum*), tying the butterfly's distribution to this dwarf heath that turns the meadows red in autumn. Although Tuolumne and adjacent meadows form the primary base, smaller colonies of Behr's sulfur have been found to the south at Mineral King and at Rock Creek.

. . .

Characteristic of the dry high meadows are pert little mammals familiar to every camper and backpacker. Belding ground squirrels (*Citellus beldingi*) signal the approach of any intruder with short piercing whistles of alarm. Standing stark upright, resting on hind feet and tail, at a distance they look very much like pickets driven into the ground to tether a horse. At closer range, the "picket pins" show bright inquisitive eyes, wiggling noses, dangling forelegs, as they gauge the threat and decide whether to dash for their burrows.

These foot-long grayish-yellow rodents with a reddish-brown band down the back fade into the background of the late summer grasses. The most terrestrial of Sierran ground squirrels, they feed primarily on grasses and depend little on the large seeds, nuts, and roots that the California ground squirrel of lower elevations eats. Along the margins of meadows, their range occasionally overlaps that of the forest-loving golden-mantled squirrel, but the golden-mantle rarely strays far into the open shortgrass country where the Belding is at home.

Named for Lyman Belding, the Stockton naturalist who first collected it in 1885, this high-elevation squirrel spends nearly eight months of the year underground, often hibernating from September to April, varying somewhat with the weather. Its young are born in July, as many as six in a litter, and on emerging from the nest are watched over carefully by the mother; at her single sharp warning note, they disappear into the burrow, sometimes all trying to crowd through the two-inch hole at once.

When they later disperse, they dig their own burrow systems, sometimes appropriating tunnels of mountain pocket gophers. One tunnel that was excavated totaled fifty-four feet in length. Soil moisture limits the lower levels; most burrows checked have been less than a foot beneath the surface.

No depth, however, is much protection from their occasional enemy the badger, once he has found a ground squirrel at home. Excavating a series of surface holes along the tunnel, he appears to see, hear, or smell his prey as he moves quickly from one opening to the other until he captures the luckless victim.

Once common in plains and mountain meadows of the West and east to the Great Lakes, badgers (*Taxidea taxus*) have been exterminated from much of their range by settlement, cultivation, and poisons. A 1915 University of California mammal survey of a cross section of the Sierra named the badger "the most numerous carnivore on Tuolumne Meadows." No recent comparable count has been made, but badgers are now neither common nor numerous in the Sierra, occurring in meadows here and there, through timberline. The California Wildlife Plan recommends that the badger, along with the scarce high-mountain red fox, be placed on the protected list.

When it comes to digging skill and speed, it is doubtful whether any American mammal can match a badger. Many naturalists have seen the animal in action; one of the prize Sierran accounts is certainly Walter Fry's.[4]

On September 2, 1912, while at Mitchell Meadow, Sequoia National Park — elevation 8500 feet — we came suddenly upon a large badger some 100 yards from his den. We shut off his return to his burrow and chased him for a few moments on horseback. No sooner did we stop our chase than the badger dug into the ground, and did the fastest job of digging I have ever seen. Although the ground was hard and somewhat crusted with sod, the badger dug himself completely from our sight and plugged the hole behind him with dirt in less than one and one-half minutes. In excavating, his whole being was brought into action. He used all four feet, as well as mouth, with great skill and determination.

The badger's equipment for digging could hardly be more superb. Built low, with short legs and a broadly flattened body somewhat on the lines of a turtle, the animal is close to the ground to begin with. Its black feet, armed with powerful claws, are backed by stout muscles. The tough hide of long grizzled hair hangs loosely behind a face marked by a conspicuous white stripe running from the nose over the head to the shoulder and contrasting black cheek patches. All of its two-and-one-half-foot length and more than twenty pounds are thrown into its search for food. Catching gophers, ground squirrels, mice, and chipmunks in one meadow until they become scarce, it then moves on to new territory, digs a burrow for shelter, and takes up the food search anew. It is courageous and powerful like its larger cousin the wolverine, knows no fear when cornered, and will use claws and teeth to devastating effect in its defense.

The wolverine (*Gulo luscus*), according to early records never plentiful in California, is now an extremely rare high-Sierran mammal, with less than fifteen pairs estimated to be living in the area from Lake Tahoe south to the Kern gap. Here in the southernmost outposts, occasional sightings of animals or tracks represent the sole human contacts of the past three decades with this solitary powerhouse of the far North.

A low-slung, heavy-bodied animal about three feet long and weighing up to forty pounds, the wolverine is generally dark brown, with a yellowish band extending along each side from shoulder to tail base and a gray patch across the forehead. It carries its head and tail low beneath a slightly humped back.

What little is known of its Sierran habits comes largely from observations in the early 1900s by trappers and naturalists, especially Walter Fry,[5] who encountered the animal at scattered intervals during thirty years of field work in the higher regions in and near Sequoia National Park. Fry rated the wolverine "king beast of the Sierras" — a creature that knows no retreat from any animal except man and "not only expects the larger animals to let him alone but requires them to give up their own prey to satisfy his gluttonous appetite." Fry saw three large coyotes that were feeding on a horse carcass vacate immediately upon the approach of a medium-sized wolverine; and he watched a large and a medium-sized cougar that were feeding on a deer they had killed give way to a medium-sized wolverine — after much growling and threatened resistance on the part of the larger mountain lion.

At Buck Canyon, seven miles east of the Giant Forest, he happened on to a rare experience. His party had just made camp when they heard the growling of bears. Making their way to a nearby cliff edge, they looked down on a small grassy opening some one hundred fifty feet away where two large bears, one black and the other brown, were standing on the decomposed carcass of a cow disputing the right of possession. After much fussing and growling, both bears settled down to eat side by side.

About fifteen minutes later a large wolverine emerged from the brush one hundred yards to the rear and above the bears. It ambled along with occasional glances to either side, lay down for a few minutes, then got up and turned over a fairly large log under which it located a few snails and ate them. From the base of a large fir it jerked off and swallowed a good-sized fungus, then caught and gulped down frogs from nearby small pools. Suddenly the wolverine sprang onto a boulder, nose pointing in the direction of the carrion, looked over at the two bears, and eyed them and the intervening space. Sliding to the ground, it sat hunched over for a few seconds, then began the advance, cautiously but quickly moving to the shelter of a large rock within thirty feet of the bears. Here it stood up, rigid, and peered around one side of the boulder. "His black, beadlike eyes glittered," recounted Fry, "while the hair on his neck and back was erect and rough like that on a dog when going into a fight, and his short, bushy tail was hoisted to an almost perpendicular angle. Then, after having bristled himself up to what appeared double his natural size, in this queer and picturesque attitude the wolverine shot down the mountainside, landed directly on top of the carcass between the two bears, and, growling ferociously, snapped his powerful jaws and teeth in their very faces.

"Never in all my mountain experience have I seen wild animals more suddenly and thoroughly frightened than were those two bears . . . Every combative impulse gave way to hysterical fright." The brown bear in three enormous leaps reached a fir and climbed to the top. The black bear turned a complete backward somersault, landing on its feet with head downhill, and departed in a cloud of dust. The wolverine began to devour the carcass, crushing and swallowing even the large bones "as if they were mere chalk."

Filling up voraciously when food is plentiful undoubtedly carries wolverines over the periods when prey is scarce or dormant. In the timberline and red fir areas, which they hunt ceaselessly, winter and summer, wolverines take whatever they can find or catch — marmots and bushytail woodrats in the rockslides, Belding ground squirrels, Sierra pocket gophers, and voles in the high meadows, even porcupines on occasion.

Rapid diggers when seeking a rodent in a burrow, they do not dig burrows for themselves but sleep, according to Fry, at random under some shelflike rock or at the base of a tree. The wolverine, shunning man, living in the remote high areas, requires only a large enough wilderness left alone. If the south-central Sierra is ever bisected by the threatened trans-Sierran highway, the resulting patchwork could well write *finis* to wolverines in the range of light.

. . .

In some parts of the wolverine's terrain, glacial action and subsequent weathering have left low rocky ridges, sinks, and shallow bogs interspersed with meandering streams and small lakes. In the high mountain spring of May or early June, these wet meadows resound with the mellow trills of Yosemite toads (*Bufo canorus*) and the *krek-it* of tiny Pacific treefrogs (*Hyla regilla*). Emerging from hibernation as soon as snowmelt pools form in the meadows, these amphibians waste no time to commence breeding. The choruses set up by male toads soon attract wandering females, which are much in demand since they are on the short end of a 10 to 1 ratio. So eager are the males that they sometimes clasp and ride the backs of other males momentarily. Despite the distinct color difference in the sexes — the larger females showing many dark blotches on a pale background, the males a nearly uniform greenish tan — sex apparently is recognized more by trial and error behavior than visually. Females submit to clasping; protest notes and escape struggles of clasped males soon win their release.

The eggs are laid in jelly-like strings in shallow water of silty pools surrounded by sedges and rushes. Treefrogs often breed in the same pools, preferring the deeper parts, while neighboring mountain yellow-legged frogs (*Rana muscosa*) select deep areas of lakes or slow streams. After the breeding season, adults of all three amphibians can be found side by side at the edges of lakes or ponds.

Temperature is known to exert a potent influence on the rate at which amphibious animals develop; at high altitudes it becomes critical. For eggs laid in water of 45° to 73° F. to hatch into tadpoles and eventual frogs and toads in the course of a short subalpine growing season requires special acceleration. The mountain yellow-legged frog takes two seasons to accomplish its metamorphosis; it overwinters as a tadpole and matures the second summer. Living in the deeper lakes and streams that do not freeze makes this possible for the yellowleg. What happens, though, to tadpoles of Yosemite toads living in shallow meadow ponds that sometimes dry up before the summer is over?

Ernest Karlstrom, who studied the toads intensively at the 9000- to 10,000-foot elevation near Kaiser and Tioga Passes, discovered a number of ways in which the growth cycle was speeded up. The toad's habit of laying eggs in water usually not more than three inches deep gives the eggs a warmer microenvironment than their cooler surroundings; both the shallow water and adjacent ground surface pick up heat from the intense high-altitude sun; the silty bottom of the pool is a good absorber of sky radiation. The tadpoles, in turn, tend to congregate during daylight hours in the warmer margins of the pond, where their black color absorbs solar heat. In years when high-Sierran temperatures remain warm at midday into September and early

October, many Yosemite toad tadpoles apparently reach adulthood before winter.

The adult toads show an equal number of adaptations to survival in the cold subalpine meadows. Unlike most toads, they are diurnal. Night's cold temperatures force them to seek shelter in rodent burrows, and on cool mornings they may not emerge until midday, spending much time at the entrance of a burrow basking in the sun.

The geography of the Yosemite toad poses an intriguing study in speciation, the way in which new species are formed. Occupying about 150 miles of the high Sierra, from Ebbetts Pass to south of Kaiser Pass, mostly above 9000 feet, it is surrounded by the western toad (*Bufo boreas*), the common dusky garden toad of wide western North American distribution. Obviously closely related, the two toads show distinct differences — the whitish dorsal stripe on the western toad and the large parotoid glands of the Yosemite toad, among others.

At only one known area, the Blue Lakes of Alpine County, do their ranges overlap. Outside the Yosemite toad's range, the western toad occupies mountain areas similar to it, thus indicating an adaptability to the terrain. In speculating on how this situation came about, Karlstrom compared François Matthes' glacial map of Yosemite with present locations of the two toads. The Yosemite toads' localities closely approximated areas that were never invaded by glaciers. From this evidence, Karlstrom drew a hypothetical historical picture.

During the late Tertiary period a generalized western toad type was probably widespread over the low mountains that composed the Sierra. The extensive uplift of the range and subsequent glacial carving of Sierran river systems fragmented the meadow habitats. Unglaciated islands suitable for toads remained between tongues of ice at intermediate elevations from 6000 to 8000 feet. On these, in geographic isolation, the Yosemite toads evolved their own specialized characteristics and later moved crestward as the glaciers receded.

There are indications of somewhat parallel developments in two other Sierran amphibians. The mountain yellow-legged frog occupies higher elevations above the foothill yellow-legged frog (*Rana boylei*) of lower western slopes. And in the central high Sierra lives the Mount Lyell salamander (*Hydromantes platycephalus*), a granite-matching rarity of rock fissures and seepages, with a more generalized relative, the limestone salamander (*H. brunus*), in the western foothills.

. . .

That high-mountain meadows, the product of centuries, can be ruined in a few years by overgrazing and trampling of stock was demonstrated amply by the sheep herds of the late 1800s. With protection, some of the meadows have come back; others have not. Many have been damaged anew in the past few decades by overuse from the more than seven thousand horses, mules, and burros that plod the wilderness trails of national parks and forests in the Sierra each summer.

Some follow the John Muir Trail that winds for two hundred miles and more through the heights, zigzagging over ten passes from Tuolumne Meadows to Mount Whitney. Others take the High Sierra Trail from the shoulder of Mount Whitney to the Giant Forest, the Yosemite high-Sierra loop, trails up the eastside canyons, or countless others.

Wherever meadows lie at the junction of several trails or provide the only handy pack-animal feed for miles around, they have usually undergone a steady, predictable pattern of deterioration. Overgrazing and pounding hoofs break up the sod. Spring meltwaters then cut through and form gullies. Gullies drain the moisture that is the essential ecological factor in maintaining the meadow. Once the water table is lowered, lodgepole pines invade.

Meadows may be invaded by purely natural means and become forests over long periods of time, but the "replacement of wilderness meadows by trees on the scale seen today is not a natural phenomenon. It began quite suddenly [about seventy years ago] . . . with the commencement of heavy grazing." [6]

Both the Forest Service and the Park Service have taken measures in recent years to prevent overuse of the high meadows — requiring operators of pack strings to provide supplemental feed for their animals in excessively used areas, installing fences to control grazing in critical regions, relocating pack trails around meadows wherever possible. In the eight years between 1958 and 1966, the Forest Service stabilized forty-two miles of gullies and carried out range revegetation and water-spreading programs over three hundred acres of high-mountain meadows which materially reduced surface-soil movement, improved cover, and secondarily reduced sedimentation downstream.

Recent ecological studies by Carl Sharsmith for the Park Service and a current ten-year program by Arnold Schultz, jointly for the Forest Service, Park Service, and the University of California, are probing the intricacies of subalpine meadow ecosystems. Like most other American habitats, high meadows are only very superficially understood.

The high country is sprinkled with lakes as well as meadows. More than 1500 lakes nestle in rocky basins scooped out by glaciers, in steep-sided cirques or behind glacial moraines. Other lakes of the past have already filled with gravel, sand, and soil from entering streams, to become in turn marshes, meadows, and eventually forests. Most of the lakes above 8000 feet are relatively devoid of life. Their "pure" waters, derived from snow and from rock drainages, largely lack the minerals essential for growth of diatoms, algae, and the minute animals of fish food chains. At some, garter snakes (*Thamnophis*) probe the grassy edges and frigid depths looking for frogs; spotted sandpipers teeter on the surrounding beach ridges calling a sharp *peet-weet* into the solitude; algae, water beetles, and other aquatic insects, along with a few crustaceans and mollusks, form a sparse but interrelated chain of life.

None of the high lakes held fish after glaciation; waterfalls excluded them, confining the native fish to the lower streams, with the probable exception of golden trout. The native fish fauna in the Yosemite and Sequoia regions totaled six species: three minnows — hardhead (*Mylopharodon conocephalus*), Sacramento squawfish (*Ptychocheilus grandis*), and California roach (*Hesperoleucus symmetricus*) — a riffle sculpin (*Cottus gulosus*), the Sacramento sucker (*Catostomus occidentalis*), and rainbow trout (*Salmo gairdneri*).

Over the entire range trout were the primary cold-water fish, with three kinds of native trout originally distributed in separate drainage systems. East of the crest in the Lahontan Basin, served chiefly by the Carson, Truckee, and Walker Rivers, abounded the cutthroat trout (*Salmo clarki*) marked by two red stripes on its lower jaw. In cool streams west of the crest swam the gamy rainbow with a reddish-violet side stripe and many black spots on the upper part of its body.

To the south in a few high streams of the Kern River drainage, fishermen of the 1870s caught a golden trout — olive-green above peppered with large black dots, a crimson line down the center of its belly, reddish lower fins and gill flap, sides a flashing crimson-gold and gray. Directed by President Theodore Roosevelt to investigate the golden trout (*Salmo aguabonita*) and make certain that it was not exterminated, Barton Evermann explored its Kern plateau waters in 1904. The fish, he theorized, had once been a Kern River rainbow trout, but had become isolated by volcanic barriers above the main Kern River. Living in Golden Trout Creek, which contains masses of lemon-yellow and orange tufa, the trout had over time evolved the colors of its native streambed.

Hybridizing readily with rainbows, the goldens produce infinite color variations in the many high-Sierran streams and lakes in which they have been planted, earlier by enthusiastic fishermen and Sierra Club members, later by Fish and Game field crews. Colonel Sherman Stevens made one of the first transplants in 1876, carrying thirteen golden trout in a coffeepot four miles from a Kern River tributary to Cottonwood Creek near his sawmill. The fish thrived in their new home and later served to stock the Cottonwood Lakes.

From the turn of the century through the 1940s, the California Division of Fish and Game extended the range of goldens one hundred miles north of the Kern drainage, hauling the trout over mountain passes by twenty mule pack trains. Specially oxygenated tank trucks now carry fingerlings and "catchable" trout from hatcheries to roadside streams; airplanes drop the fish into back-country lakes.

Where there is running water for spawning, goldens and rainbows are often self-sustaining. Brown trout (*Salmo trutta*), introduced from Europe in 1895, and the eastern brook trout (*Salvelinus fontinalis*) occur in some waters along with the natives and in some alone. The brook trout are at their best in high lakes, where they spawn in seepage areas around the shore or in springs emerging from the lake bottoms.

. . .

The streams that carry snowmelt down the western slope formerly caused heavy flooding below in the Central Valley in winter or spring. Check dams in the mountains now reduce this hazard; additional dams impound water for irrigation, hydroelectric power, and distant-city water supplies, creating artificial lakes at middle and lower elevations. Although these reservoirs with their fluctuating shorelines lack the natural beauty of mountain lakes, they often are pleasant places for family recreation and are well stocked with squirming trophies for the angler. Depending on their elevation and plantings, the reservoirs hold brown and rainbow trout, kokanee salmon, black bass (*Micropterus*), catfish (*Ictalurus*), crappies (*Pomoxis*), bluegills (*Lepomis macrochirus*), and other imports of the Department of Fish and Game;* some also live in adjacent streams.

Reservoirs usually occupy canyons or valleys, making use of the river's natural walls. Where the canyons and rivers are of special beauty, their selection as reservoir sites by cities or municipal utility districts has led at times to stormy controversy over what is the highest use of land and water. In 1914 the issue was decided in favor of a reservoir for the city of San Francisco in the sunlit meadows and oak and pine forests of Hetch Hetchy valley in the grand canyon of the Tuolumne River, twenty miles north of Yosemite Valley. Today's human demands for the precious one-by-seven-mile space of Yosemite Valley point up that earlier choice to inundate Hetch Hetchy as an action

---

* The Division of Fish and Game changed its name to the Department of Fish and Game in 1952.

against the long-term national interest — just as John Muir and the Sierra Club said it was sixty years ago. Now underneath a hundred million gallons of water, Hetch Hetchy over the years could have brought outdoor pleasure to millions of people.

A similar choice recently hung in the balance for the last wild river of the Sierran slope, the Middle Fork of the Feather River. Rising about fifty miles north of Lake Tahoe, this fork meanders through the Mohawk Valley past the resorts of Graeagle and Blairsden. Near the settlement of Sloat the river leaves civilization and for forty-five miles surges through narrow gorges, plunges over unnamed falls, smooths glistening pebbles, glides by quiet eddies until, 7000 feet below its source, it meets the other branches of the Feather near the Oroville Reservoir.

With a watershed uncrossed by power lines or roads, the Middle Fork lies in a setting of primitive beauty. Its waters — clear, cold, and unpolluted — furnish rainbow trout one of their finest streams, with breeding and hiding places and ample food.

Whether this fork of the river would remain free seemed gravely in doubt during the mid-1960s. The Richvale Irrigation District serving rice growers of Butte and Sutter Counties developed a power-and-water package which, in conjunction with Pacific Gas and Electric Company, called for two large reservoirs and a series of diversion dams and power-generating plants along the Middle Fork of the Feather River. The bonds would provide tax-free power plants for PG and E and free water for Richvale.

Three California state agencies, Fish and Game, Water Resources, and Parks and Recreation — and the United States Department of the Interior — all recommended that the Middle Fork be designated a wild river and be included in the federal wild rivers system. Despite this, the Richvale plan was approved by the California Water Commission and the State Water Rights Board. If the Board's ruling had withstood a pending court challenge, the only remaining obstacle for Richvale would have been obtaining a license from the Federal Power Commission. At this juncture, in September 1968, Congress passed the wild and scenic rivers bill, incorporating the Middle Fork of the Feather into the system, to be administered by the Forest Service.

Water competition in California has nearly always been a conflict between the public interest and private gain. The latter view, blind to man's role as a part of nature, is equally blind to his "feel" for the roar of a wild river's cataracts, the churning of its white water, its clear pools and fellow forms of life.

In such riparian haunts in the Sierra, you cannot go long without meeting a plump slate-gray bird that bobs and dips in the shallows or on some half-submerged rock in midstream. Dippers are year-round residents of most permanent streams in the mountainous West. Water is their element and they are never far from it. Over it they fly a low whirring course; within range of its spray they build their dome-shaped mossy nests; in and around and through cascades and waterfalls they whirl and flit, jumping from rocks to catch mayflies in the air, diving head-first into foaming eddies. Flying to the middle of a rushing river, the bird alights daintily on the surface, then with a quick fluttering turn of the wings disappears beneath the torrent. Walking on the bottom, it probes for caddisfly larvae, flat-worms, hellgrammites, and on bouncing to the surface flies abruptly up and away.

A songbird with unwebbed feet, the dipper claims as its chief aquatic adaptations its waterproof feathering — maintained by an oil gland ten times larger than that of most land birds — and nostril covers that can be closed underwater. Musical at any time of year, it sometimes sings out above the river's roar on winter days when snow banks a frigid land. Chained by neither temperature nor altitude, it runs the gamut of Sierran waters, equally at home along montane streams or at the margins of alpine lakes, bobbing with rosy finches.

8. In the Rain Shadow

THE WINDS THAT CARRY Pacific Ocean moisture to the Sierra Nevada drop most of it on the upper yellow pine–red fir forests of the western slope. What is left whitens the summits, leaving only a token for the east side. The lower eastern slope is consequently arid, its foothills and valleys merging inseparably into the Great Basin desert that stretches nearly a thousand miles across eastern California, Nevada, Utah, Colorado, and Wyoming to the Rocky Mountains.

This high desert — varying from 4000 feet to 6000 feet at its Sierran border, hot in summer, cold in winter — is a wide open land from which you can look up much of the year to nearby snow-covered peaks and to eastward tawny rounded mountains. Dominating the rolling expanse of space and clear dry air is the low shrubby plant community, sagebrush scrub. Composed of several species of silvery-green sagebrush (*Artemisia*), grasses, allied shrubs, and wildflowers in season, it clothes the Sierra's eastern flank for most of its four-hundred-mile length. In the deep pervious soils, basin sagebrush (*Artemisia tridentata*), the largest form, reaches heights of seven feet or more. And all the way to 9500 feet or higher, this tough aromatic shrub carries the imprint of the desert up the eastern slope, crossing over in places onto the west side of the range.

As the raven flies it, this valley-to-mountaintop distance is not very far. For the eastern escarpment is so steep in its southern section around Mount Whitney that there is a two-mile, almost vertical drop from alpine meadows to desert flats. This dramatic contrast decreases to the north, but it is the proximity of desert valleys and snow-capped peaks with all the variety of plant and animal life packed between them in the short distance that gives the eastern Sierra its uniqueness.

The eastern slope, with a gradient in places ten times as steep as the western gradient, compresses into approximately six miles plant communities whose counterparts spread out over sixty miles on the west. This makes the east-side zonation much more compact and less distinct. Plant communities sometimes jam together, or are missing, or pop out above or below their usual sequence. Variations in local topography, moisture, exposure, temperature, slope, and history determine this.

The rivers that cascade down east-side canyons, following paths once filled by glaciers, have cut through glacial moraines at nearly every bottom. Side roads now wind alongside many an old glacial path, each approach distinct from the others as it leads across the mountain's sagebrush shoulder into the foothills and forests above. From road's end trails zigzag upward to lakes lying in minaret-rimmed basins, to green meadows, snow-filled cirques, and jagged peaks of the high country; and many of the trails link with the John Muir Trail that follows the crest of the range.

The eastern heights harbor essentially the same plant and animal communities as those we have seen in the high-Sierran west. Below the alpine fell-fields grow subalpine forests of whitebark and lodgepole pine, western white pine and mountain hemlock, with foxtail and occasional limber pine (*Pinus flexilis*) to the south. Below these, red firs rise in cool deep-shaded stands, intermingling with lodgepoles, and at their lower borders with white firs and Jeffrey pines. Aspens appear in groves anywhere from sagebrush country, where they grow along streams, to the fir-lodgepole forests.

The same sounds echo throughout the red fir forests of east and west — the distant spiral of the hermit thrush, the ruby-crowned kinglet's miniature symphony, the scold of the chicka-ree. Among the red firs of the Mammoth Lakes region, only the pumice on the ground would signal that this is the eastern slope rather than the western. Pumice, a kind of grayish, feather-weight, spongy volcanic cinder, covers much of the approxi-mately twenty-five-mile area from Mammoth to Mono Lake. Hurled out of vents as a frothy lava some 5000 to 12,000 years ago, it overlies hundreds of feet of solid lava that built the twenty-four-hundred-foot-high Mono Craters, Mammoth Moun-tain, and dozens of ridges, hills, and obsidian domes. Devils Postpile National Monument represents an outstanding ex-ample of basaltic lavas that fractured into immense polygonal columns as they cooled.

Just below the fir belt, this same region contains the largest Jeffrey pine forest in the world, some two hundred square miles of superb trees. Jeffreys generally fill the role on the eastern slope that yellow pines fill on the western, occupying middle elevations slightly above the foothills. North of Lake Tahoe both species occur together in some east-side spots; but south of Tahoe, Jeffreys are the only stately pines growing from scattered patches in sagebrush up through the foothill woodlands into pure stands of open forests at the middle levels.

The orangish-brown, large-plated trunks of mature trees, sometimes smelling in the crevices of vanilla or pineapple, often rise clear of branches for many feet. In places they tower over hillsides of mixed chaparral — the varnished-leaved tobacco brush covered with sweet-smelling white flowers in early summer, currant, bush chinquapin, bitterbrush (*Purshia tridentata*), greenleaf manzanita. The story goes that a one-hundred-dollar reward was once offered to anyone who could find a piece of manzanita twelve inches long that was straight. The reward was never claimed.

The unusually large Jeffrey pine forest east of the Mammoth Lakes owes its existence to a break in the Sierran wall. The crest, which elsewhere cuts off most moisture from the east side, drops lower at the Mammoth gap. Pacific Ocean storm clouds can here move directly over the saddles of Minaret Summit and Mammoth Pass, dropping their rain and snow east of the crest. This gives the Mammoth Mountain red firs and ski slopes their deep snow cover and provides the water for the adjacent Jeffrey pine forest to thrive on what otherwise probably would be dry sagebrush-covered hills. The Forest Service currently manages the area for sustained-yield logging and recreation. Highway 395, which runs the length of the east side, winds for miles through this parklike Jeffrey pine forest on either side of Deadman Pass, 8041-foot elevation.

At Sherwin Summit and other inclines, the road bisects pinyon pine woodland, and near Leevining passes alongside Mono Lake. Mono Lake can seem a barren, weird place — "lonely tenant of the loneliest spot on earth," Mark Twain called it in the 1860s. It lies in a depressed lake plain with a treeless white-rimmed shore, the grayish-black Mono Craters rising starkly to the south, desert spreading to the east, and tufa pinnacles looming out of the water like white specters.

On days when piles of cumulus clouds reflect from its blue

surface and thousands of Wilson's and northern phalaropes spin round and round in the shallow waters trying to stir up food, the lake is far from untenanted. But life is sparse: the California gulls that migrate from the Pacific Coast each April to nest on Mono's two islands fly to Convict, June, and adjacent lakes to fish, since Mono is devoid of all fish and most other aquatic life. Although its water is temperate, the lake has no outlet, and evaporation over the centuries has left it heavily charged with minerals. The combination of sodium carbonate, lime carbonate, salt, and borax tastes soapy and bitter as well as salty and leaves a deposit of white salt on the skin. So intensely alkaline is the water that it feels slippery between the fingers.

Too briny for most life, Mono Lake is perfect for a certain few. It teems with brine shrimp, tiny crustaceans that swim and breed in the shallows and have sometimes been harvested by the California Department of Fish and Game as trout food. The shoreline darkens at times with small flies that swarm by the millions. These are the famous "koo-chah-bee" flies (*Ephydra hians*) whose pupae were relished by the Indians for food. The larval cases of the flies were attached to rocks on the bottom in shallow water. In late summer when the winds washed great quantities of pupae onto the shore, the Indians collected them in masses, dried them, and removed their cases. The inner meat, resembling yellow grains of rice, was stored and eaten as a delicacy, reputed to have a flavor like nutmeat and shrimp. William Brewer, on his survey of California geology in 1863, described the pupae as "oily, very nutritious and not unpleasant to the taste" and wrote that they would make a fine soup if one did not know the source.

Koo-chah-bee were important trading items. The band of Paiute Indians who lived near Mono Lake and traded salt, ob-

sidian, koo-chah-bee, and other articles across the Sierra, apparently became known to their western neighbors the Yokuts as
the "Monos" or "fly people" because of this food staple.

The Indians of Yosemite Valley were very fond of koo-chah-
bee. Tabuce, the Indian squaw who demonstrated tribal cus-
toms to Yosemite Museum visitors during the 1940s, occasionally used to make acorn flour pancakes for her guests. Just
before serving she would lightly sprinkle a concoction over the
top pancake, smiling and saying, "Something special." Later
they learned it was koo-chah-bee.

·   ·   ·

The foothills of the eastern Sierra are dominated by the only
one-needled pine in the world. Like spots on a leopard's back,
one-leaved pinyon pines (*Pinus monophylla*) spread in a water-
determined mosaic over the arid rocky elevations from 6000 to
8000 feet. Covering themselves when young with the stiff,
curved, sharp-pointed needles, pinyons form compact balls and
triangles of soft-toned blue-green. At maturity they stand less
than twenty-five feet tall, more flat-topped and irregular in
shape, but still usually offering scant shade. Sometimes, as near
Rock Creek, they grow in almost pure, rather lush stands; occasionally they intermingle with Sierra junipers or Jeffrey pines;
more frequently with the desert-loving Utah juniper (*Juniperus osteosperma*), desert mahogany (*Cercocarpus ledifolius*),
or bitterbrush. North of Lake Tahoe, they taper off into a ju-
niper-sagebrush woodland that persists into Oregon.

The pinyon's affinities lie primarily with the dry desert
mountains of the Great Basin and the Southwest. Pinyon-
juniper woodlands occur in the White-Inyo Mountains just east
of the Sierra, in mountains of Nevada, Utah, Colorado, and Ari-

zona. In the last three states the pinyon is mostly a two-needled species (*Pinus edulis*) rather than the one-needled tree of the Sierra. Recent fossil evidence indicates that many parts of the Mohave Desert south of the Sierra, now occupied by scanty shrubs, supported pinyon-juniper woodlands as recently as 9000 years ago.

This evidence was contributed unwittingly by the woodrat, which ranges widely throughout the deserts and mountains of the region and has done so for a long time. The woodrat by nature collects a great diversity of plant materials within a limited foraging area for its house or den which, in arid regions, is usually inside a cave or rock shelter. Here it assembles woody branches, spiny twigs, leaves, fibrous bark, old animal bones, fruits, seeds — an astonishing variety of things from available plants. Usually placed in relatively dry and secluded crevices, these plant materials have often mummified and remained well preserved for thousands of years. Studied, they provide a fairly detailed inventory of an earlier local flora. Woodrat middens from the Mohave Desert range in radiocarbon age from 4000 to 19,500 years. Nearly all of them contain records of former juniper or pinyon-juniper woodland in the abundant fossil twigs and seeds of Utah juniper, leaves, cone scales, and seeds of one-needled pinyon pine.

Pinyon pine woodland today grows in mountain areas having 10 to 20 inches of precipitation, with desert scrub of less than half that amount of rainfall at lower elevations all around it. The fossil evidence suggests that wooded corridors once existed continuously between the higher desert divides. Along these corridors, woodland trees could have migrated in wetter times to the isolated or disjunct stands where many of them occur today.

Piñon jays, probably the most characteristic birds of the

The snow reservoir that annually forms in the red fir forests at elevations of 6000 to 8000 feet in the Sierra was especially deep in the "year of the big snow," 1968–1969. More than twenty feet of snow buried the bases of these firs when photographed in February of that winter.

Such snows make the resident chickarees work hard digging out caches. During the summer seeds and cones are easier to find.

Chipmunks (above) and golden-mantled squirrels (below) are active summer rodents in the red fir–lodgepole pine forests. Eating different foods, they compete very little.

The coyote, hunting chiefly rodents, ranges widely through forests and meadows at all elevations.

Most of the meadows support populations of pocket gophers — sometimes ten or more animals per acre. The valley pocket gopher (*Thomomys bottae*), below right, occupies lower and middle elevations; the smaller Sierra pocket gopher the higher elevations.

The prominent daytime animal of the lodgepole–subalpine meadows is the Belding ground squirrel, dug out of its burrows on occasion by the badger.

A mountain lion is a rare sight in the Sierra.

Overleaf: Mule deer in a lodgepole
pine forest at 8000 feet.

Mountain hemlocks form subalpine groves at 8600 feet on Carson Pass.

Sierra junipers sometimes indicate wind direction on high outposts.

Whitebark pines at 8800 feet on the Winnemucca Lake trail are subalpine.

Right: Glacial polish reflects the morning sun beyond tree line at 10,600 feet on Mount Huxley in the Evolution Basin of the high Sierra. Only low-growing, fast-maturing flowers and grasses of the alpine fell-fields community can survive in the scanty soil and rigorous elements of these heights.

The massive granite wall of the range's highest peaks in the southeastern region towers two miles above the Owens Valley floor near Lone Pine.

Pinyon pines of the arid eastern Sierra rise out of sagebrush. The solitary needles are unique among pines.

The largest Jeffrey pine forest in the world stands on
the eastern Sierra slope near Mammoth Lakes.

Sagebrush spreads a silvery foreground for the Sierran crest
along the entire east side of the range.

pinyon-juniper groves, wander freely from one woodland area to the next much of the year. The size of robins but looking and acting more like dull blue crows, these gregarious jays forage in loose flocks of four to forty or more at all seasons. They even nest in colonies, building twiggy nests with deep felted cups in pinyons and junipers. While feeding, there is much "conversational" mewing, chattering, or nasal cawing among them. They feed their young grasshoppers and other insects, but nuts of the pinyon are their preferred food when available.

The plump sweet pinyon nuts were the staple food of the Indian tribes of the eastern Sierra until the 1860s. Trespassing on another band's pine-nut territory seems to have been the chief cause of quarreling among otherwise relatively peaceful people. Two tribes of Indians shared the Sierra's eastern shoulder. The Washo Indians occupied the area east of Lake Tahoe, from the lower tip of Honey Lake south to the Walker River Valley. North and south of the Washo, as well as east into the Great Basin, lived the Paiute. The two tribes spoke different languages, the Paiute being related by language and culture to the Shoshoni and Bannock peoples of the Great Basin, the Washo apparently to California tribes of the Hokan stock.

In appearance neither was the tall, high-cheek-boned, aquiline-nosed warrior of the Great Plains. They generally had straight black hair and a robust roundness. Both led an uncertain existence in a harsh land and both learned to know its every source of food and water through the variable seasons. In years when the pine-nut crop was good, hopes ran high in the camps for a winter when all might eat. Ground pine-nut meal formed their basic survival food; it was made into a mush to which would be added any seeds, meat, insects, berries, or other flavorful tidbits available.

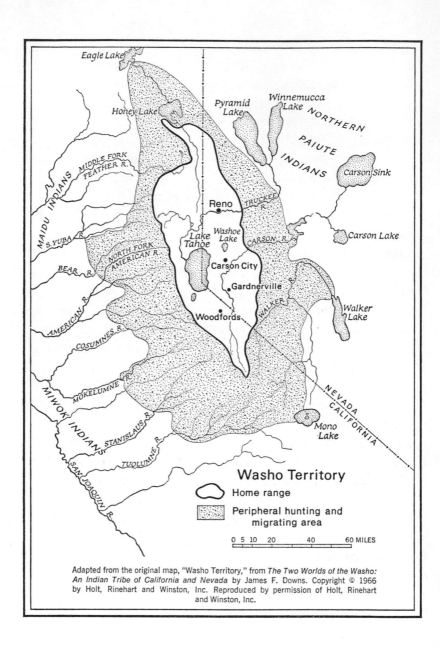

Eagle Lake

Pyramid Lake

Winnemucca Lake

NORTHERN

Honey Lake

PAIUTE

INDIANS

Carson Sink

MAIDU INDIANS

MIDDLE FORK FEATHER R.

TRUCKEE R.

Reno

Carson Lake

S.YUBA R.

Washoe Lake

Lake Tahoe

CARSON R.

NORTH FORK AMERICAN R.

BEAR R.

Carson City

AMERICAN R.

Gardnerville

COSUMNES R.

Woodfords

WALKER R.

Walker Lake

MOKELUMNE R.

MIWOK INDIANS

STANISLAUS R.

NEVADA CALIFORNIA

TUOLUMNE R.

Mono Lake

SAN JOAQUIN R.

Washo Territory

Home range

Peripheral hunting and migrating area

0 5 10   20   40   60 MILES

Adapted from the original map, "Washo Territory," from *The Two Worlds of the Washo:
An Indian Tribe of California and Nevada* by James F. Downs. Copyright © 1966
by Holt, Rinehart and Winston, Inc. Reproduced by permission of Holt, Rinehart
and Winston, Inc.

Gathering in the pinyon groves in autumn, the Indians worked in small groups, knocking the cones from the trees and gathering them in baskets. Timing was important. The cones had to be harvested before they opened and shed their nuts naturally, and before the piñon jays, Clark's nutcrackers, ground squirrels, and other nut-pickers secured too heavy a share. To open the cones the Indians sometimes spread them in the sun to dry, then beat or shook them vigorously in a basket; or they heaped brush on a pile of cones and set the brush afire. The light scorching removed the pitch and popped the cones open, exposing the large meaty brown nuts.

Pinyon nuts, rich and oily and delicious raw, will not keep long in a fresh condition. They had to be precooked to last throughout the cold weather ahead. The tribes usually spent a month intensively collecting and preparing tons of nuts to be stored against the coming winter. Then they began the trek downhill to winter camps, carrying the baskets of nuts on their backs. In good years some groups spent the fall and winter in the pinyon belt, but much of the region was subject to heavy snow and held few springs. Most families moved to the lower foothills or high ground in the valleys along the eastern edge of the Sierra, near water. Here they set up winter camps and collected firewood, great piles of it, higher than their winter houses, to combat the coming snows and cold.

Autumn was also the time for rabbit and deer hunts. The blacktail jackrabbits of the sage flats, still fat from their summer feeding, were an inviting target. Hunters sometimes shot them individually with bow and arrow, but the most productive means was a rabbit drive. Almost every Indian family owned a rabbit net several yards long and three feet wide made of sage fibers. When a number of families combined their nets and supported them on sticks, a semicircular barrier many hundred yards long could be erected. While some of the group waited behind the nets others walked across the flats toward them, scaring up and driving before them hundreds of rabbits. Once in the nets, the big jacks, weighing several pounds apiece, were killed with ease.

Hunts like this were held wherever the rabbit population was high and until the rabbits temporarily vanished. During the drives the Indians feasted on all the freshly broiled rabbits they could eat. They skinned, cleaned, and dried hundreds more into dehydrated mummies, and "during the winter these dried rabbits would be pounded into powder and added to soups or to pine nut and grass seed mushes." [1] The skins woven together provided the most important clothing and bedding that the Washo had — the rabbit-skin blanket. Soft and warm, it wore out quickly and required frequent replacement.

Both tribes hunted the mule deer that inhabited their winter range. Sometimes they stalked the deer in small groups, again individually. A Washo stalker often wore a disguise, a stuffed deer head with the skin draped over his shoulders. Keeping downwind, he approached the herd, expertly imitating the actions of a buck mingling with its fellows. When within a few feet of his quarry, he threw off the disguise and shot his arrow, aiming for the area just behind the shoulder. Here it would penetrate the lungs and usually break off, as the animal reared and plunged away with the arrowhead and foreshaft in its body. Lacking the explosive power of a bullet, even a well-placed arrow could seldom kill a deer outright. Pursued, the wounded buck might run for miles. The Washo hunter whose arrow had struck home avoided a long search by simply sitting down to wait. If he found bloodstains, he mixed the blood with saliva, made a fire, heated a stone, and put the mixture on the stone. When the liquid boiled away, he extinguished the fire and went after his quarry. He often found it a short distance away, dead or dying. Dried deer meat provided one more insurance against the long winter.

Pronghorn (*Antilocapra americana*) were more sporadic visitors but numerous when they came. In their former range over the semiarid plains of the West, they occurred in numbers comparable to the bison.[2] During the Indians' tenure in California, antelope roamed in great herds through the central and southern valleys and eastern sagebrush steppes, eating grasses and leafy plants in summer, bitterbrush and their favorite sagebrush in winter.

Keen-eyed and extremely fleet, pronghorn can detect danger at a great distance. Raising the long white hairs on the rump patch when alarmed, alerting others in the band, they dash away with these white spots bouncing. Variously clocked at thirty-eight to sixty miles an hour, they run gracefully and seemingly enjoy it. They are our fastest native mammal. At rest, their coat patterns of reddish tan marked with white and black break up the body outline so that at a distance they blend undiscernibly into the range.

Despite these defenses, the antelope has two weaknesses that allowed the Indians to hunt it successfully. It is exceedingly inquisitive and its herd members remain together even in the face of danger. Hunters today often can lure pronghorn within gun range by waving a white cloth on a stick; curiosity overrides caution, and the animals eventually move in to investigate this unusual sight.

The Indians, armed only with bows and arrows, had to bring the animals in even closer. They did it by a coralling method similar to a rabbit drive, but with refinements. When a herd of antelope was discovered in the vicinity, word quickly went out to form a communal hunt. A circular coral was built of brush or rope made of sagebrush bark, frequently with wings extending out from the opening and people on hand to fill in any spaces at the time of the hunt. Young men of the tribe then sneaked into position on the far side of the herd, away from the corral, and began to drive the antelope slowly toward the trap. Keeping out of sight, the drivers crept close. One at a time they suddenly stood up, then just as suddenly disappeared. These strange actions made the herd nervous and pushed it gradually toward the corral. As it came closer, more Indians appeared in every direction except that of the trap, until finally the antelope were stampeded into the corral and the opening closed.

Although pronghorns often leap when in flight and can broadjump twenty feet, a good three-foot fence will hold them. Once the animals were caught, the Indians usually celebrated with ritual dancing and singing that lasted all night. The confinement and the noises surrounding them panicked the antelope into running round and round the corral, until by dawn, when the slaughter began, they lay exhausted. A herd supplied food for a large group of Washo or Paiute for perhaps a week. James F. Downs writes that "one such hunt usually exhausted the antelope population in an area and would not be repeated there for several years." [3]

. . .

For their tools of bone, wood, or stone, the Indians used whatever was at hand. They made bows out of juniper or occasionally desert mahogany, arrows of willow. Obsidian arrowheads were wrapped on with sinew and glued with a sticky exudation from sagebrush. Looped willow stems furnished traps for small animals; plant fibers made nets for fishing. They wove willow baskets for every purpose — cooking, storing food, collecting food, winnowing, seed-beating, water-holding — and water-proofed them with an inside coating of pitch. With big game such as deer, antelope, and mountain sheep to furnish occasional breaks in their diet, they lived chiefly on pine nuts, small game, insects, and seeds.

Washo hunting and gathering habits were almost identical with those of the Paiute most of the year. The Washo country was perhaps the most verdant of the eastern valleys. East Sierran streams generally disappear rather quickly into lakes and sinks of the low desert. The Carson and Walker, the larger rivers in Washo territory, flowed during the entire year. There were green belts along the rivers and around the sinks. Waterfowl fed in the sinks; sage grouse, ground squirrels, gophers, and field mice abounded. Compared with the "bone dry" country to the east, Washo land was a haven. But in summer the valleys grew hot and dry very early, and Washo life moved upmountain to the blue lake they called Tahoe, meaning "big water" or "high water." Lying at 6239 feet in a basin between the main crest of the Sierra and the Carson spur range to the east, Tahoe was a revered Washo place.*

The huge rock along the eastern shore was the site of a sacred cave; the creeks flowing into the lake, certain stands of trees, and rock outcroppings were tied to the sacred myth of the creation of the Washo world. The lake itself gleamed "like an enormous gem" set among illimitable tall conifers — sugar pines

---

* Lake Tahoe ranks among the largest lakes in the world above the 6000-foot level. Approximately 21 miles long by 11 miles wide, it is 1685 feet at its deepest point.

dangling long cones full of small sweet seeds, Jeffrey pines, white and red firs, incense cedars. The waters seemed alive as they changed color during the day from emerald to cobalt blue to deep purple. Never freezing over completely in the coldest winters, they held a supply of fish vital to the Washo diet.

As soon as snow left the foothill trails in the spring, the young people of the tribe began the trek up the steep east-side passes. Arriving on the still snow-covered shores of Lake Tahoe, they lived in caves and fished for mountain whitefish (*Prosopium williamsoni*), gathered spring plants for vegetables, and brought fish back to the rest of the tribe in starvation years. As summer approached, the lowland families left winter camp and one by one moved up to the lake. By early June the entire east-side Washo population was encamped on Tahoe's shores.

They arrived in time for the spawning runs of the large lake fish. The Lahontan cutthroat trout (*Salmo clarki henshawi*) and Tahoe sucker (*Catostomus tahoensis*), in particular, swam out of the deep waters into the side streams by the thousands, sometimes so thick that their bodies filled the streams from bank to bank. Men, women, and children armed with baskets waded into the streams, scooped up the swarming fish, and tossed them onto the shore. There, others split and boned them, producing two fillets. "Female fish were stripped of their roe which was eaten raw or spread out to dry," [4] and everyone feasted on broiled fish, the first fresh protein since autumn for most of them. At the height of the run, fishing went on through the night, torchlights reflecting off the shiny backs of the fish. During the two weeks or so of the spawning runs, the Washo ate and dried enormous numbers of fish. Had they known how to smoke them, as the Indians of the northern coasts did, they could have lived nearly the year round on the resources of Lake

Tahoe's streams. As it was, the dried fish spoiled if taken into their foothill and desert valleys, hence were edible only as long as the tribe remained in the cool mountains.

This was for most of the summer. When the spawning runs diminished, families left their lakeside camps and headed into the higher mountain meadows. The meadows offered a wide variety of bulb and root plants, greens and berries. Armed with a digging stick and a burden basket, the women sought and gathered them. Granite boulders pock-marked with mortars still show where the squaws sat pulverizing dried fish roe and grinding seeds and berries.

In the higher meadows grew an early summer native sunflower whose seeds could be ground into flour. From damp spots came the new shoots, roots, and seeds of the common cattail. Before the cattail grew fluffy its seeds could be wrapped in leaves and cooked; they made a brown paste that was eaten like candy and with equal zest.

Another confection was the sugary exudation for which the sugar pine was named. Hard white crystals of "sugar" form on the upper side of wounds in the tree's wood. They contain resin and have cathartic properties, but are as sweet as cane sugar. Adults and children alike picked these "sap balls" from the bark and chewed them.

Wild strawberries and gooseberries were eaten fresh as they appeared at successively higher elevations in July and August, the strawberries sometimes mashed into a thick drink. Wild onions and "wild rhubarb" grew in profusion. Small game was available — pocket gophers in the meadows, chipmunks, golden-mantled squirrels in the open pine and fir forests. The men and boys fished wherever the lakes and streams held prospects. In the upper reaches of the Carson and Truckee Rivers, minnows by the hundreds were caught in shallow pools with winnowing baskets, and baked in an earthen oven. Water and food were plentiful, shelter and firewood readily obtainable, temperatures comfortable. Excursions to the subalpine meadows and rockslides above yielded an occasional deer or plump marmot to vary the menu.

As summer waned, many Washo dropped back down the eastern slope to the foothills and valleys where grasses were ripening and the seed harvest was at hand. Seeds of "wild mustard," pigweed (*Chenopodium*), rabbitbrush (*Chrysothamnus nauseosus*), saltbush (*Atriplex*), and certain grasses were especially prized because they kept so well; every ounce of surplus summer food that would store was a bonus against the nonproductive winter.

A few Washo families often climbed the crest above Lake Tahoe and descended to the western foothills to collect ripening acorns. Occasionally, if early snows made a return hazardous, they wintered on the western side alone or moved into Miwok villages. But most of them were back in the eastern foothills for the vital autumn pinyon-nut harvest.

The discovery of gold in the Sierra's western foothills in 1849 brought the first serious trespass of cross-country emigrants on Washo and Paiute lands. A decade later, with the finding of gold near Mono Lake and silver in the Comstock Lode at Virginia City east of Lake Tahoe, the eastern slope began to fill up with mining camps, boom towns, and "strike-it-richers." Cattlemen and sheepmen moved their stock onto the Indians' best wild-seed lands and brush slopes. The newcomers pre-empted game and fish and cut pinyon and Jeffrey pines for fuel.

The Washo accepted their fate stoically, managing to exist marginally between invader and land. Some of the Paiutes fought back in the year-and-a-half "Indian War" of 1860–1862.

Eventually, to survive, they were forced to go to work for the white man. Some took jobs at the ranches springing up in the better-watered valleys; others became drivers of the flotillas of logs that now rumbled down the Carson River each spring.

The logging boom was shifting into high gear in the Sierra. The demand for wood seemed insatiable. The first transcontinental railroad crossed the range in the 1860s, using Sierran timber and fuel from California to the Rockies. Each mile required 2500 ties; immense quantities of lumber were needed for viaducts, bridges, trestles, and tunnels. Thirty-seven miles of snowsheds alone took 65,000,000 board feet.

The mines of the Comstock and the cities that sprang up around them devoured even more wood than the railroad. William Brewer, visiting the Gould and Curry Mine at Virginia City in 1864, was amazed at the lumber hidden in the depths. The timbering to prevent cave-ins surpassed anything he had imagined: stout pieces a foot square ran across the mine in every direction, with additional braces where the pressure was greatest. Estimates went to 600,000,000 board feet buried underground in the shafts and tunnels of the silver mines — enough to build a city of six-room houses for 150,000 people. And when the towns that mushroomed on the barren hills went up in smoke, as Virginia City did on October 26, 1875, it was timber from Tahoe and Truckee that rebuilt them.

For a third of a century lumbermen went after the tall timber. The streams were bordered with their camps and choked with floating logs. At one place along the Truckee River, there were twenty-five sawmills in operation. Most east-side river canyons were too narrow and winding for logs to be floated down without catching on snags. The East Carson was an exception, and each spring, on the receding water after the spring flood, an unbroken flow of high-country logs moved downstream, kept free from obstructions by Paiutes and French Canadians maneuvering nimbly on the edges of the flotilla. Millions of board feet and hundreds of thousands of cords of wood snaked down the Carson in this manner.

Getting the big sugar and Jeffrey pines, the finest lumber, up and out of the Tahoe basin and down the eastern slope to the mills was often brutally exciting work. Skid roads made of logs were sometimes used, with teams of six or eight oxen rolling a train of logs onto the skidway, then hauling it down. Wanting a speedier way, Truckee loggers invented the chute — a well-greased gutter between skid logs. In this track the logs plummeted down self-propelled. From the mountains above each lumber center, torpedoes of pine and fir came smoking down the chutes at a hundred miles an hour, smacking into the ponds at the bottom of the slides with a bombardment like cannon, hurling spray a hundred feet.

The next step was to use water for the rapid transit itself. Taking a tip from miners who dug or built aqueducts to divert water for hydraulic mining, lumbermen built flumes. These V-shaped wooden troughs, up to three feet across, were strong and reasonably watertight. Angled at a slight incline and mounted on trestles, they could carry logs across gulches and chasms or along mountainsides for short or long distances to a mill.

By 1875 narrow-gauge railroads joined the flumes in carrying away the trees of the Tahoe region. Twelve large lumber companies worked steadily, cutting down the "colossal specimens" of pine and fir, clearing one piece of ground, then moving mill and camp to the next stretch of timber until they had nearly encircled the lake. A narrow-gauge railroad climbed the steep grade from smoke-shrouded Glenbrook on the eastern shore, "where three sawmills whined night and day" to Spooner Summit; from the summit, twelve miles of flume carried the lumber and wood down to Carson City for use along the east side.

The Tahoe destruction was part of a general logging havoc throughout much of the Sierra. By the time that public outcries reached national proportions at the turn of the century and brought about the creation of national forests and parks, Tahoe had come close to ruin. "The great expanses of naked, brush-covered mountain, the hundreds of thousands of acres of second growth, the slashings, punk and trash in young forests, the eroded gullies, the diminishing streams, the desiccated mountain lakelets. These are the souvenirs of the Comstock. What the demolition did to the Tahoe-Truckee watershed cannot be contemplated without a shudder and probably will never be assessed." [5]

· · ·

One of the consequences in which demolition had at least a hand was the virtual extinction of the Lahontan cutthroat trout in Lake Tahoe and in the lake's only outlet, the Truckee River. Native to the Truckee, Walker, and Carson River drainages of the eastern Sierra, this yellowish-olive fish with black spots on the upper body and red stripes under the jaw was also known as the Tahoe trout because of its great abundance in the lake. In its heyday, specimens up to thirty-five pounds plumbed the clear waters.

One or more of the many adverse changes in its environment killed it off. Logging, forest fires, overgrazing, and water diversions devastated its watersheds, causing stream erosion and ruining spawning beds. On the east fork of the stripped and burned Carson River, Marsden Manson in 1896 recorded a scene where summer showers had sluiced off the ashes and soil to such an extent that tons of trout were killed; he could have loaded a four-horse wagon with the dead fish.

Pollution of the Truckee River by paper mill wastes and sawdust made it at times an uninhabitable stream. In addition, insurmountable dams were built in the Truckee River, at the Lake Tahoe outlet, and on Tahoe tributaries which prevented the migratory spawning runs of the fish. Commercial fishermen pulled hundreds of tons of trout from the big lake, many of which were shipped to San Francisco; millions of trout eggs collected on Tahoe's tributaries were sent to other areas. To try to improve the fishery, various exotic fish were introduced haphazardly into the lake from the 1880s on, with little or no knowledge of the lake's ecosystem or what the foreigners would do to the natives. The introduced fish included Atlantic salmon, king salmon, silver salmon, rainbow trout, brown trout, golden trout, brook trout, lake trout, and Great Lakes whitefish. Fishing declined rapidly after 1900, long before commercial fishing of the native trout was stopped in 1916.

Nothing that was done improved the lot of the cutthroat; between 1922 and 1928, they died off in enormous numbers. Reports of the period describe windward beaches as "white with dead fish." [6] The cause of the die-off was unknown, although disease brought by the introduced fish was considered a possibility. In addition to the disease toll, lake trout took a predacious toll. By the early 1930s, the Lahontan cutthroat trout that once packed side streams from bank to bank in spawning runs was extinct in Tahoe waters.*

* A close relative, the Piute cutthroat trout (*Salmo clarki seleniris*), still exists as a limited population in several small streams of the Fish Valley drainage, eastern Alpine County. The Piute (the American Fisheries Society's spelling) evolved the purple, gold, and pink hues for which it is famous behind the isolat-

Of the introduced fish only the lake trout, or Mackinaw (*Salvelinus namaycush*), brought from Michigan in 1895, established themselves in numbers. "Frequently seen" in 1911, they were reported as "fairly plentiful" by 1923 and flourishing in 1938.[7] Today lake trout dominate the Tahoe deepwater fishery, making up about 60 percent of the total catch. Dark gray with pale spots, they patrol unchallenged the depths to five hundred feet, where the cutthroat once swam. Not needing side streams for spawning, the lake trout drop their eggs onto the loose rock on the lake bottom.

The shallow waters harbor rainbow trout on a stocked, non-self-sustaining basis. Small numbers of brown trout, native mountain whitefish, brook trout, and kokanee salmon (*Oncorhynchus nerka*) round out most of the game list. Native nongame fish such as Tui chub (*Siphateles bicolor*), Piute sculpin (*Cottus beldingi*) and the bottom-feeding Tahoe sucker largely provide forage for the lake trout.

Tahoe's shallow-water fishing has been notoriously poor for many years; anglers have had to fish six days on the average to catch one twelve-inch trout. A recent study by the California and Nevada Departments of Fish and Game on means of improving fishing in the lake recommended stocking it annually with 27,000 twelve-inch hatchery-reared rainbows to raise the fisherman's take. This is currently being done. For the long term, the Departments took steps to fill the fish and food void that exists in Tahoe's vast open-water areas deeper than five

---

ing barrier of Llewellyn Falls above the Carson River. Where rainbow and cutthroat trout have been accidentally planted in its waters, the Piute has hybridized freely. In 1964 the Department of Fish and Game embarked on a program to preserve genetically pure Piute stock by transplants into a number of trout-free streams and lakes.

hundred feet. Their hopes lie in a tiny shrimp planted in the lake in substantial numbers from 1963 through 1965. Known as mysis, or the opossum shrimp because it carries its eggs and developing young in a brood pouch, this one-inch-long, almost transparent crustacean (*Mysis relicta*) lives in the Great Lakes, New York's Finger Lakes, and a number of large lakes of Canada and northern Europe. A close relative (*Neomysis mercedis*) is one of the most popular foods of striped bass in the Sacramento–San Joaquin delta of central California.

The diet of the opossum shrimp consists of minute plants and animals, decomposing plant and animal parts, and other detritus. Shunning light, it spends its days on the bottom in the deeper parts of lakes beyond light penetration. At night it migrates vertically almost to the surface, returning to the bottom before daylight. Besides seeking darkness, it prefers cool waters. Lake, brown, and rainbow trout, as well as kokanee salmon, all feed on the shrimp where it occurs elsewhere, and their flesh is redder and tastier as a result.

The dramatic increase in the kokanee salmon fishery at Kootenay Lake, British Columbia, between 1949 and 1963 is credited by fishery biologists to the introduction and flourishing of this little crustacean. Tahoe's opossum shrimp came from the Waterton Lakes, Canada. It will probably be ten years or more before the success or failure of the introduction is fully known, but 1969 evidence indicates that the shrimp are established.

Another recent introduction (1964–1966) is the Bonneville cisco (*Prosopium gemmiferum*), a small whitefish native to Bear Lake, Utah. It feeds on plankton — the tiny, often invisible plant and animal life that floats on or near the surface. It is hoped that the cisco will serve as a middle link in the food chain from the plankton of the open-water areas to the larger game fish, especially the kokanee salmon, which prefer open water and mid-depths but at present find little to eat there.

Tahoe has always been renowned for the unusual clarity of its waters. In 1883 John Le Conte noted in the *Overland Monthly* that he could see a white dinner plate at a depth well over one hundred feet.[8] The role of this clarity in the lake's food chain has only recently been explored.

Fish and game specialists Ted Frantz and Almo Cordone discovered a number of mosses, algae, and liverworts living as far as 300 feet below the surface and forming unique deepwater plant beds of a type unknown elsewhere except at Crater Lake, Oregon. Most of the beds are at depths of 200 to 350 feet, occasionally as shallow as 20 feet, rarely as deep as 500 feet. They furnish food and shelter for the small-animal life of these depths, harboring stonefly nymphs and snails, abundant crayfish (*Pacifastacus leniusculus*), small trout, and nongame fish hiding out from the big lake trout that lurk about the greenery. The zones where the plant beds grow are the very zones where lake trout reach their maximum concentrations. Hence the ecology of the lake's major game fish may be intimately linked to the deepwater plant beds whose lifeline descends through the clear water from the sun.

If that water were to become cloudy from silt, sewage, or growth of surface algae, light would no longer penetrate to the necessary depths to keep the vital plants alive. Decaying mats of these plants on the beaches over the past years indicate that such is already happening. The growths of algae on the rocks and in pools along the shore and on the hulls of boats left in the water tell the same story. Tahoe's water is on its way to turning "from clear blue to turbid green."

Charles Goldman, Director of the Institute of Ecology at the

University of California at Davis, has been studying Tahoe for ten years. "The real problem at Lake Tahoe," he says, is a "steadily increasing fertility which will lead to more and more algae which will reduce the clarity and change the color of the water and destroy much of the lake's esthetic appeal . . . In the natural geologic aging process, lakes tend to become more fertile. Their basins gradually fill with material eroded from their watersheds and with the remains of dead aquatic plants and animals. This increase in fertility, known as eutrophication," ordinarily slow, has been fantastically accelerated by man in some regions — to such an extent in Lake Erie that it "has eutrophicated to near ruin in a single generation." [9]

If Tahoe's small watershed had been left to nature, the lake could have remained crystal-clear for thousands of years. "Every disturbance of the watershed has its influence on the lake." Lumbering, fire, overgrazing, and roadbuilding started it at Tahoe by laying bare the mineral soil. Nutrients leached out of the soil by rains flowed in creeks and tributaries into the lake, beginning the fertilizing and silting process.

The tremendous urbanization of Tahoe in the past two decades has brought with it garbage dumps, septic tanks, millions of gallons of sewage and effluent. "When the spring runoff occurs, these make their annual contribution to the ever-increasing fertility of the lake" and its resultant algae. Land disturbance has brought the erosion of roadcuts, subdivisions, ski slopes, land-leveling — the removal of soil-protecting vegetation in endless ways. This both increases the leaching of nutrients directly into runoff waters and moves tons of loose soil into the lake, causing turbidity, mud flows, and deltas at the mouths of some streams. All of this is, as Goldman puts it, too rich a diet for a primeval lake. Tahoe's "clarity is necessarily linked to its low fertility."

If further pollution is not arrested, the future of the big blue lake in the sky can be somewhat predicted by looking at Clear Lake in Lake County, California. Once well named, its waters now writhe with "pea-soup colored masses of blue-green algae," the product of fertilizing nutrients washed in from the surrounding slopes for many years. Legislative action recently taken by California and Nevada, which share the lake and its borders — and by Congress — may be able to preserve Tahoe's water quality in something like its present state for decades. An ecologically knowledgeable regional agency with the power to establish and enforce strong controls on sewage and solid waste disposal and on the deadly erosion of the watershed could slow eutrophication to a more snail-like pace.

Despite its transition from a redman's eden to a flamboyant recreation area during the past century, Tahoe is still a precious spot to the Washo Indians. Living virtually unnoticed in "colonies" in Nevada east of the lake and on homesteads in California, Washo families frequently visit the lake in summer, to look at its blue waters, to recall at the great rock and at special creeks and beaches their history and myths.

．　．　．

Many things, in addition to the lake and its second-growth forests, have changed on the east side since the Indians' day in the sun. Beavers were originally not native to the Sierra Nevada. Three geographical varieties of one species of beaver (*Castor canadensis*) occurred in California, the Sonoran beaver along the Colorado River, the golden beaver in the Central Valley, and the Shasta beaver in northern California. Trapped almost to extinction by 1900, they were given full protection from 1911 to 1946 and came back from the brink. Between 1945 and

1955, the California Department of Fish and Game transplanted Shasta and Idaho beavers into most streams of the Sierra, east and west. Today beaver colonies exist along nearly all of the streams, expanding their range wherever circumstances allow.

Needing a continuous supply of water in which to live, beavers quickly create this condition on shallow creeks by building a series of dams. Constructed of aspen, poplar, willow, fir cut by the rodent's large orange incisors, and filled in with mud, sticks, wire, rocks, the dams are often solid structures.

The pools behind them, where the beavers live, form a habitat very different from the former fast-flowing creek. As they silt in, they become suitable for cattails, sedges, rushes, water buttercups (*Ranunculus aquatilus*), pondweed (*Potamogeton*), duckweed (*Lemna minor*), and other aquatic plants — and in turn provide a haven for waterfowl, muskrats (*Ondatra zibethica*), and large trout.

The effects of beavers on trout vary in different situations within the Sierra, as they do elsewhere in the United States. In streams that ordinarily go dry in the summer, beaver ponds are the only instrument for maintaining permanent trout populations.

In Sagehen Creek near Truckee in the eastern Sierra, beavers helped to increase the total numbers of trout. When the beaver dam went in, the substrate changed considerably, from gravel to silt. Water velocities decreased; water temperature extremes lessened; fewer kinds of organisms lived in the new silty pond bottoms, but what were there occurred in much greater abundance than in the stream. Brown and brook trout supported themselves on the pond fauna, while rainbows living in the ponds still returned to the streams for forage. Trout numbers were much greater in the ponds than in the stream alone. When a flood removed the dam and returned the area to stream once more, the stream-oriented rainbows replaced brown trout as the dominant species.

In some waters in the Kern territory of the golden trout, beaver dams are reducing spawning areas. Flood waters pouring down can't get through the dams and spread over the green meadows. When the waters recede, they leave a thick layer of brown silt on the grass and stream bottoms, covering the gravel beds preferred by the trout for spawning.

Where beavers flood meadows and dam irrigation ditches that conflict with ranching, where they block culverts under highways, damage ornamental trees, domestic water supplies, and campgrounds, flood trails, and multiply beyond the carrying capacity of their area, their numbers are being controlled by trapping. About one-half the beaver plants in the state are currently giving trouble in one or more of these ways, and require some control.

Nothing less than trapping usually discourages a beaver from dam-building. The story is told of a rancher who tried several times to remove a beaver dam from a creek on his property. The animals repaired it faster than he could tear it down. Finally he hit on what seemed a foolproof idea — he drove a one-and-a-half-inch pipe through the dam to drain the water off. The next day the pool was at normal water level. The beavers had fitted a limb into the pipe and cemented it in place with sticky clay.

Since 1932 an introduced partridge, the chukar, has made itself a part of the east Sierran foothill fauna. A member of the red-legged partridge family native to the Mediterranean areas and southern Asia, the chukar is of an Indian strain. In appearance like a big pale gray quail with a white throat edged with black, black and white barrings on the sides, red beak and legs, it lives in large flocks or coveys most of the year. In summer the birds usually stay within a mile of water, coming in to drink in early morning. Chukars use the same waterholes as quail, doves, and rabbits compatibly, and seemingly do not compete with the natives for food, frequenting more open knolls and flats than the others. Their diet is broad and includes the seeds, leaves, and stems of a great variety of grasses, as well as seeds of Russian thistle (*Salsola kali*), rabbitbrush, sagebrush, buckwheat, lupine, and mountain rose (*Rosa*). Their call, repeating the bird's name — *chuck, chuck, chuck, chuckarr, chuckarr* — carries a long distance in the clear dry air. Rapid fliers and strong runners, they seem well able to take care of themselves on the rocky east Sierran slopes, in spite of loss of some eggs to ravens.

The native grouse of the region, the sage grouse, is a bird of completely different character. Confined to sagebrush country, where in fall and winter it feeds exclusively on sagebrush leaves, this largest of the North American grouse puts on one of the most unusual spring courtship displays of all game birds. In mid-March, depending on the weather, male grouse from several miles around gather on their ancestral strutting grounds. These assembly grounds, known as the arena or lek and used year after year, are usually flat areas in a meadow with good visibility on all sides. Here the cocks take up stations twenty-five to forty feet apart, occupying a swathe several hundred yards wide for as long a distance as there are birds to fill it; on large arenas, four hundred cocks may spread over half a mile, with as many hens about.

Each morning at predawn for weeks the arena is the scene of weird sounds and a kind of shadowboxing. The Crowley Lake arena often fills with more than one hundred dancing, booming sage grouse by 4:00 A.M. On moonlight nights you can see the big cocks arching their spiked, spread tails, drooping the wings stiffly, raising the white feathers on each side of the breast into a huge cape framing the dark head, and turning to right and left as they partially inflate the yellowish air sacs on the neck. Then, strutting about with the sac region bouncing, they inflate and deflate the sacs in rapid succession and produce an effect something like two lusterless large fried eggs appearing and disappearing, with curious plopping sounds as the air is expelled. During the strut the wings scrape downward over the breast with a swishing noise. A steady chorus of booms, clucks, swishes, and cackles fills the night air and continues until sometime after dawn as the cocks strut on their territories. Occasionally the birds fight at territorial boundaries, but it is a ritualized fighting, largely bluff, with feints and prolonged glaring at the rival.

Nevertheless, research of John Scott and James Simon in Wyoming disclosed that this daily fighting and displaying over a number of weeks gradually builds within the flock a social hierarchy in which a dominant cock, the best strutter and fighter, occupies the top rung. In large flocks there are several dominants. This master cock takes over the primary mating area, the territorial prize, a spot about six to ten feet in diameter which is used year after year. Here he mates with over three fourths of the hens. Half his size, they walk to his station through groups of lower-ranked males and squat with wings spread in invitation, sometimes quietly waiting their turn if traffic is heavy. Master cocks have been observed to breed twenty-one times in a single morning, forty times in a day. Flocks often display in late afternoon also.

Near the master cock stands his chief rival, the subcock, who takes over some matings when the master is occupied. Farther away the guard cocks, a step lower in the hierarchy, keep lesser-ranking males out of the select circle and sneak in an occasional mating on the side on the rare occasions when the system breaks down. Since only the most vigorous, most aggressive, and larger males attain the rank of master cock, natural selection tends to perpetuate these traits in the offspring. The breeding season lasts four to six weeks. At its end, the hierarchy crumbles. The hens move to nesting areas, the cocks to summer feeding grounds.

The fantastic displays of the sage grouse were once widespread each spring throughout the sage region of the western United States and along the eastern shoulder of the Sierra Nevada. At one time the big grouse were not infrequent on the east side of Lake Tahoe; Sagehen Creek, north of Truckee, recalls in name their former presence there.[10]

The species suffered the usual heavy decrease in numbers as livestock grazing, settlement, and agriculture engulfed its land. The tens of thousands of cattle driven into east Sierran valleys in the 1860s and the nomadic sheep bands following the "Great Circle" route up the east side from 1865 to 1907 caused complete destruction of much virgin range. Eating the palatable grasses and forbs and ignoring the sage, the stock grazed meadows to ground level. As they overgrazed and destroyed the grasses and herbs, sagebrush and unpalatable plants invaded. Years of little rain aided the sage, which can tolerate drought better than grass. What had been a sagebrush-grass country gradually came to support nearly pure stands of sagebrush.

It was 1930 before the Inyo National Forest, established in 1907, was able to achieve some control of range use and livestock numbers on the east side. And about 1934 the sage grouse, which had earlier dropped close to the extermination stage in

eastern California, began to come back. Today their best populations are in the northeastern part of the state, in the Crowley
Lake area and scattered eastward to the White Mountains. The
grouse are not found at all uniformly throughout sagebrush
range. Sagebrush may look "all alike" to motorists whizzing
through it, but it contains wide variation.

The localities that have grouse possess the four basic habitat
types the birds require: nesting areas, brood areas, strutting
grounds, and winter range. The nesting areas usually are in
sparse sagebrush from two to three feet high and within one
mile of wet meadows or streams. Brood areas, used by hens and
young as summer range, are along meadow edges near permanent water, with tall sagebrush adjacent for escape cover. Strutting grounds most commonly occur along meadow edges in short
sagebrush, where visibility is good. Winter ranges require south
slopes or rocky ridges where wind blows the snow clear from
sagebrush two to three feet high.

In the Crowley Lake area these habitats all are available
within ten miles; but they are owned by four different landowners — the Inyo National Forest, Bureau of Land Management,
City of Los Angeles, and private individuals, each of the four
with somewhat different management objectives. The range
and wildlife staff of the Inyo National Forest has worked out a
sage grouse habitat management plan for the area and is enlist-
ing the cooperation of the co-owners in implementing it. It
hopes in the future to schedule guided trips that will bring the
thrill of sage grouse on their strutting grounds to groups of visitors who have never seen the big birds' spectacular annual show.
And amid the large-scale conversion of sagebrush to livestock
range that is going on in much of the West, the Inyo
management plan calls for serious consideration of the habitat

requirements of sage grouse. It points out that the rapid destruction and conversion of sagebrush may have effects on the
total ecosystem which are at present completely unknown.

. . .

Among the other variations of the sagebrush country are the
areas, usually somewhat elevated, where bitterbrush abounds.
Growing in a great variety of rigidly branched shapes and
heights, with leaves whitish beneath and grayish bark, bitterbrush is at a distance not easily distinguishable from sagebrush
except when in bloom. In June, when the last pink glow of
desert peach (*Prunus andersonii*) is fading, bitterbrush blossoms envelop the shrub in a creamy-yellow haze. The fragrant
flowers, somewhat like miniature single roses, place it in a distinctively western North American genus of the rose family,
with two very similar species that intergrade in some east Sierran areas (*Purshia tridentata* and *P. glandulosa*).

The wedge-shaped leaves and young twigs are a favorite
winter food of the Inyo and Rocky Mountain mule deer herds
that migrate down from the high passes with the first snowfall.
They furnish the only natural food in the area that by itself
sustains deer for prolonged periods. In earlier years they were a
staple of the pronghorn; the shrub is still sometimes called antelope bush. Antelope in California are now restricted to the
northeastern corner except for a small but growing herd rein-
troduced into Mono County in the 1940s.

The seed of bitterbrush is popular with many birds and rodents. Deer mice, chipmunks, ground squirrels, pocket mice,
kangaroo rats (*Dipodomys*) and woodrats all relish it. The rodents sometimes spread the shrub by caching its seeds in shallow
burrows well away from the parent plant, but they also steal the

Forest Service "blind" in attempted new field plantings of bitterbrush by seed.

In southeastern Sierran slopes adjacent to Owens Valley, bitterbrush has proved in recent years to be a preferred food of tule
elk (*Cervus canadensis*). This light-colored and smallest race of
American elk once occurred in numbers that "darkened" the
open grassy valley of central California, its native habitat.
Herds of up to two thousand animals, containing bulls of over
seven hundred pounds carrying magnificent antlers, were described in 1846. From Gold Rush days onward, settlers and
market hunters decimated the elk, until by the early 1870s only
a remnant of the race remained, hiding out in the tules of Kern
County in the southern valley.

By good luck, they were on the large ranch holdings of Miller
and Lux. "The elk were here before we were," Miller told his
ranch hands. "Protect them."

As the elk increased in numbers over the years, they were
transplanted to more than twenty different places around the
state, including Yosemite and Sequoia National Parks, in
attempts to keep the species alive and — vainly — to find a permanent suitable home. In 1932, a Tule Elk Refuge was established by the state and Kern County near Tupman, not far from
the elk's last wild stand on the Miller ranch; this later became a
state park and today includes a semitame, artificially fed, fenced-
in herd of thirty to forty animals. A free-roaming herd today
numbering about eighty, also survived at Cache Creek in Colusa
County.

In 1933–1934, through the efforts of Walter Dow of Lone
Pine and the California Division of Fish and Game, fifty-five
tule elk were successfully transplanted to the Owens Valley.
Lying between the Sierra Nevada and the White-Inyo Moun-

tains, with plenty of open range, little ranching, and few people (primarily because the water of the area was owned by Los Angeles and carried away in its aqueduct), Owens Valley seemed ideal for animals that like dry open spaces. Dow obtained permission from Los Angeles for the elk to run free on its land.

The elk thrived. In September the bugling of the bulls could soon be heard in the willows along the Owens river bottoms. Naturally browsers and grazers of green vegetation, the elk had no trouble in finding a wide variety of food. But as their numbers grew over the years, so did the protests from a handful of cattlemen who claimed that the elk were competing for their winter cattle feed, breaking down fences in order to eat, trample, and wallow in irrigated alfalfa fields. To appease the ranchers, the California Division of Fish and Game authorized several hunts to keep the elk total between 100 and 200 animals.

Alarmed at what an epidemic might do to such a limited species stock, a citizens' group — the Committee for the Preservation of the Tule Elk — formed in 1960 to press for a larger, safer number. On the Advisory Board were such well-known conservationists as Ansel Adams, Horace Albright, Ira Gabrielson, François Bourlière, Victor Cahalane, Carl Hubbs, Jean Delacour, and others. Quoting world standards, which consider a species endangered when its numbers fall below 2000, the committee was instrumental in persuading the California Fish and Game Commission to raise elk numbers to 250 or 300 animals. The Commission sets policies for the Department of Fish and Game. The Commission reiterated its policy to manage the herd primarily for esthetic reasons, to preserve it in safe and thrifty condition, and to allow hunts for culling of poorer animals only when needed. The committee has grave doubts that the last management policy, shooting only the inferior elk, has been carried out in actual practice in the field.

Today there are five herds in the region, one of which — the Goodale herd — has become resident in the bitterbrush zone of the lower Sierran foothills. Here it forages most of the year on bitterbrush, sage, California buckwheat (*Eriogonum fascicula-tum*), and desert needlegrass (*Stipa speciosa*). In the autumn, yearlings and cows drop down to the shadscale scrub to feed on the four-wing saltbush (*Atriplex canescens* and *A. conferti-folia*), hopsage (*Grayia spinosa*), buckwheat, and sagebrush.

At higher, more remote elevations of the same region bighorn sheep also join the bitterbrush brigade part of the year. The California race of bighorn (*Ovis canadensis californiana*) once occurred along the Sierran crest far to the north. Reduced by hunting, overgrazing, and disease picked up from domestic sheep, its Sierran population is estimated today at less than four hundred, split among several herds in the craggy southeastern section. After summering in the alpine heights, the bighorns in late autumn descend the eastern scarp, only three to seven miles in distance, five thousand feet in elevation. This is the breeding season when rams fight for possession of a band of ewes. The clash of horns can be heard a long way off as the big rams rear and charge from a distance of thirty feet, colliding head-on with massive horns again and again until one of them has had enough.

On the south slopes of formidably steep Black and Sawmill Canyons, with sheer bare rock escape routes nearby, the Mount Baxter bighorn herd winters, just above normal tule elk range and in terrain not frequented by deer. Bitterbrush, mormon tea (*Ephedra californica*), California buckwheat, and desert needlegrass make up the bulk of bighorn winter diet.

Since the primary species of plants used by bighorns, deer, and tule elk are in general the same as those used by cattle, priorities have been established on national forest land. Cattlemen and sheepmen of past decades so maimed the range that much of it can never again support the game and livestock once possible.

The Forest Service closed off Sequoia and Sierra National Forests and the Sierran sector of Inyo National Forest to domestic sheep in the early 1960s. Cattle grazing continues on all Sierran national forests except one area adjacent to bighorn–tule elk range. Recent research by Dale McCullough and Edward Schneegas on the ecological requirements of tule elk and bighorns has contributed heavily to Inyo National Forest management decisions. In the Goodale region, the Service has assigned bighorn sheep and tule elk first priority, deer second, and closed the area to all livestock grazing.

History makes it unmistakably clear that the fate of the wild, free-running bighorns, elk, and deer of the southeastern region rests completely in human stewardship of the land. The carrying capacity of the available habitat will determine the number of animals that can live well on it. The Committee for the Preservation of Tule Elk backs an Owens Valley wildlife refuge that will support a larger number of elk as the wisest long-term use of the area; the present elk-cattle ratio is about 300 tule elk to 15,000–40,000 cattle. McCullough, after a three-year study of the elk, sees "little justification for creating an inviolate sanctuary in Owens Valley." He feels that higher numbers of elk might be reached at the expense of the general health of the herds and that if elk populations were allowed to become distributed continuously, closing the gaps between the herds, anthrax or other infectious diseases could sweep from one end of the valley to the other. He argues for diversity, spreading the resource, as the best hedge against species loss.[11]

On one point all seem agreed. The exceptional beauty of Owens Valley as a natural area must be maintained, with the tule elk an important component of a healthy, natural ecosystem.

9. Imprints

THE MASSIVE EARTH movements that thrust the Sierra Nevada to its present height one to two million years ago even then carried traces of earlier life. On the high metamorphic peaks lie fossils of marine mollusks embedded when the range was below the sea. The geological impacts produced the steep eastern escarpment, the singular granite domes, and the glaciated river canyons. The combination of these in a great single block range is uniquely Sierran.

Equally characteristic is the sequence of plant communities that we have traced up and over the range. Sierran plants of today are the survivors of past migrations from the north and from the south and of major land and climate changes. These plants have been isolated long enough to develop individuality. Sierran boreal forests differ from Rocky Mountain and northern boreal forests in that they have no spruce trees. Sierran forests contain the only groves of giant sequoia on the planet, as well as sugar pines, incense cedars, and red firs of a distribution virtually limited to California.

The interplay of plant and animal life — and the effect on this of man-made environmental change — is pointed up vividly by the mule deer's role in Sierran ecosystems. Mule deer are just as linked to black oak seedlings and other green plants that they eat as they are to mountain lions, which in turn consume them. Deer are linked to logging and to new highways, which produce edge openings and fresh browse. Deer are also tied to livestock and rodents that compete for food, to periods of good seedling reproduction, to heavy winter snows, to campers who feed them scraps and trample down green shoots and kill the snakes that would have reduced the ground squirrels that compete with deer for food. They are linked to trampling of any origin — people, cattle, sheep, themselves; trampling affects water infiltration into soil and inhibits root growth of young green shoots. They are linked to disease that comes from crowding and malnutrition; they are linked to fire, which stimulates new green growth on a rich mineral-ash soil, and to many more processes that we haven't yet discovered.

Under wilderness conditions a more or less closed food chain probably existed in the Sierra. Minerals were absorbed from the soil by plants, passed on into ground squirrels, pocket gophers, deer, and other plant eaters, transferred to grizzly bears, cougars, coyotes, badgers, and other carnivores when they ate the herbivores, and were returned to the soil through the death of the carnivores. The Indians fitted into the food chain at several points. What they took as food was usually consumed nearby; when they died, their bones enriched the soil. Their numbers were few, their imprint on the land was light and primarily in the form of annual burning that kept meadows open and slowed succession in some areas.

The miners, loggers, and stockmen who followed them left a different mark. In addition to their devastation, all these reversed the natural pattern of returning to the soil vital minerals borrowed for a lifetime. Logs that were shipped away left no decaying elements to nurture saplings. Sheep and cattle by the

millions each autumn carried off to the lowlands minerals acquired in mountain meadow grasses. Erosion added to deminer-
alization. Mountain soils gain new minerals only from the
weathering and breakdown of rocks, an exceedingly slow process. The mineral drain from Sierran national forests has gone
on for more than one hundred years — and continues.

Other men left as their legacy Yosemite, Sequoia, and Kings
Canyon national parks, the national forests, the giant sequoia
groves, the state parks, the John Muir Trail. Some handed
down Hetch Hetchy reservoir, where a beautiful mountain valley had been. Today's conservationists continue the battles on
many fronts: to keep the national parks inviolate; to keep Lake
Tahoe blue; to end the threat of a Minarets trans-Sierran highway by establishing an unbroken high-Sierran wilderness from
Tioga Pass to Walker Pass; to ensure that the United States
Forest Service shows as much interest in wildlife, recreation, and
wilderness as it does in grazing and logging.

The day of sophisticated ecological knowledge of our earth
is here. The place to do this type of research is in the national
parks (and some national forests), almost the only places left
where there is enough virgin forest to provide a true picture
of natural forces at work.

The influx of today's concerned youth into university and
college programs offering a major in ecology holds hope for the
production in this decade of a core group of the best-informed
young ecologists in our history. As these graduates add their
up-to-date expertise and depth of view to state and federal wildlife and forestry agencies, planning boards, community and state
colleges and universities, conservation organizations, and the political arena, we can look forward to wiser ecological insights
along a broadening plane. We can expect a citizenry sufficiently

informed and aroused to demand, among other things: (1) fish
and game managers who develop management policies built on
ecological knowledge; (2) foresters who view trees not just as
board feet but as living links in an ecosystem; (3) state and
county parks in the western Sierran foothills that preserve woodland and chaparral in their natural forms and include sound
use of fire, buffer areas, and hiking trails; (4) an ecological rather
than a merely political solution for regional problems such as
the Tahoe basin; (5) protection for all wilderness areas; and (6)
regulation of our numbers and wastes so that there will always
be room in the Sierra to renew our ties to the earth.

What will happen to the Sierra Nevada, as well as to the rest of
our planet, over the next few decades depends primarily on our
attitude — whether we view man as a part of the natural world
or as a thing apart. If the latter prevails, our imprint on the land
and wildlife will weigh heavier and heavier and become increasingly irreversible. If the former wins out, there are many ways
to achieve a minimal human interference with natural evolu-
tionary processes. The first step is to recognize the natural
cycles, the way things interlace. John Muir learned years ago
that when you try to pick out anything by itself, you find it
hitched to everything else in the universe.

Appendixes, Notes, References

Appendix I: Plant Communities and Life Zones

ELEVATIONS of plant communities and life zones on a west-to-east trip over the central Sierra Nevada. Each plant community reaches higher elevations in the south than in the north. The elevations used are central averages, allowing for an ecotone, or overlapping border, on the west.

Approximate Elevation (in feet)	Plant Community	Life Zone
400–2000	foothill woodland; chaparral	Upper Sonoran
2500–6000	yellow pine forest; mixed evergreen forest	Transition
6500–8000	red fir forest; lodgepole pine forest	Canadian
8500–10,500	subalpine forest	Hudsonian
11,000–14,495	alpine fell-fields	Arctic-alpine
	(descending eastern slope)	
11,000–9000	subalpine forest	Hudsonian
9000–8000	red fir forest; lodgepole pine forest	Canadian
8000–7000	northern juniper woodland; Jeffrey pine forest	Transition
7000–6000	pinyon-juniper woodland; sagebrush scrub	Upper Sonoran
6000–5000	sagebrush scrub; shadscale scrub; alkali sink (Mono Lake)	Lower Sonoran

The life zone names were first applied in 1898 by C. Hart Merriam, Chief of the United States Biological Survey, to the zones or bands of vegetation that appear at different elevations in the high mountains of the western United States. Like the system, the names are generalized, roughly equating increasing altitude with increasing latitude from the state of Sonora, Mexico, north to the arctic tundra. The zones actually consist of intricate plant and animal communities living at altitudes where temperature, moisture, soil, slope, and other environmental conditions meet their needs — and where circumstances of evolution and history have put them.

Plant communities, named for their dominant plants, provide more specific ecological units for describing plant distribution and are supplanting zones in most recent work. The Sierran plant-community names used are those generally accepted by California botanists and ecologists and are from *A California Flora* by Munz and Keck. There is one addition: the Jeffrey pine forest. Storer and Usinger's *Sierra Nevada Natural History* recognizes the extensive forests of Jeffrey pine on the east side as the Jeffrey pine belt; I include them here as Jeffrey pine forest.

Appendix II: Finding Your Way

THE ROADS over the northern and central Sierra offer a cross section of the range's plant communities, which differ considerably with each highway. On some roads the foothills stretch out for twice as many car miles as on others, where you gain altitude sooner and enter yellow pine forests more quickly.

The highest road across the range and a route that, if followed from one side to the other, goes through all plant communities except alpine fell-fields, is the Tioga Pass road (Route 120) in Yosemite National Park. Yosemite can be entered from the west by any of three main highways (see map): Route 41 (out of Fresno), 140 (at Merced), or 120 (at Manteca). These all cut for miles through woodland and chaparral of the western foothills. Route 140 follows the Merced River canyon in its approach to Yosemite, and on reaching the park entrance at Arch Rock Ranger Station passes through mixed evergreen forests of Douglas fir, nutmeg, canyon oak, and California laurel. All three roads lead to Yosemite Valley's meadows and yellow pine forests at 4000 feet.

The road from Yosemite Valley to Glacier Point, which overlooks the valley from 3200 feet, gives close views of sugar pines, white and red fir forests, lodgepole pines, and the mixed Jeffrey pine–chaparral areas that blue grouse, mountain quail, and Townsend's solitaires like. A branch of the Glacier Point road goes to the Mariposa Grove of giant sequoias at the southern end of the park. Another road from Yosemite Valley is the Tioga Pass road mentioned above. The Tioga road winds through red fir forests, around granite domes, past glacial polish on the rocky borders of Tenaya Lake (best seen

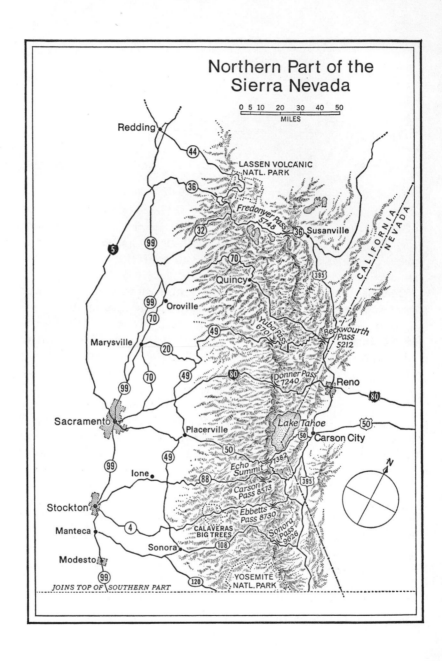

Northern Part of the
Sierra Nevada

0 5 10   20   30   40   50
MILES

Redding

44

LASSEN VOLCANIC
NATL. PARK

36

Fredonyer Pass
5748

32

36 Susanville

5

99

70

Quincy

395

99 Oroville

70

49

Yuba Pass
6701

Beckwourth
Pass
5212

Marysville

20

70

49

80

Donner Pass
7240

Reno

99

80

Sacramento

Placerville

Lake Tahoe

50

50 Carson City

49

50

Ione

88

Echo
Summit 7382

395

99

Carson
Pass 8513

Stockton

Ebbetts
Pass 8730

Sonora
Pass
9626

Manteca

4

CALAVERAS
BIG TREES

108

Modesto

Sonora

99

JOINS TOP OF SOUTHERN PART

120

YOSEMITE
NATL. PARK

CALIFORNIA
NEVADA

N

Southern Part of the
Sierra Nevada

JOINS BOTTOM OF NORTHERN PART

120

YOSEMITE
NATL. PARK

Tioga Pass
9941

Merced

140

Mono Lake

MARIPOSA
GROVE

DEVILS
POSTPILE
NATL.
MONUMENT

Mammoth Lakes

Lake
Crowley

99

41

Huntington
Lake

Kaiser Pass
9200

6

Fresno

Bishop

KINGS
CANYON
NATL.
PARK

NEVADA

CALIFORNIA

Visalia

SEQUOIA
NATL.
PARK

Lone Pine

395

N

Bakersfield

178

Walker Pass
5250

58

99

14

TEHACHAPI
SUMMIT 4032

0 5 10   20   30   40   50
MILES

Sam! H. Bryant

in early morning and late afternoon light) to wide-open Tuolumne Meadows at 8600 feet and over Tioga Pass among subalpine whitebark pines at 9941 feet. In the Tioga Ranger Station area, a climb of a thousand feet on foot will bring you above timberline into alpine fell-fields. Ask the rangers for a suggested route. From Tioga Pass, the road makes a quick eastern descent through pinyon pines and sagebrush to Mono Lake.

The Sonora, Ebbetts, and Carson Pass roads also offer largely unspoiled Sierran cross sections reaching into subalpine forests. Donner Pass is now a freeway, and Echo Pass almost is one. The northern passes all are lower, as is the most southerly pass, Walker. For visiting giant sequoias, the largest groves are in Sequoia National Park, in the Mariposa Grove of southern Yosemite National Park, and in Calaveras Big Tree State Park on Route 4.

Notes

1. THE RANGE

1. Quoted by Francis P. Farquhar in *History of the Sierra Nevada* (Berkeley: University of California Press in collaboration with the Sierra Club, 1965), pp. 15–16. Distant snow-capped mountains to the east had been observed from the Central Valley in 1772 by Captain Pedro Fages and padre Fray Juan Crespi and mentioned in their diaries. Crespi had even made a quaint drawing of rivers emerging from the mountains. Pedro Font, in 1776, was the first to map the range and to give it a name, a descriptive one that took.

2. François E. Matthes, *The Incomparable Valley*, edited by Fritiof Fryxell (Berkeley: University of California Press, 1956), p. 43. Reprinted by permission of The Regents of the University of California.

3. John Muir, *The Mountains of California* (Garden City, N.Y.: Doubleday, 1961 reissue), pp. 2–3.

4. Appendix I gives elevations of plant communities and life zones on a west to east direction across the central Sierra Nevada.

2. THE WESTERN FOOTHILLS

1. Quoted by W. W. Robbins in "Alien Plants Growing without Cultivation in California," *Bulletin* No. 637 (July 1940) of the University of California Agricultural Experiment Station at Berkeley.

2. John Woodhouse Audubon, *Audubon's Western Journal: 1849–1850* (Cleveland: Arthur H. Clark Company, 1906), p. 219. Reprinted by permission of the publisher.

3. Named for Johann Friedrich Eschscholtz, surgeon and naturalist on two Russian expeditions to explore the western coast of North America, including California, in 1816 and 1824. The dance has been observed and described by Robert C. Stebbins in *Amphibians of Western North*

America (Berkeley: University of California Press, 1951). Since 1951 the Sierra Nevada salamander has been designated a subspecies of the ensatina.

4. This information about chamise was reported by Z. Naveh in "Mediterranean Ecosystems and Vegetation Types in California and Israel," *Ecology*, Vol. 48 (Late Spring 1967). James K. McPherson and Cornelius H. Muller found that the toxins accumulated on the surfaces of chamise leaves as a result of normal metabolism during the summer months and washed into the top inch of soil with the first rains. ("Alleopathic Effects of *Adenostoma fasciculatum,* 'Chamise,' in the California Chaparral," *Ecological Monographs*, Vol. 39 [Spring 1969]).

5. Howard L. Cogswell, "The California Chaparral," *The Bird Watcher's America,* edited by Olin S. Pettingill, Jr. (New York: McGraw-Hill, 1965), p. 110.

6. Quoted by Lowell Sumner and Joseph S. Dixon in *Birds and Mammals of the Sierra Nevada* (Berkeley: University of California Press, 1953), p. 38. Reprinted by permission of The Regents of the University of California.

7. Tracy I. Storer and Lloyd P. Tevis, Jr., *California Grizzly* (Berkeley: University of California Press, 1955), p. 17. Reprinted by permission of The Regents of the University of California.

8. A debatable exception is the tule elk of Owens Valley and the eastern Sierra Nevada foothills; see Chapter 8, p. 231.

9. In addition to being cleared for pasture, foothill land is being converted increasingly into subdivisions. Heavily grazed oak woodlands contain few or no replacement trees. Only one national park — Sequoia — includes a minimally reasonable percentage of both foothill woodland and chaparral within its boundaries; state parks preserve inadequately distributed amounts. Whatever is to be saved as natural areas, fire-managed samples, game preserves with "edge" openings, hiking trails, and recreation areas for the burgeoning populations of cities and valley must be set aside soon.

3. MIDMOUNTAIN FORESTS

1. Cited by Arthur Cleveland Bent in *Life Histories of North American Birds of Prey,* Part 2, Bulletin 170 of the U.S. National Museum (Washington, D.C., 1938), pp. 415–19.

2. Lowell Sumner and Joseph S. Dixon, *Birds and Mammals of the Sierra Nevada* (Berkeley: University of California Press, 1953), p. 67. Reprinted by permission of The Regents of the University of California.

3. William M. Longhurst, A. Starker Leopold, Raymond F. Dasmann, *A Survey of California Deer Herds: Their Ranges and Management Prob-*

lems, Game Bulletin No. 6, California Department of Fish and Game (Sacramento, 1952), p. 14.

4. *Survey of California Deer Herds,* p. 73.

5. Quoted by Ferris Weddle in "A Cougar Is Killed — a Deer Is 'Saved,' " *Sierra Club Bulletin,* 50 (September 1965):14.

6. William P. Dasmann (U.S. Forest Service, San Francisco), letter to author, August 1968.

4. GIANT SEQUOIAS

1. Quoted by Francis P. Farquhar in *History of the Sierra Nevada* (Berkeley: University of California Press in collaboration with the Sierra Club, 1965), p. 87.

2. Quoted by Walter Fry and John R. White in *Big Trees* (Stanford University: Stanford University Press, 1938), p. 27.

3. Both species of redwoods have been widely planted over the world since the 1850s. They have thrived especially in Europe, Britain, and Australia, where some individuals are nearing an age of 120 years. Most are specimen trees. (From a University of the Pacific Faculty Research Lecture given by Ernest E. Stanford at Stockton in 1958, pp. 1–27.)

4. Richard J. Hartesveldt, letter to author, October 7, 1969.

5. Lowell Sumner and Joseph S. Dixon, *Birds and Mammals of the Sierra Nevada* (Berkeley: University of California Press, 1953), pp. 98–100. I have quoted in the text on page 83 from pages 99 and 100 of *Birds and Mammals* by permission of The Regents of the University of California.

6. Ibid., p. 406. Reprinted by permission of The Regents of the University of California.

5. FIRE ECOLOGY

1. The legend is told by Jean-Pierre Hallet in *Congo Kitabu* (New York: Random House, 1965), pp. 120–21.

2. From Theodora Kroeber, *Ishi in Two Worlds* (Berkeley: University of California Press, 1962), pp. 185–87.

3. From Thomas Morton's *New English Canaan* (1637), quoted by Emil F. Ernst in "Forest Encroachment on the Meadows of Yosemite Valley," *Sierra Club Bulletin,* 46 (October 1961):26–27.

4. From Omer C. Stewart, "Barriers to Understanding the Influence of Fire by Aborigines on Vegetation," *Proceedings, Second Annual Tall Timbers Fire Ecology Conference* (Tallahassee: Tall Timbers Research Station, 1963), p. 123.

5. Galen Clark's letter of August 30, 1894, to the Commissioners of Yosemite Valley is quoted by Ernst in "Forest Encroachment," p. 27.

6. The Miwok practices are described by Irene D. Paden and Margaret E. Schlichtmann in *The Big Oak Flat Road: An Account of Freighting from Stockton to Yosemite Valley* (Oakland: Emil P. Schlichtmann, 1955), pp. 121, 158.

7. H. M. Towne is quoted by Edwin V. Komarek, Sr., in "The Natural History of Lightning," *Proceedings, 3rd Tall Timbers Conf.* (1964), p. 139.

8. James W. McFarland, "A Guide to the Giant Sequoias of Yosemite National Park," *Yosemite Nature Notes*, 28 (June 1949):75.

9. Floyd L. Otter, *The Men of Mammoth Forest* (Ann Arbor: Edwards Brothers, 1963), p. 36.

10. W. Storrs Lee, *The Sierra* (New York: Putnam, 1962), pp. 204–6.

11. Quoted by Linnie Marsh Wolfe in *John of the Mountains* (Boston: Houghton Mifflin, 1938), pp. 173–74.

12. Longhurst, Leopold, and Dasmann cite C. H. Merriam (1899) as the source of these facts in *A Survey of California Deer Herds*, p. 15 (see "Principal References" for full documentation). The *Survey* has furnished valuable other information for this chapter.

13. Mark Twain, *Roughing It* (New York: Harper, 1871), p. 140.

14. John Muir, *The Mountains of California* (New York: Doubleday, 1961 reissue), pp. 113–14.

15. Galen Clark, "A Yosemite Plea of 1907," *Yosemite Nature Notes*, 6 (February 1927): 13–14.

16. E. Richard Toole, "Fire Damage to Commercial Hardwoods in Southern Bottom Lands," *Proceedings, 4th Tall Timbers Conf.* (1965), pp. 145–51.

17. Harold Weaver, "Observations of Short Time and Long Time Effects of Prescribed Burning in Ponderosa Pine" (manuscript read at Teaford Forest Field Day, May 1966), p. 12.

18. Richard J. Hartesveldt, letter to author, April 10, 1967.

19. Quoted by Edwin Way Teale in *The Wilderness World of John Muir* (Boston: Houghton Mifflin, 1954), pp. 221–22.

20. Richard J. Hartesveldt and H. T. Harvey, "The Fire Ecology of Sequoia Regeneration," *Proceedings, Calif. Tall Timbers Conf.* (at Hoberg, California, 1967), pp. 65–77.

21. Richard J. Hartesveldt, letter to author, October 7, 1969.

6. RED FIRS AND LODGEPOLES

1. Parkinson's story is quoted by Joseph Grinnell, Joseph S. Dixon, and Jean M. Linsdale in *Fur-bearing Mammals of California* (Berkeley: University of California Press, 1937), 1:223–25.

2. Lloyd G. Ingles, *Mammals of the Pacific States* (Stanford University: Stanford University Press, 1965), p. 96.

3. Ingles, "Territoriality of Shrews and Men," a lecture given at Fresno State College, Fresno, California, 1964.
4. David Brower, "The Tuolumne Spraying Debate," under "Letters" column, *Sierra Club Bulletin*, 48 (September 1963):12. Reprinted by permission of The Sierra Club *Bulletin*, © 1963.
5. Conrad L. Wirth, "The Tuolumne Spraying Debate," under "Letters" column, *Sierra Club Bulletin*, 48 (September 1963):13. Reprinted by permission of The Sierra Club *Bulletin*, © 1963.
6. James O. Keith and Merlin L. Killpack, "Malathion Applications in Yosemite," an annual progress report of the U.S. Fish and Wildlife Service, Davis, California, 1964 (mimeographed).

7. TREE LINE AND BEYOND

1. Harold E. Broadbooks, "Ecology and Distribution of the Pikas of Washington and Alaska," *American Midland Naturalist*, 73 (April 1965): 299–335.
2. Orland Bartholomew, "A Winter in the High Sierra," *Sierra Club Bulletin*, 15 (February 1930):71.
3. Charles Albert Harwell, "Some Birds of the Sierra Nevada," *The Sierra Nevada: The Range of Light,* edited by Roderick Peattie (New York: Vanguard Press, 1947), p. 308.
4. Walter Fry, "The Wolverine and the Badger," *Sierra Club Bulletin*, 15 (February 1930):50–63.
5. Ibid.
6. Lowell Sumner, "Our Sierra Meadows," *The Living Wilderness*, No. 30 (Autumn 1949), pp. 20–21.

8. IN THE RAIN SHADOW

1. James F. Downs, *The Two Worlds of the Washo* (New York: Holt, Rinehart, 1966), p. 27.
2. Alexander C. Martin, Herbert S. Zim, and Arnold Nelson, *American Wildlife and Plants: A Guide to Wildlife Food Habits* (New York: Dover, 1961), p. 274.
3. Downs, *The Two Worlds,* p. 31.
4. Ibid., p. 14.
5. George H. and Bliss M. Hinkle, *Sierra Nevada Lakes* (New York: Bobbs-Merrill, 1949), p. 321. This material is reprinted by permission of the publishers. Copyright, 1949, by the Bobbs-Merrill Company, Inc.
6. *Angler's Guide to Lake Tahoe* (Reno: Nevada Fish and Game Commission, 1968), p. 4.

7. Almo J. Cordone and Ted C. Frantz, "The Lake Tahoe Sport Fishery," *California Fish and Game*, 52 (October 1966):242.
8. John Le Conte's account is recorded by Charles R. Goldman in "The Bad News from Lake Tahoe," *Cry California*, Vol. 3 (Winter 1967).
9. Ibid., p. 13.
10. George Wharton James, *Lake Tahoe* (Chicago: Charles T. Powner Co., 1956).
11. Dale R. McCullough, *The Tule Elk: Its History, Behavior and Ecology*, University of California Publications in Zoology, 88 (1969): 161.

Principal References

other than those cited on page xiii

1. THE RANGE *and* 2. THE WESTERN FOOTHILLS

Axelrod, Daniel I. "Evolution of the Madro-Tertiary Geoflora," *Botanical Review*, Vol. 24 (July 1958).
——. "Late Tertiary Floras and the Sierra Nevadan Uplift," *Bulletin of the Geological Society of America*, Vol. 68 (January 1957).
Biswell, Harold H. "Ecology of California Grasslands," *Journal of Range Management*, Vol. 9 (January 1956).
——, and J. H. Gilman. "Brush Management in Relation to Fire and Other Environmental Factors on the Tehama Deer Winter Range," *California Fish and Game*, Vol. 47 (October 1961).
Dasmann, Raymond F. *The Destruction of California*. New York: Macmillan, 1965.
Ellis, Gene, and Frank Kester. "The Rape of the Elfin Forest," *Sierra Club Bulletin*, Vol. 51 (June 1966).
Gankin, Roman, and Jack Major. "*Arctostaphylos myrtifolia*, Its Biology and Relationship to the Problem of Endemism," *Ecology*, Vol. 45 (Autumn 1964).
Hanes, Ted L. "Ecological Studies on Two Closely Related Chaparral Shrubs in Southern California," *Ecological Monographs*, Vol. 35 (Spring 1965).
Ingles, Lloyd G. *Mammals of the Pacific States*. Stanford University: Stanford University Press, 1965.
Lawrence, George E. "Ecology of Vertebrate Animals in Relation to Chaparral Fire in the Sierra Nevada Foothills," *Ecology*, Vol. 47 (Early Spring 1966).
Shelford, Victor E. *The Ecology of North America*. Urbana: University of Illinois Press, 1963.
Stebbins, G. Ledyard. "The Ione Island of Plant Life," in the monthly newsletter of the California Native Plant Society, Vol. 3 (July 1967).

——, and Jack Major. "Endemism and Speciation in the California Flora," *Ecological Monographs*, Vol. 35 (Winter 1965).

Stebbins, Robert C. *Amphibians and Reptiles of Western North America.* New York: McGraw-Hill, 1954.

Wolfe, Linnie Marsh. *John of the Mountains.* Boston: Houghton Mifflin, 1938.

3. MIDMOUNTAIN FORESTS

Belisle, Anne M. "Death of a Scorpion," *Yosemite Nature Notes*, Vol. 30 (September 1951).

Bryant, Wayne W. "1950 Wildlife Census of Yosemite Valley," *Yosemite Nature Notes*, Vol. 29 (August 1950).

Dasmann, William P. *Big Game of California.* Sacramento: California Department of Fish and Game, 1965.

Deer-coyote incident in "Nature Notelets" column, *Yosemite Nature Notes*, Vol. 25 (April 1946).

Ernst, Emil F. "Some Observations on Showy Flowers and Deciduous Plant Reproduction in Yosemite Valley," *Yosemite Nature Notes*, Vol. 31 (September 1952).

Garth, John S., and J. W. Tilden. *Yosemite Butterflies.* Arcadia, Calif.: Lepidoptera Foundation, 1963.

Gibbens, Robert P., and Harold F. Heady. "The Influence of Modern Man on the Vegetation of Yosemite Valley," *Manual*, No. 36 (July 1964). University of California Agricultural Experiment Station at Berkeley.

Grinnell, Joseph, and Tracy I. Storer. *Animal Life in the Yosemite.* Berkeley: University of California Press, 1924.

Ingles, Lloyd G. *Mammals of the Pacific States.* Stanford University: Stanford University Press, 1965.

Leopold, A. Starker, Stanley Cain, Clarence Cottam, Ira Grabrielson, and Thomas Kimball. "Wildlife Management in the National Parks: A Report to the Secretary of the Interior," *Audubon Magazine*, Vol. 65 (May–June 1963).

Leopold, A. Starker, Thane Riney, Randal McCain, and Lloyd P. Tevis, Jr. *The Jawbone Deer Herd.* Game Bulletin No. 4, California Division of Fish and Game. Sacramento, 1951.

McLean, D. D. "Mountain Lions in California," *California Fish and Game*, Vol. 40 (April 1954).

Muir, John. "Proceedings of the Meeting of the Sierra Club" [Nov. 23, 1895], *Sierra Club Bulletin*, Vol 1 (January 1896).

Parker, Harry C. "Mammals of Yosemite National Park," *Yosemite Nature Notes*, Vol. 31 (June 1952).

Ritter, William E. *The California Woodpecker and I.* Berkeley: University of California Press, 1938.

Roth, Hal. *Pathway in the Sky.* Berkeley: Howell-North Books, 1965.

Sequoia and Kings Canyon National Parks. "Natural Resources Management Plan," manuscript sent to author by Sequoia Park Naturalist Russell Grater in July 1966.

"Sequoia and Kings Canyon National Parks Natural Sciences Research Plan," edited by Lowell Sumner, George Sprugel, Jr., and Robert M. Linn. Mimeographed. National Park Service, Washington, D.C., April 1966.

Walker, Ernest P. *Mammals of the World,* Vol. 2. Baltimore: Johns Hopkins Press, 1964.

Young, Stanley P., and Edward A. Goldman. *The Puma.* New York: Dover 1964 reissue.

4. GIANT SEQUOIAS

Beidleman, Richard G. "Summer Vertebrates of Mariposa Grove," *Yosemite Nature Notes,* Vol. 29 (May 1950).

Berland, Oscar. "Giant Forest's Reservation: The Legend and the Mystery," *Sierra Club Bulletin,* Vol. 47 (December 1962).

Grinnell, Joseph, and Tracy I. Storer. *Animal Life in the Yosemite.* Berkeley: University of California Press, 1924.

Hartesveldt, Richard J. Letters to author, May 11, 1966, April 10, 1967, and January 3, 1968.

Ingles, Lloyd G. *Mammals of the Pacific States.* Stanford University: Stanford University Press, 1965.

Lawrence, George E. (Bakersfield College, Bakersfield, California). Letter to author, 1967.

McFarland, James W. "A Guide to the Giant Sequoias of Yosemite National Park," *Yosemite Nature Notes,* Vol. 28 (June 1949).

Otter, Floyd L. *The Men of Mammoth Forest.* Ann Arbor: Edwards Brothers, 1963.

Peattie, Donald Culross. *A Natural History of Western Trees.* Boston: Houghton Mifflin, 1953.

Sequoia and Kings Canyon. National Park Service, Washington, D.C., 1963.

Stebbins, G. Ledyard. "The Chromosomes and Relationship of Metasequoia and Sequoia," *Science,* Vol. 108 (July 30, 1948).

Sumner, Lowell, and Joseph S. Dixon. *Birds and Mammals of the Sierra Nevada.* Berkeley: University of California Press, 1953.

Teale, Edwin Way. *The Wilderness World of John Muir.* Boston: Houghton Mifflin, 1954.

Waldo, Allen W. "A Seldom Observed Feeding Habit of the Pileated Woodpecker," *Yosemite Nature Notes,* Vol. 33 (May 1954).
Wood, Richard Coke. *Tales of Old Calaveras.* Angels, Calif.: Calaveras Californian, 1949.

5. FIRE ECOLOGY

Arnold, Keith. "Project Skyfire Lightning Research," *Proceedings, Third Annual Tall Timbers Fire Ecology Conference.* Tallahassee: Tall Timbers Research Station, 1964.
Barrett, S. A., and E. W. Gifford. *Miwok Material Culture.* Milwaukee Public Museum Bulletin, Vol. 2 (March 1933).
Biswell, Harold H. "The Big Trees and Fire," *National Parks Magazine,* Vol. 35 (April 1961).
——. "Man and Fire in Ponderosa Pine in the Sierra Nevada of California," *Sierra Club Bulletin,* Vol. 44 (October 1959).
——. "Prescribed Burning and Other Methods of Deer Range Improvement in Ponderosa Pine in California," *Proceedings of the Society of American Foresters,* 1959.
——. "Research in Wildland Fire Ecology in California," *Proceedings, 2nd Tall Timbers Conf.,* 1963.
——. "Research Project at the Whitaker's Forest." Mimeographed. Berkeley: University of California Agricultural Experiment Station, 1964.
——, Hayle Buchanan, and Robert P. Gibbens. "Ecology of the Vegetation of a Second-Growth Sequoia Forest," *Ecology,* Vol. 47 (Summer 1966).
Burcham, L. T. *The Influence of Fire on California's Pristine Vegetation.* Berkeley: University of California Extension Forestry Office, Agricultural Extension Service, 1960.
——. *Planned Burning as a Management Practice for California Wild Lands.* Sacramento: California Division of Forestry, 1959.
Colby, William E. "Yosemite — Then and Now," *Yosemite Nature Notes,* Vol. 32 (March 1953).
Dudley, William R. "Forest Reservations: With a Report on the Sierra Reservation, California," *Sierra Club Bulletin,* Vol. 1 (January 1896).
Elliott, Wallace W., & Co. *History of Tulare County, California.* San Francisco: Wallace W. Elliott & Co., 1883.
Givens, Lawrence S. "Use of Fire on Southeastern Wildlife Refuges," *Proceedings, 1st Tall Timbers Conf.,* 1962.
Hallenbeck, Cleve. *Alvar Nuñez Cabeza de Vaca: The Journey and Route of the First European to Cross the Continent of North America, 1534–1536.* Glendale, Calif.: Arthur H. Clark Co., 1940.

Harper, Roland M. "Historical Notes on the Relation of Fire to Forests," *Proceedings, 1st Tall Timbers Conf.*, 1962.

Hartesveldt, Richard J. "Fire Ecology of the Giant Sequoias," *Natural History*, Vol. 73 (December 1964).

——. "Sequoias and Human Impact," *Sierra Club Bulletin*, Vol. 48 (December 1963).

Jepson, Willis L. *The Trees of California*, 2nd ed. Berkeley: Sather Gate Bookshop, 1923.

King, Clarence. *Mountaineering in the Sierra Nevada*. New York: Norton, 1935 reprint.

Kinney, A. S. "Electro-Germination," *Annual Report of the Massachusetts Agriculture Experiment Station*, Bulletin No. 43 (1897).

Komarek, Edwin V., Sr. "Fire Ecology," *Proceedings, 1st Tall Timbers Conf.*, 1962.

Kroeber, Alfred L. *Handbook of the Indians of California*. Berkeley: California Book Co., 1953 reissue.

Larson, Geraldine B. "Whitaker's Forest," *American Forests*, September 1966.

Lehmann, V. W. "Fire in the Range of Attwater's Prairie Chicken," *Proceedings, 4th Tall Timbers Conf.*, 1965.

Leopold, A. Starker, Stanley Cain, Clarence Cottam, Ira Gabrielson, and Thomas Kimball. "Wildlife Management in the National Parks: A Report to the Secretary of the Interior," *Audubon Magazine*, Vol. 65 (May–June 1963).

Longhurst, William M., A. Starker Leopold, and Raymond F. Dasmann. *A Survey of California Deer Herds: Their Ranges and Management Problems*, Game Bulletin No. 6, California Department of Fish and Game. Sacramento, 1952.

Manson, Marsden. "Observations on the Denudation of Vegetation — a Suggested Remedy for California," *Sierra Club Bulletin*, Vol. 2 (June 1899).

Marshall, Joe T., Jr. "Fire and Birds in the Mountains of Southern Arizona," *Proceedings, 2nd Tall Timbers Conf.*, 1963.

Mason, Herbert L. "Do We Want Sugar Pine?" *Sierra Club Bulletin*, Vol. 40 (October 1955).

Muir, John. "God's First Temples: How Shall We Preserve Our Forests?" *Sacramento Record-Union*, February 5, 1876.

——. "Hunting Big Redwoods," *Atlantic Monthly*, Vol. 88 (September 1901).

——. "Proceedings of the Meeting of the Sierra Club" [Nov. 23, 1895], *Sierra Club Bulletin*, Vol. 1 (January 1896).

Phillips, John. "Fire — as Master and Servant: Its Influence in the Bioclimatic Regions of Trans-Saharan Africa," *Proceedings, 4th Tall Timbers Conf.*, 1965.

Phillips, Walter S. "Fire and Vegetation of Arid Lands," *Proceedings, 1st Tall Timbers Conf.*, 1962.

Reynolds, Richard. "Effect upon the Forest of Natural Fire and Aboriginal Burning in the Sierra Nevada." Master's thesis, University of California, Berkeley, 1959.

Sauer, Carl O. "Grassland Climax, Fire and Man," *Journal of Range Management,* Vol. 3 (January 1950).

Spurr, Stephen H. *Forest Ecology.* New York: Ronald Press, 1964.

Stoddard, Herbert L., Sr. "Bird Habitat and Fire," *Proceedings, 2nd Tall Timbers Conf.*, 1963.

Stone, Edward C. "Climate and Vegetation of the Upper Sierra." Mimeographed. Conference on Research and Land Management in the Upper Sierra. Berkeley: University of California Wildland Research Center, 1962.

Thompson, Glenn A. "Fires in Wilderness Areas," *Proceedings, 3rd Tall Timbers Conf.*, 1964.

Weaver, Harold. "Effects of Burning on Range and Forage Values in the Ponderosa Pine Forest," *Proceedings of the Society of American Foresters.* Salt Lake City, 1958.

———. "Fire and Management Problems in Ponderosa Pine," *Proceedings, 3rd Tall Timbers Conf.*, 1964.

6. RED FIRS AND LODGEPOLES

Cofer, Howard H. "The Great Gray Owl," *Yosemite Nature Notes,* Vol. 37 (April 1958).

Crenshaw, Elisabeth C. "Slow Freight to Tuolumne," *Yosemite Nature Notes,* Vol. 24 (October 1945).

Dahlsten, Donald L. Letter to author, April 22, 1968.

———. "Nesting Boxes for the Encouragement of Insectivorous Hole-Nesting Birds in California," *Bulletin* No. 60 of the California Christmas Tree Growers, 1967.

———, and Steven G. Herman. "Birds as Predators of Destructive Forest Insects," *California Agriculture,* Vol. 19 (September 1965).

Eissler, Fred. "Pesticide Fallout in Tuolumne Meadows," *Sierra Club Bulletin,* Vol. 48 (September 1963).

Ingles, Lloyd G. "The Ecology of the Mountain Pocket Gopher, *Thomomys monticola,*" *Ecology,* Vol. 33 (January 1952).

———. "Mammals of Mountain Meadows," *Pacific Discovery,* Vol. 11 (January–February 1958).

———. "A Quantitative Study on the Activity of the Dusky Shrew," *Ecology,* Vol. 41 (October 1960).

Leopold, A. Starker, Stanley Cain, Clarence Cottam, Ira Gabrielson, and

Thomas Kimball. "Wildlife Management in the National Parks: A Report to the Secretary of the Interior," *Audubon Magazine*, Vol. 65 (May–June 1963).

McKeever, Sturgis. "The Biology of the Golden-mantled Ground Squirrel," *Ecological Monographs*, Vol. 34 (Autumn 1964).

Oosting, Henry J., and W. D. Billings. "The Red Fir Forest of the Sierra Nevada," *Ecological Monographs*, Vol. 13 (July 1943).

Orr, Robert T. *Mammals of Lake Tahoe*. San Francisco: California Academy of Sciences, 1949.

Roth, Hal. *Pathway in the Sky* (Berkeley: Howell-North Books, 1965).

Stocking, Stephen K., and Jack A. Rockwell. *Wildflowers of Sequoia and Kings Canyon National Parks*. Three Rivers, Calif.: Sequoia Natural History Association, 1969.

Struble, George R. "Effect of Aerial Sprays on Parasites of the Lodgepole Needle Miner," *Journal of Economic Entomology*, Vol. 58 (April 1965).

——. "Insect Enemies in the Natural Control of the Lodgepole Needle Miner," *Journal of Economic Entomology*, Vol. 60 (February 1967).

——. *Lodgepole Needle Miner*. Forest Pest Leaflet No. 22, Forest Service, U.S. Department of Agriculture. Washington, D.C., 1958.

Sumner, Lowell, and Joseph S. Dixon. *Birds and Mammals of the Sierra Nevada*. Berkeley: University of California Press, 1953.

Telford, Allan D. "Features of the Lodgepole Needle Miner Parasite Complex in California," *Canadian Entomologist*, Vol. 93 (May 1961).

——. "Lodgepole Needle Miner Parasites: Biological Control and Insecticides," *Journal of Economic Entomology*, Vol. 54 (April 1961).

——, and Steven G. Herman. "Chickadee Helps Check Insect Invasion," *Audubon Magazine*, Vol. 65 (March–April 1963).

Tevis, Lloyd P., Jr. "Pocket Gophers and Seedlings of Red Fir," *Ecology*, Vol. 37 (April 1956).

——. "Stomach Contents of Chipmunks and Mantled Squirrels in Northeastern California," *Journal of Mammalogy*, Vol. 34 (August 1953).

Wentz, Charles M. "Experimenting with a Coral King Snake," *Yosemite Nature Notes*, Vol. 29 (August 1950).

7. TREE LINE AND BEYOND

Clausen, Jens. "Population Studies of Alpine and Subalpine Races of Conifers and Willows in the California High Sierra Nevada," *Evolution*, Vol. 19 (April 1965).

Colby, William E. "Jean Baptiste Lembert — Personal Memories," *Yosemite Nature Notes*, Vol. 28 (September 1949).

Dawson, William Leon. *The Birds of California*. Los Angeles: South Moulton Co., 1923.

Garth, John S., and J. W. Tilden. *Yosemite Butterflies.* Arcadia, Calif.: Lepidoptera Foundation, 1963.

Grinnell, Joseph, Joseph S. Dixon, and Jean M. Linsdale. *Fur-bearing Mammals of California.* 2 vols. Berkeley: University of California Press, 1937.

Grinnell, Joseph, and Tracy I. Storer. "The Yosemite Cony," *Sierra Club Bulletin,* Vol. 10 (January 1917).

Hubbs, Carl L., and Orthello L. Wallis. "The Native Fish Fauna of Yosemite National Park and Its Preservation," *Yosemite Nature Notes,* Vol. 27 (December 1948).

Ingles, Lloyd G. *Mammals of the Pacific States.* Stanford University: Stanford University Press, 1965).

Karlstrom, Ernest L. *The Toad Genus* Bufo *in the Sierra Nevada of California,* University of California Publications in Zoology, Vol. 62, No. 1 (1962).

Kendeigh, S. Charles. *Animal Ecology.* New York: Prentice-Hall, 1961.

Klikoff, Lionel G. "Microenvironmental Influence on Vegetational Pattern near Timberline in the Central Sierra Nevada," *Ecological Monographs,* Vol. 35 (Spring 1965).

Ochsner, David C. "A Badger Secures His Meal," *Yosemite Nature Notes,* Vol. 31 (August 1952).

Orr, Robert T. *Mammals of Lake Tahoe.* San Francisco: California Academy of Sciences, 1949.

Roth, Hal. *Pathway in the Sky.* Berkeley: Howell-North Books, 1965.

Schneegas, Edward R., and Others. "Habitat Management Plan for Native Golden Trout Waters, Inyo National Forest." Mimeographed. Bishop, Calif.: U.S. Forest Service, 1965.

"Sequoia and Kings Canyon National Parks Natural Sciences Research Plan," edited by Lowell Sumner, George Sprugel, Jr., and Robert M. Linn. Mimeographed. National Park Service, Washington, D.C., April 1966.

Seymour, George. *Furbearers of California.* Sacramento: California Department of Fish and Game, 1960.

Sharsmith, Carl W. "A Contribution to the History of the Alpine Flora of the Sierra Nevada." Doctoral thesis, University of California, Berkeley, 1940.

——. "A Report of the Status, Changes and Ecology of Back Country Meadows in Sequoia and Kings Canyon National Parks." Mimeographed. National Park Service, Washington, D.C., 1958.

Simpson, George Gaylord, and William S. Beck. *Life.* New York: Harcourt, 1965.

Sumner, Lowell, and Joseph S. Dixon. *Birds and Mammals of the Sierra Nevada.* Berkeley: University of California Press, 1953.

Teale, Edwin Way. *The Wilderness World of John Muir.* Boston: Houghton Mifflin, 1954.

U.S. Forest Service, California Region. Letter to author, January 26, 1966.

Wales, J. H. *Trout of California.* Sacramento: California Department of Fish and Game, 1957.

8. IN THE RAIN SHADOW

Bakker, Gerhard. *History of the California Tule Elk.* Los Angeles: Los Angeles City College Press, for the Committee for the Preservation of the Tule Elk, 1962.

Barraclough, Mary Edith. "A Trip to Mono Lake and the Mono Craters," *Yosemite Nature Notes,* Vol. 30 (August 1951).

Calhoun, Alex. "Research Dividends at Lake Tahoe," *Outdoor California,* Vol. 28 (May–June 1967).

Cordone, Almo J., and Ted C. Frantz. "An Evaluation of Trout Planting in Lake Tahoe," *California Fish and Game,* Vol. 54 (April 1968).

Dasmann, William P. *Big Game of California.* Sacramento: California Department of Fish and Game, 1958.

Frantz, Ted C., and Almo J. Cordone. "Observations on Deepwater Plants in Lake Tahoe, California and Nevada," *Ecology,* Vol. 48 (Late Summer 1967).

Gard, R. "Effects of Beaver on Trout in Sagehen Creek, California," *Journal of Wildlife Management,* Vol. 25 (July 1961).

Hamilton, Andrew. "A Sanctuary for the Little Elk," *Westways,* Vol. 59 (October 1967).

Hanson, Jack. "Mysis: Shrimp Cocktails for Lake Tahoe," *Outdoor California,* Vol. 26 (January 1965).

——, and Almo J. Cordone. "Age and Growth of Lake Trout in Lake Tahoe," *California Fish and Game,* Vol. 53 (April 1967).

Harper, Harold T., Beverly H. Harry, and William D. Bailey. "The Chukar Partridge in California," *California Fish and Game,* Vol. 44 (January 1958).

Johnsgard, Paul A. "Dawn Rendezvous on the Lek," *Natural History,* Vol. 76 (March 1967).

Jones, Fred L. "A Survey of the Sierra Nevada Bighorn," *Sierra Club Bulletin,* Vol. 35 (June 1950).

Lee, W. Storrs. *The Sierra.* New York: Putnam, 1962.

McCullough, Dale R., and Edward R. Schneegas. "Winter Observations on the Sierra Nevada Bighorn Sheep," *California Fish and Game,* Vol. 52 (April 1966).

McLean, Donald D. *Upland Game of California.* Sacramento: California Department of Fish and Game, 1958.

Manson, Marsden. "Observations on the Denudation of Vegetation — A Suggested Remedy for California," *Sierra Club Bulletin,* Vol. 2 (June 1899).

Nord, Eamor C. "Autecology of Bitterbrush in California," *Ecological Monographs,* Vol. 35 (Summer 1965).

Orr, Robert T. *Mammals of Lake Tahoe.* San Francisco: California Academy of Sciences, 1949.

Peterson, Roger Tory. *The Birds.* New York: Time, Inc., 1963.

Rogers, William R. "Plumas County Beaver Survey." Mimeographed. Sacramento: California Department of Fish and Game, 1966.

Schneegas, Edward R., and Staff. "Bighorn Sheep Habitat Management Plan." Mimeographed. Bishop, Calif.: Inyo National Forest, U.S. Forest Service, 1964.

——. "Sage Grouse Habitat Management Plan." Mimeographed. Bishop, Calif.: Inyo National Forest, U.S. Forest Service, 1966.

——. "Tule Elk Habitat Management Plan." Mimeographed. Bishop, Calif.: Inyo National Forest, U.S. Forest Service, 1965.

——. "Wildlife Habitat Management Plan." Mimeographed. Bishop, Calif.: Inyo National Forest, 1966.

Schumacher, Genny. *Deepest Valley.* San Francisco: Sierra Club, 1962.

——. *The Mammoth Lakes Sierra.* San Francisco: Sierra Club, 1959.

Scott, John W. "Mating Behavior of the Sage Grouse," *The Auk,* Vol. 59 (October 1942).

Seymour, George. *Furbearers of California.* Sacramento: California Department of Fish and Game, 1960.

Wales, J. H. *Trout of California.* Sacramento: California Department of Fish and Game, 1957.

Wells, Philip V., and Rainer Berger. "Late Pleistocene History of Coniferous Woodland in the Mohave Desert," *Science,* Vol. 155 (March 31, 1967).

Index

Index